O.S. Nock with his own model railway layout at his home, Silver Cedars. (The locomotive is the North British Atlantic No 877, Liddesdale, *being prepared to back on to its train).*

Line Clear Ahead

75 YEARS OF UPS AND DOWNS

O.S. NOCK

BSc, CEng, FICE, FIMechE,
Past President and Honorary Fellow,
Institution of Railway Signal Engineers,
Past President, Old Giggleswickian Club

 Patrick Stephens, Cambridge

First published April 1982
Reprinted June 1982

British Library Cataloguing in Publication Data

Nock, O.S.
    Line clear ahead.
    1. Railroads—History
    I. Title
    385'.09'04   HE1021

    ISBN 0-85059-545-2

Front endpaper *A place of many memories, extending back to LNWR days: the gorge of the River Lune, just south of Tebay before the construction of the M6 motorway. Amid this splendid mountain scenery, a converted 'Royal Scot' is speeding southwards with a Glasgow–Manchester express. This engine, the* Scots Guardsman, *is now preserved* (Derek Cross).

Rear endpaper *Steam in South Australia: a special, consisting of vintage rolling stock, leaving Adelaide hauled by the preserved 4-8-4 locomotive, No 520,* Sir Malcolm Barclay-Harvey. *The author rode on the footplate on this occasion* (South Australian Railways).

Text photoset in 10 on 11 pt English Times by Manuset Limited, Baldock, Herts. Printed in Great Britain on 100 gsm Fineblade coated cartridge and bound by The Garden City Press, Letchworth, Herts, for the publishers, Patrick Stephens Limited, Bar Hill, Cambridge, CB3 8EL, England.

Contents

Preface

It is sometimes said that everyone has the material for at least one book within his grasp, the story of his own life; because no two of us are alike, and no two of us think exactly alike. At the time of beginning *Line Clear Ahead* my own score stood at one hundred and ten books, but few of them have more than a random scattering of purely personal reminiscence amid the facts of railway engineering, history and biography that they contain. And even this one, which promised to be much more personal than any of its predecessors, is far from being an auto-biography. I am nevertheless taking recollections back to very early childhood, and to my parents and grandparents. Biographers usually try to discern hereditary influences leading to traits of interests or enthusiasms in their subjects; but in the great family bible that I inherited from my father, and in which he traced the family tree back to 1735, there is not a clue to account for my own interest in railways, which dates almost to my cradle, and which makes the year 1907 the starting point for this book.

Nevertheless railways were then subjects of general public interest. They were then the only form of long-distance land transport available to the general public, and men like my own father and my Uncle Fred were interested in railway development as part of their business in keeping in touch with current affairs. As to my uncle, my mother used to recall an occasion when he took her to the platform end of some major northern station to see a new engine with *ten foot driving wheels*! Careful cross examination of my mother in much later years established fairly certainly that what she actually saw was one of the first Aspinall 'Atlantics' of the Lancashire and Yorkshire Railway. How 10 feet came into it I do not know, unless someone took the actual diameter of 7 feet 3 inches, and added the feet and inches together to make 10!

When one begins to edge beyond that time of life vaguely described as 'middle age' there is a dangerous tendency to reminisce, and to degenerate into an old bore; but I nevertheless recall the phrase Joseph Tatlow quoted at the beginning of an autobiography entitled *Fifty Years of Railway Life*. He had been General Manager, and later a director of the Midland Great Western Railway of Ireland. He quoted: 'We lose a proper sense of the richness of life if we do not look back on the scenes of our youth with imagination and warmth'. I certainly look back with gratitude to the way in which my father and mother nourished my interest in railways. Had it not been for their encouragement I might never have been gripped as I was by the fascination of the steam locomotive. That in later years we came to disagree over some facets of life is no more than the workings out of human nature; but my gratitude remains, not least for the splendid education they gave me, as a first step to my professional career.

At the time I suppose few boys really enjoy their days at boarding school, unless they rise to heights of glory in sport, or become prefects—or *praeposters* as we knew them at Giggleswick. Certainly my own affection for the school, and my appreciation of what it had done for me, grew as my years there receded into the past. Of one thing, however, I am very sure; it is that the excellent health I have enjoyed through my life is in no small measure due to the five years I had of toughening up amid the mighty hills and dales of Craven. As will be told later the steps my parents proposed to take for me in further education received no approval from the Headmaster, and there were no indications of any scholarships that might be open for me to compete for. My father paid my fees at Imperial College in full, even to the extent of giving me a post-graduate year. In business the list is long of those to whom my gratitude is due: to those who gave me my early opportunities; to those who worked with me as close colleagues, and to those who in my later years worked for me.

Nor must I forget in my gratitude the dozen or so publishers who have taken my literary work. Two, who have published much of my work, have, with abounding enterprise and success in a difficult age, been established no more than recently; but I am proud to have been associated with three men whose family firms have been acknowledged leaders in the business, each for considerably more than a hundred years—Archie Black, the late Harry Batsford, and Ronald Ian Nelson. Each, in very different ways, I found as outstanding railway enthusiasts. It was Batsford who in a single half-hour on the floor of his office showed me how to select and arrange the illustrations for a book. Archibald Adam Gordon Black, President of the family firm whose name he bears, commissioned the series of books on overseas railways that has taken me over much of the world, and made the years after my retirement from Westinghouse some of the most enjoyable of my life. For Ronnie Nelson, a co-enthusiast of the stop-watch, whether on or off a locomotive, I did books containing many intimate details of locomotive performance, but none so treasured as that I did in collaboration with my great friend, the late Bishop Eric Treacy, *Main Lines Across the Border*.

There is one, however, whose help, encouragement and devotion surpasses all. It is now 48 years since I first met Olivia Ravenall, and 46 years since I asked her to marry me. To say that she has been behind me in everything I have undertaken in the intervening years would be the merest platitude. In many of my books I have sometimes lightheartedly, and always very sincerely, acknowledged her help; but that is no more than the outward façade. I think now of the countless occasions when absorbed by the day's problems I have come home testy and remote; when the children had to be 'shushed', because Daddy was busy, and I was far away, although in the same house, when she needed me most. I recall the occasion, when after one such admonition Trevor was heard muttering: 'Daddy has no sense of a humour'! But Olivia has never failed *me*. Quite apart from the work-a-day chores like housekeeping, the countless things that a good mother and housewife does, not to mention typing my books (!) and, in her case, very often in conditions of great physical disability and pain, there have been times when we have had to take great, and sometimes grave decisions, and then always we were solidly one.

It is certainly true that at times it was a case of *toujours les chemins de fer*, as our great friends from Nogent-sur-Marne, Yves and Janot Paris, were in the habit of expressing it; nor must I forget the junior schoolboy of immortal memory who translated *chemin de fer*, as chimney on fire! But once embarked upon reminiscences, of whatever kind, one could continue gossiping by the hour, and it is time to stop, and roll the years back to 1907 when I was just beginning to distinguish between South Eastern and Chatham, and Great Western locomotives.

O.S. Nock, Batheaston, Bath, April 1981

This was the result of an invitation to supply an apt caption for the drawing which appeared on the back of the menu at the Annual Dinner of the Cambridge University Railway Society in 1980! O.S. Nock was one of the guests of honour.

Chapter 1

Gauge 1 in the nursery, 1907–1914

The year was 1905, and it was just three weeks old when I was born at Sutton Coldfield, Warwickshire. Many times afterwards I have been asked who, or what, first sparked off my interest in railways and I have usually replied that it stemmed from my cradle, because I cannot personally remember a time when I was not interested. This, however, cannot be strictly true, because naturally I do not remember much about the first two years, except that at the age of about 1½ I am reputed to have tried to interest my infant sister in my favourite toys— without success.

There were no engineers in our family. My father was securities clerk at the Midland Bank in Temple Row, Birmingham, within the shadow of the beautiful 18th century Palladian-style church of St Philip's, which was chosen as the Cathedral when Birmingham attained the status of a city. My mother often spoke in after years of the controversy there had been over the choice of St Philip's. Many of the older residents would have preferred St Martins, in the Bull Ring which, although a newer church than St Philip's, was built on a site that had been consecrated ground from at least the 14th century and was in a traditional Gothic style with a magnificent spire. But St Philip's standing on its own (in a green oasis in the business heart of the city) was unquestionably the better choice.

My father was descended from a very old Worcestershire family and from him I inherited a colossal family bible, which included a family tree dating back to the year 1735. My grandfather, James Nock, of whom I retain quite vivid memories, was an apothecary practising from an address in the Coventry Road. He was one of those amazing self-taught men who had a genius for prescribing potions to suit all ills. Among the poor of the district where he lived, and there were very many of them, he was known affectionately as 'Doctor' Nock. Those were the days of large families. My father was the youngest of eleven, but that was nothing compared to some of my earlier progenitors on that family tree. At the time of my birth only one of my father's two brothers was still living, and he was a permanent invalid.

Lawrence Frederick was some 13 years older than my father and, before the paralysis that struck him about the time of my birth, he had been a most vigorous, versatile and widely read man. He was a surveyor at the General Post Office in Birmingham but had already established himself as a freelance journalist. Being on the Post Office staff he could not write under his own name, but he neatly adapted his initials 'LFN' into the pen name of 'Elfin'.

Left *James Nock (1824-1915), paternal grandfather.* **Right** *Thomas Stevens, maternal grandfather.*

Unfortunately little of his work survives among the family records. Even during the years when he was prostrate his interests remained limitless and his books on learned subjects were packed with press cuttings and annotations of his own. From him I inherited a first edition of Foxwell and Farrer's classic *Express Trains English and Foreign* with my uncle's own observations on the likely contributing causes to the wreck of the West Coast 'Tourist' express at Preston, in 1896.

My maternal grandfather, Thomas Stevens, was the nearest of all my progenitors to being a railwayman, because he was manager for Pickford & Co at Curzon Street, goods station of the London and North Western Railway. Curzon Street had been the original passenger terminus of the London and Birmingham Railway and it is good to know that its splendid classic portico, a modest northern counterpart of the Doric Arch at Euston, is to be preserved. Thomas Stevens, *en famille*, was the gentlest and kindliest of men, and I should think it is from him more than any other of my ancestors that I have inherited my sense of humour; but down at Curzon Street he could be a holy terror. My Uncle Fred, of whom I shall write much later in this book, told me the tale of how one Sunday the Stevens family was walking demurely home from church when a typical Birmingham artisan of the day with his wife, both decked in their 'Sunday best', passed nearby, and he said, in a stage whisper: 'That's 'im; that's our gaffer. Goes raving mad, 'e does!'. I am told that my grandmother, who was the most straitlaced of all my immediate forebears, wished that the earth could open and swallow her up!

Before her marriage my mother was a schoolmistress—a headmistress in fact; and it so happened that her greatest friend, Mary Richmond, was also one. After the death of my grandmother the two were inseparable, although there would be no point in mentioning this particular friendship were it not for an earlier association of the Richmond family with the London and North Western

Railway. Mary's father had been a draughtsman in the locomotive works at Crewe, but at an early age decided there were more lucrative occupations, and he became a house and estate agent. But connected in some way with the Richmonds was a very old lady of the name of Bland, who had the most vivid and precise memory. As a teenager she had been locked in her room to prevent her going to the opening ceremony of a new railway in the district. But she had forced the window, shinned down three stories of drain pipe, and enjoyed the opening ceremony as much as anybody. Railways were evidently in her blood. She married one John Bland, another draughtsman in Crewe Works, and it was he who first suggested the idea of water troughs. The idea was passed upwards through the hierarchy of the locomotive department, and the great John Ramsbottom was glad enough to give it a trial. Whether John Bland ever got any formal recognition of his idea I do not know. But I was told that in her great old age his widow always spoke of it with pride, rather than with any sign of rancour that Ramsbottom had become the universally accepted 'inventor' of water troughs.

After my mother became engaged to be married, Mary Richmond decided to go abroad. In the work of rehabilitation in the Transvaal after the end of the Boer War there was a call for experienced English school teachers and Mary decided to go. For a time her home was in Pretoria. By the oddest of coincidences, while one of the two bosom friends became a Mrs Nock, the other shortly afterwards became a Mrs Lock! My father and mother were married quietly at Colwyn Bay on September 3 1903 and returned to a little house named 'Grasmere', in Sutton Coldfield, where I was born 16 months later. By that time it was evident that my father's chances of promotion in so large a concern as the Midland bank in Temple Row were remote, and with the promise of a manager-ship in the near future he transferred to the then-Birmingham District and Counties Bank. Shortly afterwards he was appointed to open an entirely new branch of that bank in Reading.

A house went with the job—but what a house! The bank, No 6 Broad Street was—and still is today!—in a terrace of variegated and very tall buildings, none of them then less than five storeys high. The frontage of each was so narrow that only one room on each storey looked out over Broad Street. The result was a series of 'tower blocks', cheek by jowl with each other, and an all-pervading perpendicular motif. In ours the bank occupied the whole of the ground floor. On the first floor were—as I remember it—just two living rooms, and as one progressed upwards there were the nursery, various bedrooms and, on what must have been the fifth floor, the servants' bedrooms. Such were the conditions of life in those days that although my father's salary was only around £250 per annum we had *three* resident maids! The bank house had one feature that the others in that terrace did not possess. This was a round turret standing high above all the neighbouring roof tops. It was glazed all round, and had a conical pointed roof. One got up to it by a somewhat precarious ladder, but once there it gave a marvellous view of the town and the country beyond. It was naturally some years before I was allowed to go up there, but I remember going up with my father when he was fixing an enormous Union Jack to fly at the time of King George V's coronation in 1911. That, however, is taking the story six years ahead of our first arrival in Reading and I must go back to earlier days, and get down to the real business of running 'Gauge 1' trains in the nursery.

I soon passed beyond the stage of crude clockwork toys that cost a shilling

Broad Street, Reading, in the early 1900s. The turreted building in the centre was the family home from 1905 until the end of 1910. Note the horse-cab rank in the middle of the road (Reading Museum and Art Gallery).

each in those days, though when one uncle presented me with a 0-gauge live steamer my parents decided that to run this was much too risky, with the chance of 'meths' being spilt and then a fire. We stuck to clockwork and changed early from Gauge 0 to Gauge 1. There was plenty of room in that nursery. There were several toy shops in Reading where the cheap mass-produced German trains could be bought. I think it was Bing of Nuremberg that marketed a Gauge 1 0-4-0 tender engine, with outside cylinders. It was supplied in LNW, Midland, or Great Northern Colours, and my own first engine, in black, carried the name *King Edward VII.* At a vague stretch of the imagination, supplying in thought the bogie that was not there, it did bear a passing resemblance to the LNWR *Alfred the Great* Class compound 4-4-0. It remained the work-horse of the nursery line until 1910, and then one day my father brought upstairs a copy of the September issue of *The Railway Magazine* which was a special issue in celebration of the Diamond Jubilee of the Great Northern Railway. I devoured the pictures, and from that time onward the Ivatt large-boilered 'Atlantics' became my No 1 'pin-up' engines. At Christmas that year the GNR version of the Bing 0-4-0 was added to the stud and became the pride of the nursery line.

In the meantime my mother was contributing to the early build-up of my railway interests. She had been brought up in the country and it was natural enough that she found constraint amounting to something near claustraphobia amid the closely piled bricks and mortar of central Reading. Fortunately, however, the town is well furnished with pleasant open spaces. There are the Forbury Gardens, less than 10 minutes walk from the Bank House. They are not very large and are laid out in the grounds of Reading Abbey, with the fragmentary ruins of the abbey itself near at hand. The central feature of the

Forbury is a huge lion, a memorial to the men of the Royal Berkshire Regiment
who fell in the battle of Maiwand on July 27 1880 in the Afghan war. But far
more important from my point was the view obtained of the railway lines; and
there from the infantile pleasance of a bassinet I did my earliest train spotting.
Palmer Park on the eastern fringes of the town was another fine open space,
though a walk of about two miles from home. It was not so attractive as the
Forbury from the railway point of view for, although it was bounded on one
side by an embankment, it was only that of the SE & CR, whereas from the
Forbury we had an excellent view of the Great Western main line, in addition to
all the local activities in the South Eastern station.

Encumbered with a bassinet there was no way of getting to any of these
'parks' other than by walking, and this my mother did in full measure. Things
became easier when I graduated from the bassinet to a push chair, for that could
be taken on the trams. It was from the tram terminus on the Bath Road that my
mother somehow found her way down the country lane that led to the lines⁴ at
Southcote Junction. How she contrived it I never found out, and I was then far
too young to do any map reading for her, even if I had known or even guessed at
the Valhalla that awaited us at the end of that lane! For our first expeditions
there were made in 1906 not long after the opening of the shortened route to the
West of England, via Westbury, and there I saw some of the first three-hour
Exeter expresses.

For summer holidays we fairly rang the changes on the south coast holiday
resorts going to Ryde, Folkestone, Eastbourne, and Margate in my very early
childhood. I remember nothing of Eastbourne, except the occasional telling of
an old family joke against my father: of how, in changing from the SE & CR
train at Redhill he ushered us into the wrong connecting train and how we ended
up at Brighton instead of Eastbourne. Of Ryde, where we stayed in a house
overlooking the pier I remember watching the trains coming off the pier then
diving into a tunnel beneath the promenade. But it is of Folkestone, where we
went in 1909, that I have the first clear recollections, of how I found walks along
the harbour pier promenade much more attractive than digging sand castles,
and was fascinated by the coming and going of the cross-Channel steamers. It
was during that holiday, at the age of 4½ that I was first taken abroad, on a day
trip to Boulogne.

The business of obtaining seaside lodgings then was simplicity itself, in
theory. There was never any question of booking in advance. We just went to
our chosen resort, left the luggage at the station, and then my mother went to
find accommodation, while my father took me, and later my sister also, to the
beach. One never dreamt of booking rooms until they had been seen.
Occasionally things came unstuck, as when we lighted upon Margate, and found
it unexpectedly crowded. We had less satisfactory quarters that year, 1910; but
for me the holiday was highlighted by a present of the first edition of *The
Wonder Book of Railways* and this brings me to the interesting way in which
one's education in railways could be fostered, in days when the popular
literature was practically non-existent.

The South Eastern and Chatham Railway had quite a flair for publicity, and
while, as I discovered later, other railways issued their own series of picture
postcards those of the SE & CR were all in colour, and very attractively
produced. Once luggage was assembled, and there was nothing left to do on the
station platform but to wait for the train, my father always gravitated towards

the bookstall, and there nicely displayed were dozens of colour cards, showing locomotives, trains, stations, steamers and such like. Who could resist? Not my father anyway, and he made a considerable collection, which used to be shown to me at discreet intervals. It quickened my interest intensely, and having what my wife likes to call a 'photographic memory' I began to build up quite a picture of what the whole SE & CR was like.

Home again in Reading, and less than five minutes walk from the Bank House, I discovered something more exciting still. In a stationer's shop in Queen Victoria Street they sold the famous 'F. Moore' coloured cards of the Locomotive Publishing Company, and before I was six years of age I was learning the colours of many distant railways. I found that the Midland had red trains; that the Caledonian had huge blue engines, and that the locomotives of the LNWR were black. Even before that, however, the London and North Western was much more than a name to me. My mother talked of it frequently; her own father had been so closely associated with it in Birmingham, and for the family holidays of her youth it was used to get from Birmingham to North Wales, or to Blackpool. And from that stationer's shop I too began to build up a collection of coloured railway postcards. My pocket money was then one penny a week, and that meant one postcard a week! The trouble was choosing, and the man in that shop used to get very impatient when I could not make up my mind which one to have that week. There was an almost bewildering choice.

Of the maids who lived at the Bank House I can recollect only two. One was a very competent and pleasant nurse who came to look after things when my sisters were born, and who visited us when professional nursing help was needed. The other was the nursery maid, a delightful girl who was very popular with us children. Her real name was May Hayward, but to all of us, parents and children alike she was never anything but 'Ningey Nur-Nur'! She was the devoted slave of this tiresome young man, already with something of a railtrack mind, and she once incurred the high displeasure of my mother by having herself and her charge photographed, when according to 'high authority' I was not suitably dressed. I am glad she did, because it is nice to be able to include her portrait in this book.

My mother was always very susceptible to environment. If she did not like a district nothing would make her come to terms with it; and in Reading it was the trams. They passed just beneath the Bank House from early morning till late at night, and after five years of it she persuaded my father to give up the Bank House, put in a resident caretaker, and take a small villa in the village of Mortimer, and involving him in daily travelling by train into Reading. Although I was only about six years old when we went to live there I have some very clear recollections of Mortimer Common. Even in those days it was not entirely a rural community, and in travelling daily to Reading my father soon made the acquaintance of several business men who were regular commuters. Beyond the confines of the village there was gloriously open country in every direction, which my mother soon began to explore. We rented a small detached villa at the end of a lengthy cul de sac named St Mary's Road. The owner was one of the local butchers, and the road terminated in gates which led down a steep hill to some stabling where he kept the horse that did his supply round. Our garden led down the hill beside the road to the stables, and beyond the stream that marked the end of the property the land rose steeply again to a row of fine poplar trees, which gave the name to our house 'The Poplars'. The stream, the stables, and

*The once-banned photo-
graph—not properly
dressed! With May
Hayward ('Ningey Nur-
Nur') about 1908.*

the paddock beyond, to which we had free access, all came to play a part in the life we led in the next few years.

The first problem was that of transport. A trap was purchased, and the first form of motive power was a most lovable grey donkey, which had the strongest objections to hurrying. Most of our 'running' was made at little more than walking pace, and one day when my mother was in a hurry, and gave some encouragement with the stick, 'Jenny' just lay down in the middle of the road. How my mother got things moving again I cannot remember; but it was by this uncertain form of transport that I used to be taken to a little private school at Padworth. After a while we exchanged Jenny for a little Exmoor pony, but before telling of some of our adventures with that fiery little animal I must recall an occasion when my mother did succeed in making some quite record running—not with a donkey, I hasten to add. My Uncle Fred, with my aunt and cousin, came to spend a short holiday in the village, and one day it was arranged that we should make an excursion. A smart cob and quite elegant trap was hired for my uncle, while my mother hired a shaggy, nondescript grey pony and trap from one of the grocers on the Common. The contrast was extraordinary: a gleaming well groomed, smartly harnessed horse, and a scruffy unkempt thing that looked as if it had spent most of its life roaming the heaths and woodlands. Route having been settled the 'right away' was given, and without any encouragement from my mother that scruffy grey pony went off like a bomb, leaving the smart cob literally standing. Off we dashed towards Aldermaston, and at each curve in the road we had to stop, for the *concours d'elegance* that was following to catch up! My uncle was not amused, and he and my aunt were quite sure that the old pony had been heavily belaboured to produce such 'running'. But as one of the passengers in that old trap I can tell that it was quite an unsolicited effort. It was a pity it was before my stop-watching days.

The Exmoor pony 'Mary' was a flyer too, but in a wild and disconcerting way. I am afraid she was very much under-utilised, and used to work off her energy in unexpected places. Occasionally my mother used to drive into Reading, for a shopping spree. Where 'Mary' was garaged during the day I don't know, but one such trip remains vividly in my memory. We had come down Burghfield Hill, and were approaching the place where the road crossed the Berks and Hants line of the GWR, not long after it had been promoted to become the West of England main line, when sweeping eastwards in all its glittering elegance came a Dean 7 foot 8 inch 'single' hauling a horsebox special from Newbury Racecourse. Our return to Mortimer that afternoon was uneventful until we were nearing the foot of Burghfield Hill, when Mary, who had been trotting placidly along until then, suddenly broke into a tearing gallop and thundered up the hill like *Papyrus* winning the Derby! But her energies became too exciting to be nice, and after she had tried to crash the trap backwards on Silchester Common she was sold into farm service where her vigour could be expended in hard work!

Reverting to railways, the 'Hants' fork of the Berks and Hants railway line ran along the valley about a mile east of the high ground of Mortimer Common and we saw the trains sometimes when we went to a house where I received some of my 'kindergarten' lessons. It was called Brocaslands Farm, but it was not until I was actually writing these memoirs that I realised the deep significance of that name. I was looking up Silchester, and referred to a favourite source in my own library, the *Highways and Byways* series. Near Silchester was Beaurepaire, the home for many centuries of a family named Brocas who could trace their ancestry back to the time of the Norman Conquest. The association of that old house, where the farmer's daughter gave elementary lessons, was thus explained; but it would seem that when I went there, trundled along by the lackadaisical grey donkey, Jenny, it was in a poor state of repair, because we children always called it 'Hole in the wall Farm'!

So we came to the year 1913, one that became very important to me in a diversity of ways. For the summer holiday we went to Weymouth that year, and in recollections of a crowded month it is difficult to decide which of my developing interests made the greatest impression. There always seemed to be so much going on at Weymouth. From the sands there were always ships to be seen in the bay. Battleships were at anchor; the Channel Islands packets and cargo boats were going and coming, and to add to the variety there was a courtesy visit from a Russian battleship, the *Rurik*. I was keen enough to visit Portland, where many more ships of the Royal Navy lay anchored in the Roads, but my interest in the Navy was quickened in another way. In one of the shops there was a great display of waterline models, little small-scale masterpieces arranged to depict a review of the fleet, and these little models could be bought in sets of four, each comprising a battleship, a cruiser, a destroyer and a submarine. They were made, I believe, by Brittains, the celebrated manufacturers of lead soldiers. I have always been an insatiable collector, and I began collecting warship models. While we were at Weymouth we were able to see over a battleship, HMS *Hindustan*; it was an old pre-Dreadnought type, but interesting enough for all that.

Our evening walks frequently took us along the Backwater, where a path led between the railway yards and that pleasant sheet of water. There was always plenty to see on the line, with both Great Western and London and South Western trains coming and going. It was there that I began to recognise the different types of locomotive, and to read their names. Most of the Great Western passenger engines were either 'Bulldogs' or 'Atbaras', with an occasional outside cylindered 'County'. The LSWR engines were mostly of the Adams outside cylindered 4-4-0 type. Then one day my railway interest, which had been running level with that in the Royal Navy since we arrived in Weymouth, received a very powerful 'shot in the arm'. We were passing a tobacconists shop in the town when my eye caught sight of a little card in the window: 'Complete model railway, for sale; enquire within'. My mother said, 'Go in and ask how much it is'. I did, and received the non-committal reply that a shopkeeper might have been expected to give to a small boy of eight years old. But later in the day my father went to investigate, and came back with a large parcel. There and then the tinplate '1' gauge railway in Mortimer, that had hitherto boasted no more pretentious rolling stock than two German made clockwork 0-4-0s, and a few 4-wheeled coaches, suddenly became possessed of a Bassett-Lowke scale model of an 'Atbara' 4-4-0 No 3410 *Sydney*, and three bogie clerestory coaches. I could scarcely wait to get home and run that lovely train.

But the holiday at Weymouth was not yet over, and there were other pleasures to be experienced. There were band concerts on the promenade, the amusement of seeing parties of Russian sailors from the *Rurik* sightseeing in the town, and then a well remembered visit to the theatre in the pier pavilion. From a very early age I had been taken to the pantomime at Christmas, but this was something quite different—a musical comedy, none other than *The Arcadians* and even at that young age I remember my delight in the gay and catchy music. It has always remained one of my favourites, and I have thought that if anyone ever asked me to name my eight 'Desert Island Discs' the overture to *The Arcadians* would be one of my first choices. But as the end of that memorable holiday of 1913 drew near, there was a cloud on the horizon. Soon after we returned home I was going to school—real school this time, and the prospect was daunting.

Marlborough House was I suppose, typical of many private preparatory schools of that time. In these more forthright days it would have been called a 'snob school' catering only for 'the sons of gentlemen'. Fathers who were in trade of any kind could not get their sons entered, much as they tried, because for some reason it was regarded—or regarded itself!—as a prestige school. On reflection more than 65 years later I cannot for the life of me think why! The headmaster, and owner, was a rather flamboyant individual and his staff were a strangely assorted lot. There was a tall and handsome young games master who taught geography, two elderly women who took the most junior classes, but the king-pin as in so many schools large and small, was the second master—a man wonderfully at home with boys of all ages, and a wise and sympathetic teacher. I went there very much as the 'square peg'. I am told that in my babyhood I was very delicate. In later years indeed my Aunt Emmie told me that Uncle Fred once returned to Bradford after a visit to us in Reading and declared roundly:

'That child will never live!' But the care and affection that was bestowed upon me in my early childhood was continued long after I had developed normal health and strength, and my mother continued to dissuade me from any form of exercise that might have taxed my strength unduly. I was indeed ill prepared for the life of a boys' school, and particularly one where sport formed almost as much of the day's routine as learning. It would not have been so bad if the school had not recently made a change from soccer to rugger, and the total strength was barely enough to make up two XVs. Consequently every boy who was medically fit was pressed into one side or the other, and beginners like myself, small in stature and weight, played in the same game as hefty young teenagers. I must admit to not liking those early scrums! In class I began to learn Latin and French, but enjoyed the drawing and geography lessons most. Discipline under that flamboyant headmaster was harsh. Misdemeanors were punished by caning in front of the whole school.

To reach Marlborough House from Mortimer meant daily travelling by train, and at the age of eight I became a season-ticket holder on the Great Western Railway. I used to travel to Reading West Station, whence it was about ten minutes walk to the school. But it was the return home that provided the major interest for me. On certain days, in deference to my tender years I was allowed to leave at mid-afternoon, and then I travelled by a steam rail motor car that left Reading Central, as it was then called, at 4.15 pm. This was a highly significant time, for that 'motor' left immediately after the passage of the 3.30 pm West of England express, which passed Reading West about 4.9 pm. There was another good reason for getting down to the station a little before the 'motor' was due, because at about 4.6 or 4.7 pm the up Cornish Riviera Express came through. And so, on those homeward journeys from Marlborough House I saw many of the Churchward 4-cylinder 4-6-0s in all their original glory: *Red Star, Shooting Star, Knight of the Golden Fleece, Queen Berengaria* were names that I well remember from my train spotting of 1913. That year was also to prove another veritable milestone in my life, though in a way not to be known until many years later; for it was in October that the girl who was to become my beloved wife 24 years later, was born in Walthamstow, Essex.

The winter of 1913–14 was our last at Mortimer. My father felt the strain of daily commuting with a trek of more than two miles each way between our house and the station, and while he had no desire to see my mother's health reduced to the state of nervous debility that five years at the Bank House had produced he sought something a little more accessible, while still in the country. He lighted upon Hurst, a little village five miles east of Reading, and took, unfurnished, an old Georgian farmhouse. It lay some little distance from the village itself, but within ten minutes walk from Sindlesham and Hurst Halt, on the South Eastern Line from Reading to Guildford and Redhill. The house lay back from the road with a garden in front. There were extensive outbuildings at the back, which we never used, and a two-acre meadow, surrounded by a ring of enormous elms. But joy, oh joy for me, there was a pond. On its fringes I built little harbours, floated various forms of craft, and blissfully passed many an hour, steadily contracting a throat infection that was to be with me for nearly a year. But there were disquieting things as well as happy ones in the few months we lived at Lea Cottage. First of all there was the chronic and almost unbelievable unpunctuality of the SE & CR trains. Where the train that took me into Reading in the mornings originated I have no idea; but every morning down at the Halt

Trains of early childhood: **Above** *GWR, one of the two-hour Bristol expresses, composed of clerestory roofed carriages, and hauled by one of the 'Saint' Class 2-cylinder 4-6-0s in non-superheated condition.* **Below** *LSWR, a London bound train just after leaving Weymouth and passing the 'backwater'; hauled by an Adams outside-cylinder 4-4-0.*

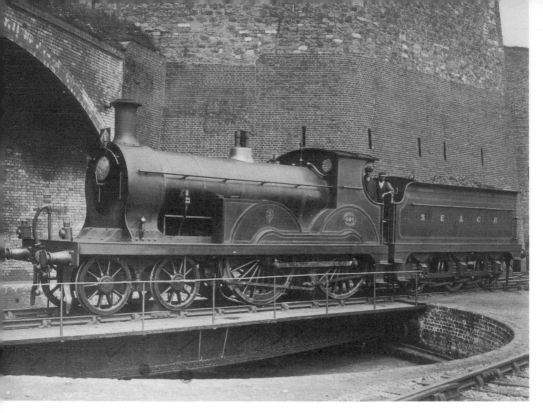

Trains of early childhood: **Above** *A Stirling 'B' Class express passenger 4-4-0 of the South Eastern and Chatham* (BR). **Below** *GWR 'City' Class 4-4-0, No 3402* Halifax.

we spent ages waiting for it, with the awful thought of how those intolerant folks at Marlborough House were going to react to my quite regular late arrivals. I was met with questions such as 'Why can't you catch an earlier train?' and suggestions that I had been dallying among the shops in Reading, instead of boarding the first tram that came. The image of the SE & CR shrunk to negligible proportions in my eyes.

At the age of nine I was beginning to become aware of affairs beyond school, the village and Reading itself. I was learning history, and history—dramatic history—was being enacted before our very eyes, as it were! I became aware of the dangers that were looming up in Ireland, where Home Rule was a highly explosive topic. Then one Saturday, catching the midday train from the South Eastern station I was suddenly aware of a highly tense atmosphere. I looked up to the Great Western main line and saw a sight that was not repeated before my eyes for more than another 50 years—the immediate aftermath of a railway collision. Tilted at a precarious angle was a 'Bulldog' Class 4-4-0 which had received a glancing blow by an express from Worcester to Paddington and, farther on, lying on its side and partly buried by wreckage from the leading carriage of its own train, was the *County of Leicester*, sadly battered in its fall. It was a sight I shall never forget, even though I had no more than a passing view of it, from the South Eastern. It was 53 years before I saw another railway accident—a marvellous tribute in itself to the safety of railway travel. Then, however, I was a passenger in the train that crashed! ·

Shortly before the end of school summer term the infection from that pond of ours caught up with me, and I was put to bed with a high temperature and a throat that seemed as though it was all but closed up. The doctor's medicine soon began to get my temperature down, but one day my father returned from Reading in the evening and entered the bedroom where I lay. He looked grave, and said: 'There's going to be a war'. With my mind instantly switched to Ireland I said, 'Civil?', and he replied 'No France and Russia, and probably ourselves, against Germany, Austria and Italy'. I remember how newspapers for the next few days were full of banner headlines, estimates of the relative strengths of the combatants and then, after our own declaration of war, maps of the North Sea, showing where the anticipated battle between the British and German fleets would take place. My mother took us children into Reading very soon after the declaration of war, and I can recall the rumours that rent the air of the result of the great fleet encounter which, of course, never took place. One result I remember hearing that day was that five English and 25 German ships had been sunk! Another report was even more favourable, putting the figures at three against 35—while a third spread wild alarm reversing the result at 25 English and five German.

At this moment of national crisis Father could not get away for a holiday, but my mother took us to Weymouth once more. It was a very different place from that we had known a year ago—alive with service men bound on urgent missions, the evenings punctuated by recruiting meetings, and expressions of patriotic fervour; by that time also news of the continued retreat of the British Expeditionary Force after the Battle of Mons filled the newspapers. Each morning I used to go before breakfast to a newspaper shop on the promenade to collect our copy of *The Daily Mail*, and one morning I saw to my delight, splashed across the front page 'Great Franco-British Advance'. It was the first news of the Battle of the Marne, the action that saved Paris. I cannot remember that we ever returned to Hurst. Quite apart from that pond there were other disadvantages. Our evacuation must have been sudden because we had no other house to go to, and spent the next few months living in lodgings in Reading. My attendances at Marlborough House were spasmodic. Every three weeks or so my temperature would go soaring up and my throat became half closed; and in between times I went with my mother visiting house after house in the search for more permanent quarters. Eventually we found anchorage in a fine Victorian semi-detached house in Maitland Road, a cross connection between the Bath Road and Tilehurst Road. It was named Keston, and we moved in about a month before Christmas 1914.

The recurring throat infection continued—in fact I spent Christmas 1914 in bed—and it was decided that I should not go to school again for at least one term. The period between Christmas and Easter that year was just misery. The slightest thing, it seemed, would send my temperature up and there was nothing for it but to go to bed. Be that as it may have been, arrangements were made for me to start at Reading School after Easter, and to try to get a break before then we went to Bournemouth for a short holiday. My father was able to get some leave, for the first time since the summer of 1913, and he came with us. For my mother that 'break' was a disaster. First I, and then my sister went down with influenza, and of the three weeks we were there she had two days free of the sick room! But as far as I was concerned it was the final 'kick' from that throat infection contracted at Hurst, and from then onwards I became fit and well again.

Chapter 2

Wartime—transition from Reading to Barrow

I had barely begun to settle down to the life of a day boy at Reading School than we learned that the bank of which my father had been manager for ten years, and whose name had in the meantime been changed to the 'United Counties' was to be taken over by Barclays. There was already a large branch of the latter in Reading, and the manager there was of far more senior status than my father. It was an anxious time, for my father became virtually redundant in Reading. In due course he was summoned to head office in London, and late that same afternoon a telegram arrived with the single phrase: 'Barrow-in-Furness'. There was a dash for the school atlas, for neither my mother nor I were quite sure where Barrow was. She had a haunting fear of being sent to somewhere on the east coast, which had already been bombarded by enemy 'tip and run' raiders. She was relieved to find it was on the west coast; but there was not much relief otherwise. She had been comfortably ensconced at 'Keston', Maitland Road, and hated the idea of a move.

With an increasing amount of homework from Reading School, time for my older hobbies became less, and I must admit that the possession of that splendid Gauge 1 Great Western train and some goods vehicles did not prove enough to sustain my interest in model railways at that time. After all when one was limited to making the circuit of a single, not very large oval, and the changes could be rung only between the three-coach passenger train and the three-wagon goods, there was a sameness about it that inevitably palled. It was not in the nature of a boy of 11, or his parents, to realise that he had there a period piece of model engineering potentially of very considerable value; and, sad to relate, those models were sold at a knock-down price to raise funds to buy a more elaborate Meccano outfit.

Not long before we moved to Barrow I came down to breakfast one morning to read, in huge letters across the front page of *The Daily Mail*, 'HEAVY LOSSES IN NAVAL BATTLE', and together my mother and I read the news of the Battle of Jutland, which had taken place on the previous afternoon. I remember how shocked I was, even as a boy of 11, at the loss of several of our great battle-cruisers, each with the loss of more than a thousand lives, and adding up the losses on both sides it seemed that this great sea fight, which had been anticipated from the very first day of the war, had ended in nothing better for the Royal Navy than a draw. The details were discussed in every home, every shop, every café, every classroom at school, and I remember a friend of my parents who was then manager of the Reading Waterworks saying, 'The only good thing about it is that the Germans ran away'. As we came to appreciate afterwards it was everything.

From the first weeks of the war the dashing exploits of Vice Admiral Sir David Beatty, commanding the battle-cruiser squadron, had thrilled the nation; and some older men of the fleet who served under him were moved to whisper: 'Nelson has come again'. But of the Commander-in-Chief, Sir John Jellicoe, little was known or heard. In moments of frustration men and women in England were inclined to ask: 'What *is* the Navy doing?'. And then, after Jutland, we learned that the great battle fleet had arrived too late to slaughter the German High Seas Fleet that had so mauled our battle-cruisers. Jellicoe waited all next day, in case there was any disposition on the enemy's part to resume; but the Germans had fled, never again to venture out of port. A commentator afterwards remarked that the British Commander-in-Chief could well have signalled—in the Nelson idiom—'We have swept the enemy from the seas'. He had done just that. But Jellicoe was not the man for heroics. Had the German fleet been annihilated in the process it would have been a tremendous boost to British morale, but it would not have shortened the war by a single week. On the other hand, if a great battle had gone the other way, well, it was Winston Churchill who said that Jellicoe's responsibilities were such that he was the one man on either side who could have lost the war in a single afternoon!

I remember well, however, the keen disappointment that was generally felt over Jutland at the time, and we had hardly recovered from it when there came another profound shock, the sinking of the cruiser HMS *Hampshire* with Lord Kitchener on board. To my mother and to many others of her generation, with girlhood memories of the Sudan and South African campaigns, Kitchener was a legendary figure, and her immediate reaction on reading of his death in the papers was: 'Now we shall lose the war!'. But by that time all our personal concerns were concentrated on the impending move to Barrow. My father had gone on ahead, but was finding great difficulty in locating a likely house for us, and at the end of a somewhat despondent post card to my mother he had scribbled, almost as an afterthought 'Can you come and have a look?'. Up to now we had always rented houses, except for the bank house in Reading; there was no bank house at Barrow, but once my mother was on the spot with every day to do the searching, she found a house which the bank agreed to purchase for its manager in Barrow and duly rented it to us. And so, in June 1916 we said farewell to Reading.

There is no doubt that my interest in railways cooled off considerably in the last year we were at 'Keston'. After that visit to Weymouth just after the outbreak of war we did little travelling by train. I have told how the Gauge 1 model railway came to be sold, and with my creative instincts satisfied by Meccano, and my collecting urge given a new facet by an introduction to postage stamps, railways slipped into something of an eclipse. But, with the prospect of our move to Barrow, those earlier interests revived with a rush, especially as I realised our journey north would be over the London and North Western Railway. Of the precise manner of our leaving 'Keston' I have no recollection, but we went by train to Paddington and crossed by cab to Euston. There our train was none other than the 2 pm West Coast Corridor express, which conveyed two through coaches for Whitehaven. At that time it always left from No 6 platform at Euston, and having found seats I remember the long wait for departure time, in the semi-darkness at the back end of that platform,

Furness Abbey: home station, from 1916 to 1930, looking towards Carnforth. In the left foreground can be seen the shelter for the subway from the down platform.

adjacent to the arrival cab yard. We had seats on the right-hand side of the carriage, and so I missed the most entertaining railway spectacles of the journey, such as the running sheds at Camden, Bletchley, Stafford and Crewe. With only my mother and a faithful 'abigail' of Mortimer days, who travelled to help get us settled into our new home, I was not allowed to wander, and so did not see the engines that hauled us on that momentous journey.

At that period the Whitehaven coaches were detached from the 'Corridor' at Preston, and taken forward as far as Carnforth on the 6.40 pm Liverpool and Manchester 'Scotsman'; but on arrival at Carnforth I was disappointed to find that we were leaving the LNWR. I was vaguely conscious that somewhere in these regions there was a Furness Railway, but until we actually landed up there I was quite unaware of its extent. Although by that time in the evening I was getting very tired I remember how much I enjoyed the run along the coastal stretch from Arnside, but I did not realise at this time that this fast evening train from Carnforth also conveyed a through Midland carriage from Hellifield, and slipped a coach at Grange-over-Sands. At Furness Abbey my father was on the station to meet us, and until our house was ready it had been arranged for us to stay at the Furness Abbey Hotel. This was a new experience of a most fascinating kind. The hotel itself was set in a pleasance adjacent to the ruins of the abbey, in the strangely named 'Vale of Deadly Nightshade'. But there was nothing deadly nor poisonous about it. One could scarcely have imagined a more charming place. The weather was fine, we often had tea out on the hotel lawn, and there was little suggestion that a large industrial town, hell-bent night and day on the production of war material, was so close at hand. The constant passage of trains of all kinds was an added attraction for me, and the Furness engines, very smartly turned out in their iron-ore red livery, soon joined the ranks of my firm favourites.

Furness Railway: stopping train leaving Carnforth hauled by one of the large Pettigrew 4-4-0s, '130' Class. The chimney of the long-dismantled ironworks is in the background.

Life in the hotel was interesting. It was the recognised overnight lodge for men of affairs visiting the Vickers Works. I remember one elderly and apparently very senior naval officer, with a vast amount of gold braid on his cuffs, who discovered I was interested in stamp collecting. He took our new home address and not long after we settled there a large packet arrived full of stamps of all kinds. It was nice to think that a man so obviously concerned with war duties of high importance could find time to stimulate the interests of so youthful a chance acquaintance. I have, unfortunately, long since forgotten his name. On arrival in the north, of course, my sister and I were all agog to see our new home. It was no more than ten minutes walk from Furness Abbey in a district known as Croslands Park. The house itself was a smart little semi-detached villa called 'Abbey Holme'—no allusion to its being a 'home' near to the abbey, but actually named after the small Cumberland town of Abbeyholme, near Wigton. When we arrived the previous owner was still in residence, and not due to leave for a week or so; but we received a friendly enough welcome and were shown round.

It was the smallest home in which we had so far lived, even including 'The Poplars' at Mortimer. It was entered through a greenhouse, which led into a spacious tiled hall; but the rooms were small and, as one of the four bedrooms had to be allocated to a resident maid, childlike activities such as building in Meccano had to be done in one of the bedrooms. The garden was interesting. It was long and rather narrow, and led down to a strip of woodland that ringed the original estate of Croslands Park. In the 'Wood', as we called it, there was an attractive fernery containing many unusual plants, while beyond was open country giving a distant view towards the sea. On a clear day one could see right across Morecambe Bay to where the Tower marked the position of Blackpool. It was not until after the war, when the blackout regulations were lifted, that Blackpool showed up as a line of shimmering lights at night. Nearer at hand was

Piel Island, with its ancient castle, and the five chimney stacks of the salt mines at the southern end of Walney Island showed up prominently. All this was to become a pleasant area of exploration in due course. Such was the outlook from the garden of 'Abbey Holme', which remained the family home for the next 14 years.

Having seen the house on that first morning, the next thing was to visit the town and, walking to the end of Croslands Park Road, as it then was, my first sight of one of the Barrow trams was something of a surprise. Instead of the smartly painted, scrupulously clean street-cars of Reading the thing that came along was every inch an essentially utilitarian job. There was evidently no time for such things as cleaning; the frames did not seem straight, and it was driven by a woman. By 1916 we had conductresses on the trams in Reading, but in Barrow there were very few male *drivers* left by that time. The car rattled and swayed its way down the Abbey Road, and so into the town, which I saw at once was built almost entirely on the rectangular plan. It was, of course, a growth of the latter part of the 19th century, and looked, like its trams, wholly utilitarian. Walking towards the bank, to see my father in his new office, I saw a huge tram, carried on two four-wheeled bogies, that excited my curiosity still further. It seemed to be sagging in the middle, and its end platforms tipped down until the 'cow-catcher' device almost touched the ground. I did not have to wait long to find the reason for that peculiar shape.

Just as we were about to leave my father's office the 12-noon hooters sounded. They were more like deep-toned buzzers than the sirens familiar in the South of England; but in a minute or more the street was alive with greatly hurrying men. Some were scorching along on bicycles, others running, but all in haste to get home to lunch. Then came the trams! It would be no exaggeration to say that every square inch of foothold was packed. They were massed like a rush-hour Underground train inside; the open-tops were equally packed, while

Barrow: Island Road station, used for munition workers' specials during the First World War (R. Sankey).

The historic Bury 0-4-0 engine, No 3, Coppernob, *which was enthroned in a glass case at Barrow Central station, is now in the York Railway Museum. It is shown here on exhibition at Carlisle.*

others hung on up the stairways, on the back platforms and even on the fenders outside. No wonder those trams sagged in the middle and dropped at their ends. How the girl conductresses managed to collect any fares I have no idea. One after another they came, some four-wheelers, rocking and swaying more than ever, and then a great bogie car driven by a stout middle-aged matron, who seemed to have friends to greet all along the route. In less than ten minutes, however, this incredible 'rush hour' was over and we were able to board, and get seats, on one of those shop-soiled and battered trams, to return to the Abbey Road terminus and to the monastic-like calm and seclusion of the Furness Abbey Hotel.

As a town Barrow was dull. As a growth of the Victorian era it had no buildings of any architectural interest; but over the tops of the houses there were glimpses of far more exciting things, the great dockside cranes of the shipyard, and it was not long before our rides on the trams went further than the Town Hall. Beyond that large edifice, the main tram route turned a right angle to the right and entered upon the High Level Bridge. This crossed the waterway between the Devonshire and Buccleugh Docks and gave splendid panoramic views of all that was going on in them. When I first rode that way, in the early summer of 1916, some of the great ships that had fought at Jutland were in for repairs, and the sight of shell holes, and steel plating torn like paper, was a most vivid presentation of the tremendous power of naval gunnery. The tram route passed between workshops with no windows or doorways open to the road, and then swung round again in another right angle. Coming into this roadway from the left were standard-gauge railway tracks, with points leading into some of the workshops; while in the opposite direction to which we were travelling was the shipyard station. This was little more than an open platform, but it was from there that workmen's specials were run, morning and evening, to bring in the many men living in the neighbouring towns who commuted daily to 'The Yard'. These trains were made up of old six-wheeled non-corridor stock obtained from the LNWR. The characteristic white upper panels had been painted over, and I was told they were known as 'munition workers' flea boxes'!

Near the end of this public road between various parts of the great Vickers works was the 'shell shop'. The end doors of this were usually open and something of the tremendous activity inside could be glimpsed. Its output of shell cases was colossal. Beyond here the road passed outside the works area and swung round to the left to cross the bridge over the tidal channel on to Walney Island. Until the beginning of the 20th century communication across the water had been by steam ferry. Walney was then a narrow strip of an island, 10 miles long, and was little more than sand dunes; but for the shipyard workers an extensive housing estate called Vickerstown had been developed, and it was then that the bridge was built and the tram route extended on to, and across the island. In 1916 most of Walney was a prohibited area. There were defences against invasion, and against the risk of bombardment from the Irish Sea. At the south end, near to the derelict salt mines, was an extensive gullery, and during the worst days of food rationing in the war, seagull's eggs became something of a delicacy in Barrow. New ships built in Vickers yard were launched into the Walney Channel but, because of its narrowness and the mud banks on the farther shore, the largest ships were launched sideways.

I was fascinated by the view southward from our own garden, because some distance away we could see the southern tip of Walney Island, the ancient ruin of Piel Castle and, occasionally, ships passing up the channel towards the Barrow docks and shipyards. On Roa Island was the village of Piel. A causeway ran out from Rampside to Roa Island, with a road and a single line of railway running alongside. This causeway had, at the time of its origin, been the subject of one of the most amusingly-worded engineering projects I have ever known. A certain Abel Smith sought Parliamentary powers to construct a causeway from Roa Island to the neighbouring island of Great Britain! That single line railway was still being used for a local train service from Piel to Barrow, in 1916; but at one time it had been of quite considerable importance. On Roa Island had been established the rail and steamer terminal of Piel Pier, which was the connecting point for steamers to the Isle of Man and Belfast, before the construction of Ramsden Docks in the Barrow complex. The foreshore at Rampside was only five miles from 'Abbey Holme', and occasionally my father and I would walk it, out and home, on a Sunday morning.

My next area of exploration was the system of railway junctions north of Furness Abbey. This can best be explained to a modern reader by a map (over); but in 1916, with few roads, a few field paths and all set in very hilly country, it was a perplexing business trying to trace out where the various lines led to. I knew the main line from Furness Abbey that led through Dalton-in-Furness, and ultimately to Carnforth, but I was very surprised the first time I saw a heavy freight train coming up what I thought to be a branch line, with its engine pounding hard, and then another engine working equally hard, pushing in rear. It was some little time before I discovered that this was the Barrow avoiding line, used by through freights. Another puzzle was the track of a disused line, from which the rails had been lifted, that diverged from the main line to the south, less than a mile from Furness Abbey. Still more curious was the design of the signal box at what had at one time evidently been a junction—a tall circular

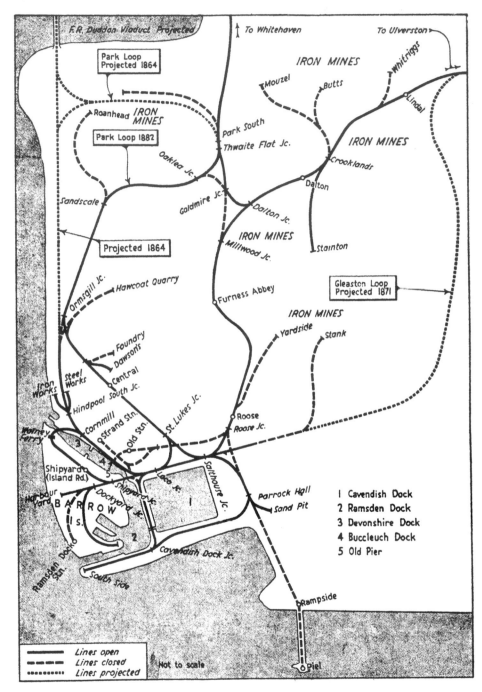

Diagrammatic map, not to scale, of railway development in the neighbourhood of Barrow-in-Furness, showing routes projected, but not built, and lines that have been abandoned.

tower, with a conical pointed roof, that reminded one of a mediaeval watch-tower on the Rhine, rather than an English signal box. As the map shows, however, that disused track had once been part of the original main line of the Furness Railway. As I recall it the conical roofed signal box was still being used as a block post.

Then there was the country on the western side of the peninsula. The ridge west of the Abbey Road was crowned by the little village of Hawcoat, and up there was a small out-look tower. It was a favourite turning point on some of our shorter walks from 'Abbey Holme', and that little tower commanded a magnificent view over the estuary of the Duddon. At low tide it was just one vast expanse of red sand, with the iron-working town of Millom across the water, and the fine mountain, Black Combe, towering up behind. But sloping down to the shore from Hawcoat, perched so elegantly on its height, was a tumbled beckoning countryside, simply asking to be explored, especially in that it seemed to end in a vague, quite depopulated shore of long sandy beaches. So, to this shore also I pointed my bicycle. The intervening lanes were, if anything, narrower and more hazardous; but I eventually found my way to the sand dunes of Roanhead. One had to take it on trust that the place where the lane ended *was* Roanhead, because there was precious little there when one arrived except the dunes, and Roanhead was the name on the signpost!

While these expeditions were made alone, for my sister was not then old enough to ride a bicycle, as a family we explored farther afield by the Furness Railway. In 1916 fares and cheap excursions facilities were little changed from those of peace time, and we visited Windermere and Coniston lakes, and journeyed up the Cumberland coast as far as Seascale and St Bees. In those days there was something very appealing to me about the lonely seashores of the north. They were so different from the sophisticated seaside towns of southern England. St Bees, with a pebbly beach beneath the lofty headland, featured in every geography book of the day, seemed the least attractive and having taken

The Furness Railway steam yacht Lady of the Lake *arriving at Lake Bank pier, at the foot of Coniston Lake.*

Above *Seascale station, destination of wartime holidays, showing a southbound stopping train hauled by 4-4-0, engine No 37* (R. Sankey).

Left *The up evening mail train on the Furness Railway at St Bees. This train, during the First World War, was regularly hauled as far south as Millom by one of the bright green Maryport and Carlisle Railway engines, as in this picture, by 0-4-2, No 15. An M & CR travelling post office van is next to the engine* (R. Sankey).

Below *Miniaturisation of the Eskdale Railway: the Bassett-Lowke 4-4-2 express locomotive* Sans Pareil, *as received at Ravenglass in 1915. This engine is believed to have been first used on an exhibition railway in Norway in 1913 and at that time named* Prins Olaf.

one look at it we headed back to the station and caught the first train back to Seascale. A true appreciation of the remarkable geological formation of the great headland, and the quiet charm of the little village that led uphill from the station came much later in my exploration of the district. Seascale we liked so much that in 1917 and 1918 when holidays further afield were taboo we obtained lodgings and stayed there for several weeks in each summer. Seascale had the added attraction that it was near enough to the Ravenglass and Eskdale Railway to make an occasional excursion possible. But in those explorations during our first summer at Barrow we did not visit that strange and fascinating little line.

The love of geography as a subject, which seems to have been born into me, naturally made visits to places of rare beauty like Windermere and Coniston positive red letter days. It was the first time I had seen real mountains, and that indefinable 'something' that grips all mountaineers and fell-walkers undoubtedly began to take hold of my boyish imagination; and the sight of the Fairfield massif grouped beyond the head of Windermere, of the Langdale Pikes, and of Coniston Old Man, made me impatient to explore deeper into the hill country. But in a day, or sometimes no more than an afternoon, one could not penetrate beyond Ambleside, or Coniston village, and deeper exploration had to wait. There was plenty of incentive to sharpen the keenness of anticipation; because on the railway station bookstalls, and in every stationer's shop there were scores of exquisite picture postcards taken by Abraham's of Keswick, and these I collected as eagerly as I had done the 'F. Moore' coloured cards of locomotives and trains when we lived in Reading. There were coloured cards of scenes in the Lake District, published by the Furness Railway; but in my boyhood I did not appreciate the style of the artist. It was not until ten years later that I became captivated by the work of that great Lakeland artist, A. Heaton Cooper, and avidly collected books containing reproductions of his work.

In the interest and novelty of settling down in a home and surroundings so different from that which I had hitherto known, the unpalatable fact that I should sooner or later have to start school again was pushed into the background. I had left Reading School in the early months of the summer term, and I was delighted to know that my parents did not intend me to restart school until the autumn. But the summer was slipping by. Among our new-found neighbours in Croslands Park there was natural curiosity as to where I should be sent. The nearest Public School was St Bees, but for reasons not vouchsafed to me, this did not seem to be recommended; then one day, a neighbour whose friendliness seemed, to my mother's natural reticence, to be rather excessive, called, and extolled the merits of Giggleswick. To be quite honest none of us had ever heard of it; but the days were slipping by, and my father wrote for information. It meant going there as a boarder, but in view of the scholastic situation in Furness that seemed to my parents inevitable. Having found it on the map, if I *had* to board, Giggleswick seemed no bad place for a railway enthusiast. It was itself on that cross-country line of the Midland that ran eastwards from Carnforth, but it was also relatively near to the Midland main line to Scotland, which I found later ran within sight of the school. We journeyed to Giggleswick, were shown around, and my parents were delighted with all they saw. Arrangements were made for me to start in September. But that was still six weeks or more away, and I returned lightheartedly enough to the various explorations around Barrow.

Looking back on those August and September days of 1916, I can see now that they marked the end of a very definite first phase in my life, a time when the only appreciable and lasting influences were those of my father and mother. I had not been long enough at any one school, kindergarten or otherwise, for teachers to make any lasting impressions, and because we moved house so often then, friends of my childhood were there today and gone tomorrow. Now I write the next few paragraphs in an atmosphere of hindsight, for I was much too young for the significance of it to strike me at the time. I came to appreciate, not so many years later, that not all members of our family shared my own happy interest in those first few months at Barrow, nor indeed of the whole time that we lived at 'Abbey Holme'. My mother was absolutely devoted to us children, and at times lived for little else than our welfare and education; but her outlook on life was based almost entirely on the precepts of her own mother and father, with not infrequent references to her brother (for advice and help), my Uncle Fred who, for many years, held the eminent position of Town Clerk in the City of Bradford. It can thus be well imagined that her Victorianism, for such it certainly was, went against the grain with neighbours, and associates of my father, and in those early years we had few family friends.

She hated Barrow, and just lived for the time when my father might get a transfer to another branch of the bank. Unfortunately there were times when she made little attempt to conceal her disapproval of northern ways. It was lucky that I went away to boarding school so soon, and that little of this rather stiff-necked attitude rubbed off on me, for her influence at times was over-poweringly strong. That her attitude to life was bred from a deep and continuing conviction there is no doubt, and she tried to mould my life and that of my sister in the only pattern she really knew. She encouraged my home-based hobbies to the utmost. Cycling had been a pastime of her own girlhood, and we children rode with her full approval. It was when things began to get slightly unorthodox that friction developed. Nevertheless at this stage in my life I remember her as nothing but a most devoted parent. My father's interest and encouragement was of a more casual kind. He was constantly urging me to study and, in my later school days, felt that my interest in railways was swamping everything else, and would eventually do me no good. But up to the time I went to Giggleswick he had shared, as far as time permitted him, my interest in exploring the country—though he himself never rode a bicycle; we shared an interest in postage stamps, and in books and pictures, though he was at times impatient and over-critical of my early attempts in drawing landscapes and buildings.

My most outspoken critic in those years was my sister, 3½ years my junior, and sceptical of everything I did! She remained at home for the first four years at Barrow, fervently sharing my mother's dislike of it, but nevertheless making quite a few friends of childhood. She, too, came under the strong influence of my mother, at a very impressionable age, and I think her persistent criticism of me was a case of letting off steam. She would not have dared to criticise my mother—or father for that matter; and she found in me someone who would take it. It was good for me too, because she had a most disconcerting way of saying: 'How do you know?', and on countless occasions I had to think hard to justify my statements on this and that. So against this family background the last weeks of August passed in feverish preparation for my departure, and in collecting items for my outfit that were then unusual in our family circle.

Chapter 3

Giggleswick, 1916–1921

My journey to Giggleswick in September 1916 was an occasion of high comedy, although I did not appreciate the very funny side of it until years later. The only school cap that I possessed was that of Reading, and that did not seem appropriate to wear even briefly on my first appearance at my new school. Sunday headgear at Giggleswick was that of a bowler for the winter terms, unless any intrepid souls cared to continue wearing a straw boater, even when there was deep snow on the ground. So to get over the problem of wearing an alien cap on the first day my mother decreed that the obvious course was to wear a bowler. But while a regiment of boys of ages from 8 upwards all wearing bowlers on Sunday was nothing new to the residents of Giggleswick village or of Settle, the sight of a young thing of 11 in a bowler hat sitting demurely in the train beside his mother was too much for two teenage girl passengers. It was a non-corridor carriage so there was no escape. Askance looks and nudges led to giggles; one touched off the other, until before their own journey's end, they were well on the way to hysterics. I can quite imagine what a comic little sight I must have presented that day.

I shall never forget the sense of bewilderment in being left to board at school. Being under 13 years of age I was placed at the junior boarding house, Bankwell, a large stone house with a fine garden in Giggleswick village, and about 10 minutes walk from the main school buildings. There was no segregation so far as lessons were concerned; we all trekked up to the main school daily, and I found myself placed in a class rather above the general average of the Bankwell boys. The master in charge of Bankwell was away on active service in 1916, and in his place we had the school's 'second master', H.M.F. Hammond. In after years I have often reflected upon how much schools, and particularly Giggleswick, have owed to their 'second master'. I am writing at a time when another outstanding second master, L.F. Dutton, has just retired. But to revert to my own years at school, Hammond was one of the first people outside my own family who was to have an appreciable influence on my life. When I first went to Giggleswick he was the kindly housemaster, well enough aware of the feelings of a new boy fresh from home; and I was in his class for Latin. But I learned to know him as one of the very finest types of schoolmaster—he was a classical scholar, a fine cricketer and possessed a very pretty wit and the knack of always turning up at the moment we boys were up to mischief. It was this propensity that earned him his nickname of 'The Little Nipper'. But it was when I had climbed to the Upper Fifth Form, of which he

Nowell House, Giggleswick, July 1921. Immediately behind Ernest Grant, the Housemaster, is P.A. Scott, who subsequently became Senior Partner of the world famous civil engineering firm of Sir William Halcrow & Partners. Fifth from right in the back row is E.J.L. Wooler, subsequently Lord Mayor of Leeds. The author is second from the left (seated row).

was Form Master, and I was sitting for the School Certificate, that I came to realise to the full his skill and charm as a teacher.

The Headmaster, Robert N. Douglas, I found a strange character; as a new boy I looked to him with a degree of respect, but it was a respect due more to his position than to his actions. He took the junior French set that I was in, and in spells of oral translation if a boy was stuck for a word, and went silent, he was immediately branded as a coward. It was an insidious form of bullying, which had a contrary effect; for once outside the class we delighted in calling each other cowards! In later years 'Bob', as we called him, lost our respect in more lasting ways. In retrospect one could have every sympathy with him in his administrative difficulties during the war years, for a number of his best masters had been called up, and substitutes were hard to obtain. One who did step into the breach was Hammond's wife. She was a tall and extremely handsome woman, with a brilliant science degree, but from my point of view she was more successful as a private tutor than as a class teacher. She taught 'science' to the most junior boys taking that subject and my father kept, for many years after, a school report in which I was listed as 'rock bottom' of the whole school in science. But my parents were more concerned about my first 'maths' report— *Very weak.* The master who took the set to which I was assigned was one of the wartime stand-ins. He was a distinguished looking old gentleman with a long-flowing beard. We called him 'Noah'. In all probability he was a skilled mathematician, but towards the teaching of a class of high-spirited youngsters he had not a clue. I am afraid his lessons were regarded as something of a rag. To supply the deficiencies so far as my own education was concerned, my parents arranged for me to have private coaching from Mrs Hammond, and she certainly set me on the right road.

The last of the staff to be mentioned at this stage was the music master, who

was then away on active service; but his name was printed on the school list as
A. Claughton, FRCO, and the name excited the imagination of this young 'man
with a rail track mind'. It was not until later, when he returned to school and I
began music lessons, that I learned the significance of his name; but having
returned to railways, it is time for a digression, away from purely scholastic
affairs. Bankwell had a small, but adequately stocked library. Many of the
books were of exciting, but entirely wholesome, adventure; but a few years
previously a former pupil had died and his parents had presented his own books
to Bankwell by way of a memorial. These included a number of the then-latest
books on railways, including the two bound volumes of W.J. Gordon's part-
work, *Our Home Railways*. I soon discovered the boys who were interested in
railways, and within the little group allegiance seemed to be equally divided
between the Midland and the Lancashire and Yorkshire. Adherents of the last
named were mostly those who lived in towns like Accrington, Burnley, Padiham
and so on, while the Midland fans came from Leeds and Bradford. There was
little support for the LNWR and, as for the Great Western, it was practically
unheard of. When partisanship reached its height, and I was asked which side I
was going to support, I was much tempted to reply: 'A plague on both your
houses', and to play my trump card in the locomotive line, *The Great Bear*.
Unfortunately the north country boys needed not a little convincing that such an
engine really existed; but the pages of *Our Home Railways* came surely to my
rescue!

Giggleswick was a 'rugger' school and at Bankwell, playing entirely with boys
of my own age and weight, I soon began to enjoy the game, and memories of
those purgatorial afternoons at Marlborough House faded into the background.
We played twice a week, except on those days when there was a school match,
and then Bankwell, like everyone else not in the 'XV', was under orders to
watch, and cheer. The principal school playing fields, for rugger at any rate,
were on level ground beside a lane that led from the village to the station; but on
the far side was a very steep and high bank that formed a natural grand stand.
The boys from the main school were massed along the touch line, but Bankwell,
decreed to remain in splendid isolation out of lesson times, used to occupy the
top of this bank, and incidentally have a superb view of the game. Looked at
from above one could begin to appreciate the finer points of attack and defence,
far better than when involved personally in the rough and tumble.

But there were other things that some of us looked forward to seeing from
that highly elevated viewpoint. Early in the afternoon the eyes of one or two of
us suddenly strayed from the dog-fight in progress immediately below, for,
across the valley, the down Scotch Express went thundering through Settle
station. I found out many years later that it was the 9.30 am from St Pancras to
Glasgow, and it was always worked by one of the handsome '999' Class 4-4-0s.

There was a second master attached to Bankwell, socially as it were. He had a
room in the village, and took his meals with us. His personality was as striking
as his queer appearance. Sydney Harris Kenwood taught modern languages,
and was a widely travelled and well read man. In stature he was bulky rather
than athletic, and being exceedingly short sighted he wore enormously thick
glasses. I regret to add that our name for him was 'Bleary Bill'! At free periods
he would enthrall us with tales of adventure, and the whole of Bankwell would
gather round in rapt attention. I believe these yarns were of his own
composition, though to outward appearances he would have seemed the most

unlikely author for such stirring tales, being himself about the most un-athletic man imaginable.

That small library at Bankwell included another volume that gripped my attention—*The Boy's Book of Locomotives* by the Rev J.R. Howden. It was profusely illustrated and gave me a wider introduction to the locomotives that ran on railways that I had not yet seen. I must admit that in my early days at Giggleswick there must have been many times when homesickness possessed me, as I suppose it did to most boys boarding away from home, and it is of the journeys to and from home that I retain the clearest memories. These, it is true, amounted to no more than three in each direction in most of the years I was at school; but then there were holiday visits to boys who lived elsewhere, and when the war was over the family began to move further afield in my father's annual leave from the bank. Looking back on the five years I was at Giggleswick I feel that I was very fortunate in seeing the northern railways at an extremely interesting and historic time.

During term time we boarders had very little free time, and on Sundays in the hour or so between morning chapel and lunch there were no trains to be seen either on the Settle and Carlisle main line, or on the line through Giggleswick. After the war on those Sunday mornings many boys used to make for the Kendal road to watch the cars of those days, and vintage motor-cycles, struggling up the steep gradient to the crest of Buckhaw Brow. For my own part I found it rather dull. I was not car-minded in those far-off days. At Sunday lunch our house-master, Ernest Grant, would often ask how we had enjoyed our morning 'inhaling petrol'! The ambition of many boys was to own their own motor bike and, very often after leaving school, they would take the first opportunity of riding back under their own power, and showing off what Nipper Hammond in his dry humorous way once referred to as 'the new toy'! The favourite circuit was to climb the extremely steep hill between the school buildings and the gatehouse to the chapel field, and then to make a noisy perambulation of the path that led to the cricket pavilion.

Stepping aside from locomotion for a moment, no old Giggleswickian could recall, with anything but bursting pride, the utterly magnificent school chapel bequeathed by the millionaire governor, Walter Morrison, to celebrate the Diamond Jubilee of the reign of Queen Victoria. Morrison, a bluff old Yorkshireman who lived in a mansion on the high moors east of Settle, by Malham Tarn, was a widely travelled man, and most of the building materials were imported from far overseas, notably the pink stone which forms the main fabric of the building. The dome, in copper, had not weathered to any great extent when I was at school, only 20 years after the chapel was built; but it is now, as Morrison no doubt envisaged it, a brilliant green. The stained glass of the windows is superb, though the decoration at the east end, above the altar, was severely plain. I had not appreciated the significance of this until some years after I had left school, and I went back with my great friend, 'Tubby' Clayton, the Founder Padre of Toc H, who was to preach at matins next morning. He was a high churchman, and I shall not forget the shock with which he first saw that very plain east end. But as I then realised, and I hope he did too, anything more elaborate, or sectarian, would have been inappropriate in a school chapel in which boys of all religious denominations were taught to worship.

The year 1917 opened with some of the most prolonged severe weather I had yet experienced in my young life. Even in Barrow the snow lay on the ground

Giggleswick: the magnificent school chapel, gift of the multi-millionaire governor, Walter Morrison, in commemoration of the Diamond Jubilee of Queen Victoria's reign.

from Christmas to Easter, and at Giggleswick, with wartime scarcity of fuel for heating, things were a bit grim at times. At voluntary woodwork we made sledges, and careered up and down the slopes in the Bankwell garden, while at one time the ice was so firm as to induce the headmaster to grant the school a skating half-holiday and convey us all in horse-drawn vehicles to the lake at Wigglesworth, three or four miles away to the south of the railway. As term-end approached, however, I learned that at home my sister was ill with influenza, and it was arranged that I should spend the first part of the holidays with my Uncle and Aunt in Harrogate, where, incidentally it was colder than ever, except that their home was very comfortably heated.

Although I was then no more than 12 years old I cannot remember having any qualms about finding my way by train to Harrogate, unaided. After term-end chapel, with other boys bound for homes in the West Riding towns, I dashed down to Giggleswick station to catch the first eastbound train, which left soon after 8 am. This was the Morecambe to Bradford 'residential', which at one time carried one of the famous 'club' carriages. So far as I can remember it was the only Midland service to do so, but at one time they were very popular on the Lancashire and Yorkshire, from Manchester to both Blackpool and Southport, and on the LNWR from Manchester to Llandudno. One had to be a member of the travelling 'club' to ride in one of these cars, which had an attendant who served drinks and other refreshments. On the early morning Bradford train those of us who were bound for Leeds had to change at Shipley. We did not have to wait long before a London express came in, and we finished that part of the journey in what was then the luxury of a corridor train.

At that time engines working on the Midland north-west from Leeds were a very mixed lot. The Scotch Expresses were mostly worked by the Class '4' '999' 4-4-0s, but other than that we had the beautiful Johnson 2-4-0s, often working in pairs on the Morecambe trains and rebuilt Class '2' 4-4-0s. Some of these were of the Fowler superheated series, but many were in the intermediate stage of rebuild, with large non-Belpaire, non-superheated boilers. At Hellifield shed, and we saw them on various activities, were some of the very beautiful unrebuilt Johnson 4-4-0s. The ever-famous Midland three-cylinder compounds, of which

Midland in the North Country: Edinburgh and Glasgow to Manchester express approaching Aisgill summit, hauled by rebuilt non-superheater, 6 foot 6 inch 4-4-0, No 442 and 2-4-0, No 253. Wild Boar Fell makes an impressive background (R.J. Purves).

there were then only 45, were rare birds in the north. The first time I ever saw one was on an occasion I am not likely to forget. It was in 1919, and I was being taken into Leeds for an operation for appendicitis. My mother and I caught the up afternoon Scotch Express at Hellifield, and our engine was No 1003, looking very shabby as I remember it.

Reverting, however, to that trip to Harrogate, two years earlier, I was charmed by my first sights of North Eastern locomotives. From my 'F. Moore' postcards I knew that they were green, but the colour rendering was varied and led me to expect something considerably darker than what I eventually saw in Leeds, a truly beautiful pale leaf green—like trees in their fresh spring foliage; and all so marvellously *clean*. On the Midland at that time one rarely saw an engine in really spanking condition. Most of them looked travel stained, if not exactly dirty; but the North Eastern trains were an absolute joy to behold. I remember, however, being puzzled and a bit alarmed on that first journey to Harrogate, on which I had a non-corridor compartment to myself, and was feeling a bit lonely, having said goodbye to my school friends. I thought the train was going the wrong way!

I should explain however that this was not my first visit to Harrogate. Shortly after moving into our new home at Barrow, to ease the job of settling in for my parents, it was arranged that my sister and I should spend a fortnight with my uncle and aunt in Harrogate. My mother took us by train as far as Skipton, and there my aunt and the chauffeur were waiting with the car to complete the journey by road. It gave me my first experience of a really wild North Country road over the Blubberhouse Moor. But while staying in Harrogate we would often take an evening drive to Otley to meet the Midland train by which my uncle travelled home from Bradford. I was intrigued by the rather complicated railway geography of the area and saw that trains from Leeds came up through

Bramhope Tunnel, of which I had an 'F. Moore' postcard. Consequently, when my train, allegedly for Harrogate, started off eastbound from Leeds, and passed an enormous engine shed (Neville Hill) I began to wonder just where on earth we were going to. Remember, I was alone in that compartment! But then we stopped at a station called Crossgates; a porter shouted 'Harrogate train', and I relaxed. We were taking the Wetherby route, of which at that time I knew nothing. I cannot remember any of the engine types I saw on that first trip on the North Eastern Railway, except that they were all rather small. There were no 'Atlantics', or 4-6-0s, of which I had read about in J.R. Howden's book in the Bankwell library.

Apart from this one lonesome expedition I used the Midland station in Leeds, the 'Wellington'. From its platforms I could see the goings and comings of London and North Western trains at the western end of the big joint station just alongside. By then, despite memories of the Great Western in Reading, I was an out-and-out North Western fan, and I eagerly spotted 'George the Fifth' and 'Prince of Wales' Class engines at Leeds, though from the outermost ends of the Wellington platforms they were too far away for even my young eyes to read their names. I think my allegiance had been swung from the Great Western to the North Western in 1913, when some of the autumn issues of *The Railway Magazine*, unusually well illustrated with Mackay photographs, included pictures of the first 'Claughtons'; and although I realised they were black there was a 'something' about them that took my youthful fancy. Very many years later I was to write enthusiastically of their work and still more recently to meet some of the surviving members of their great designer's family.

A pre-war service discontinued afterwards: the morning Leeds–Lake District express, which ran via Giggleswick and Ingleton, joining the LNWR main line at Low Gill. The train, here seen hauled by a rebuilt, non-superheater, 7 foot 0 inch 4-4-0, No 360, is taking water at Tebay troughs.

Leeds–Glasgow and Edinburgh express approaching Helwith Bridge, just north of the Stainforth Gorge, hauled by a 2-4-0, piloting one of the famous Midland compounds. The second vehicle in the train is a through Lancashire and Yorkshire coach from Manchester (J. Maynard Tomlinson).

In my school-time journeys, of course, Carnforth was the station to see the North Western *in excelsis*. For everything except locomotives, however, it was the last station on earth at which to linger. Grimy, draughty, devoid of any architectural pretentions, it was just a place where one changed trains, and left as quickly as possible! With two other Giggleswickians who lived at Barrow I used to travel back at the end of the holidays on a train that left about 5 pm. It involved quite a long wait at Carnforth before the connecting Midland train departed; but for me there was always one supreme thrill—the passage of the down 'Corridor'. Even on its most decelerated wartime schedule it was still made up of the magnificent 12-wheeled coaches that were exclusive to this train, but apart from coaches there was, for me, the breathtaking spectacle of its passage. There was a bell on the platform, the ringing of which announced the approach of a train that did not stop at the station. The signals were lowered, the bell began ringing continuously, and then the 'Corridor' came tearing through, always hauled by a 'Claughton'. I do not suppose that in those days the speed would have been much over 60 mph; but in the confined space, with the accoustical accompaniments, the sensation to a teenage boy was terrific!

At school, while my childish ambition to be a locomotive engineer was tempered to the extent of aiming more generally for something to do with railways, my inborn love of geography made me appreciate how supremely fortunate I was to be at school in such sublime mountain country. I will not pretend that full appreciation came at once, or even when I was nearing the end of my years at Giggleswick; but not many years after I had left school, and was

Midland through Giggleswick: a Leeds-bound express climbing the bank between Bentham and the moorland Clapham Junction. The engine, No 311, is a very historic survival for, although S.W. Johnson built 263 of these very elegant 4-4-0s between 1877 and 1900, it was only the first two batches of 1877 that were not subsequently rebuilt out of all recognition. Those with 7 foot coupled wheels, of which No 311 is one, were still in regular use on the line through Giggleswick until they were more than 50 years old. Some of them were used as pilots to the Scotch expresses between Hellifield and Aisgill summit.

feeling my way as a spare-time freelance journalist, I contributed an occasional article on topographical subjects to the motoring papers. I had to be careful about authorship because my immediate boss at Westinghouse, as will be told in more detail later, could not abide anything being credited to any of his staff. If he had realised any member of his staff was writing articles, however far removed from ordinary business, it would have been quite in his nature to appeal to higher authority to have the activity stopped. So I juggled my name and initials to produce a *nom de plume*, not so neatly as my Uncle Lawrence had done in producing 'Elfin', but these topographical articles were written under the name of 'C.K. Stevens'. Looking through my book of cuttings it would seem that one of them could well have passed as a summary of the places we rambled and scrambled to in our free time at Giggleswick. I titled it 'The Call of the Hill Country', and it opened: 'The extreme north-west of the West Riding of Yorkshire contains some of the highest and wildest country in England. From the mountain mass centred round the three great peaks of the Pennines, rivers flow in all directions . . .'

At that time Giggleswick was a school definitely orientated towards the classics. In addition to the Headmaster and Nipper Hammond there were two other masters who were experts in Latin, if not in Greek. Looking back on some of my contemporaries it would seem that many of them had careers ensured for them in prosperous family businesses, and did not need school-learning to be necessarily the foundation for making a career of their own. As one grew older and came to know something of their family background, one could appreciate that it did not matter much whether the 'art of learning' was acquired in the classics, modern languages, or science. And in the higher forms the art of learning could be absorbed very thoroughly at Giggleswick. I remember, nevertheless, the row there was at home when I had reached the level when a third language was to be added to my syllabus. All boys from the most junior upwards took Latin and French as a matter of course; but then it came to a choice of Greek or German. The war was then at a grim and critical stage, and I shall not forget my father's indignation at anyone wanting to learn 'that filthy language'—as he put it. But for me it was 'Hobson's choice', with my future career in mind; and I am glad that it was so. Classic Greek, though fascinating in its calligraphy alone, and equally so in the history it revealed, would have been useless to me in the future.

In quite lowly forms we got our first introduction to Shakespeare. We were fortunate in having a form master in A.H. Montagu who could make it *live*, and could make us feel the true comedy of *Twelfth Night*. He was a comedian in himself, too, who had temporarily taken over the house mastership of Shute while E.D. Clark, 'The Bear', was on active service. It so happened that 'Monty' and I both developed appendicitis at the same time, and both were taken to the same nursing home in Leeds for the operation, and were both under the care of that great surgeon who was afterwards raised to the peerage as Lord Moynihan, of Leeds. 'Monty' was done first, and was just becoming convalescent when I had barely passed the stage of 'coming round'. Very soon notes began to arrive from his room, hilarious perversions of the school rules, which would have sent me into fits of laughter, had not the healing of my wound not made laughing such a painful process. Soon he came to see me, and although I was then no more than 14 years old, and in his form at school, we had some merry half hours, before duty called him back to school.

The Easter holidays were just at hand so I did not return to school until the summer term. Before leaving the care of the nursing home I was encouraged to go for increasingly long walks, and needless to say one day found me at a railway station—Central this time, where the Great Northern, and Lancashire and Yorkshire trains came in. While in the nursing home I had a batch of the 1918 and 1919 numbers of *The Railway Magazine* to browse over, and in the variety of photographs and articles I was able to get fairly established in my mind the locomotive workings of most of the British main line railways. I studied the articles of Cecil J. Allen avidly, and began to form assessments in my own mind as to the relative merits of many well-known locomotive types. On visiting the Central station at Leeds I was disappointed to find that the mid-afternoon London express on the Great Northern was hauled by a big 4-4-0, and not an 'Atlantic'.

Back at school for the summer term I learned, not for the last time in my life, that the aftermath of a major surgical operation can have some lingering effects; and I had a bad first month. But there was every need to pull myself into normal line once more, because the ensuing school year beginning in September 1919 was the lead-up to School Certificate in the following summer. School learning was taking on a more serious form, and I was certainly not at my best in the summer of 1919. On the other hand it was the first year since the outbreak of war that my father could take his proper holiday and, with the return of peace, my mother was anxious to take us to an East Coast resort that she had enjoyed very much with her own parents many years previously—Bridlington. For my own part, and except in one respect, I found it rather dull, especially for a whole month.

Bridlington was a typical English seaside resort of the late Victorian and Edwardian age. The 'front' was in two parts, separated by the picturesque fishing harbour. On the north side was the rather 'grand' Royal Princes Parade, and on the south side the Spa. Both had resident orchestras that played every evening, but the Princes Parade on a fine Sunday morning presented an incredible sight. Seating along the sea wall was continuous, and every inch of space was occupied, while on the 'parade' itself, folks of all ages, all in their Sunday best, marched sedately up and down. On the Princes Parade it seemed that on Sundays at any rate collars and ties were *de rigeur* for the men often, however, backed up by immaculate white flannel trousers, while the variety in ladies' hats . . .! After a few visits to the Princes Parade we found the Spa more congenial. The orchestra there was conducted by a man who later became a household name with Radio listeners, as the leader of the Gershom Parkington quintette. We spent many evenings at the Spa listening to the pleasant light music he dispensed. I must admit, however, that I frequently looked beyond the sophisticated promenades of Bridlington to the wild, appealing Flamborough cliffs to the north and wished I could explore them as I did the country round Giggleswick. I have told elsewhere how I broke away from parental gaze and found my way to the locomotive running sheds, and how even a little 'box' camera proved a passport to an invitation 'over the fence' and on to the tracks; but my earliest adventures in photography were hardly propitious.

For some reason my parents first presented me with a little box camera of the Ensign type, instead of the more usual Kodak 'Brownie', and it was a disaster. I had it during the summer term of 1919 at school, and had no success with it. The shop where it was bought seemed to have some interest in Ensign products generally, emphasising the importance of using Ensign film, which at Bridlington was impossible to obtain. With the camera itself virtually a 'write-off' mechanically we substituted a standard 'Brownie' with excellent results, except for one catastrophic occasion in the school dark room at Giggleswick. Two of us photographic enthusiasts decided to make use of a little free time by developing some films. Developer and hypo were duly made up, and the light extinguished. But in the dim illumination provided by the little red lamp the dishes got mixed up, and my friend's film, already developed went in a second time, while mine went into the hypo. Only when his film was going blacker and blacker, and nothing at all was appearing on mine was the extent of the disaster realised!

The year leading up to the School Certificate examination in the summer of 1920 was, scholastically, the most interesting so far, at Giggleswick, because of the deepening insight into the beauty and fascination of English literature. As Form Master of '5A' Nipper Hammond took us for English, and while a Shakespearean comedy had been great fun with 'Monty', *The Tempest* with Nipper was altogether more revealing. Our second English book, for the examination, was the Essays of Addison, again delightful, beginning with the inimitable stories of Sir Roger de Coverley, as published in the earliest issues of *The Spectator*. Hammond's rare wit and sense of fun was never more vividly displayed than in the way he led us through those famous essays, and how he drew out our own appreciation of them in some of the subjects he set for our week-end essays. One, was to write in the Addison style, 'Sir Roger at the Pictures', and what he thought of Charlie Chaplin. I can still chuckle over the book, liberally marked with my school-time annotations.

One of the masters returning from war service in 1919 was the senior music master, A. Claughton. My own efforts on the piano were never very serious, but I always had an ear for music, and my parents had arranged for me to have lessons, more with the idea of being able to play light music than to take it up seriously, as it was hoped that my young sister would do. For a time I played the piano of the school chaplain, the Rev W. Byron-Scott, whose tuition was for a hobby rather than serious music playing. When Claughton returned to school and was taking up his duties once again, as a music pupil of a sort I had to report to him, and in his cottage over the piano was intrigued to see a splendid framed photograph of the LNWR engine *Sir Gilbert Claughton.* A few discrete enquiries brought out that he was a keen locomotive enthusiast himself, and that he was a nephew of the LNWR Chairman, after whom the engine was named. He himself was a Fellow of the Royal College of Organists, and used occasionally to delight us with his performances on the organ in 'Big School'. His particular friend among the masters was Ernest Grant, my own house-master, and he always came with Nowell House on our Ascension Day excursions. Several times I was able to engage him in chat on railway topics.

I passed through the School Certificate examination, and duly advanced to the Sixth Form in September 1920. 'Bob' himself was of course form master, and our English books were *King Lear* and, by way of utter contrast, the plays of Sheridan. Bob had, to me, a particularly interesting way of taking us through a play. To each of us boys was allocated a character to read, and entrances and exits were signalised by our rising from, or resuming our seats. While *King Lear* was grim, and Bob was expert in hammering home the tragedy that lay behind every line, we all enjoyed *The School for Scandal*, and still more the rumbustious language of some of the characters in *The Rivals.* Our third English book was *The Iliad of Homer*, 'done into English prose' as the sub-title expressed it. We got as much amusement from the quaint literal translations of battle-pieces as we did from Sheridan, and one boy wrote a clever parody in its style describing a rugger match, featuring prominently several well-known members of the Giggleswick first XV, thinly disguised by Iliadesque variations of their names and football attributes. It was published at term-end in the *Giggleswick Chronicle;* but while all of us currently in the Sixth Form enjoyed it hugely, it is to be feared it did not mean much to the rest of the school.

The Christmas term of 1920 really marked the end of what could be called the 'settled' period of my time at Giggleswick. Most boys entering the Sixth Form were expected to stay for at least two years more, preparing to take Higher Certificate as a prelude to University entrance at Oxford or Cambridge. But in our case family funds did not run to such an extending of my general education, and it was vaguely intended, at the end of 1920, that I should go for an engineering degree at one of the non-resident universities, though at term-end at Christmas the realities of the situation had not begun seriously to loom up. Time, however, was beginning to run out.

Chapter 4

The broadening scene, 1921–1924

The year 1921 opened with uncertainties on every hand. While it was generally agreed that I should aim for a career in engineering, preferably to do with railways, there were few ideas in our family circle as to how one would set about it. Among our friends in Barrow there was only one thought, an apprenticeship at 'The Yard'. Already, however, the wartime boom at Vickers was over, and we knew of young men who had completed their apprenticeships and were just turned on to the streets. Then, I cannot remember quite how, my parents met a lady whose son was at the City and Guilds (Engineering) College in London, and who strongly recommended it. We obtained a prospectus, and decided to go for it. It seemed a more logical step to go from school to continue ones academic studies, and get a degree in engineering, rather than embark on an apprenticeship, and confine theory to evening classes. Not being very bright we all felt this latter would put a heavy strain on my capacity. With the City and Guilds in view I was registered for the London Matriculation Examination, in June, and thereby incurred the deep and lasting displeasure of Bob Douglas. He was one of that generation of headmasters who held the view that a degree at Cambridge or Oxford, preferably in the classics, was the only worthwhile 'entrée' to any profession.

At the start of the Easter holidays I went to Leeds to stay with John Moore's family for a week. From his home at Chapel Allerton near Leeds, we cycled to Arthington, to watch the trains, to Bolton Abbey and someway up Wharfedale to the Strid to enjoy the lovely river scenery, and also to York. We didn't have much luck with the trains there because, encumbered with our bicycles, we could not go on to the station. There was a coal strike on at the time, and train services were much disrupted. When the time came for me to go home to Barrow the train we had looked out was cancelled, and I had a long wait at Leeds for the first one that was going to Carnforth. Back at Giggleswick after the holidays, the probability that I would be leaving school only a year after taking the School Certificate introduced uncertainties in other ways. I could not be considered for a praeposter for the autumn term of 1921, nor as a possible NCO in the Corps. Of course I might not pass London Matriculation, and so have to return to school in September. That would be just too bad. Then, at the start of the summer term the uncertainty as to whether I was leaving or not, led to my not receiving an invitation, extended to other boys who were definitely leaving, to attend a talk about Toc H, which, in the event, came to play a big part in the next dozen years of my life.

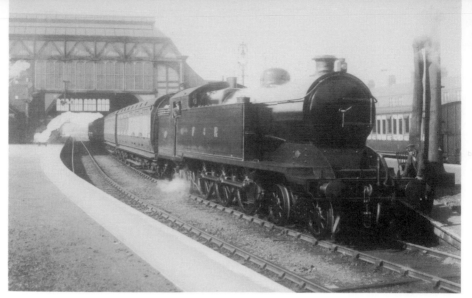

Furness Railway: one of the new 4-6-4 tank engines of 1921 on an up stopping train (LNWR stock) at Barrow Central station (R. Sankey).

In travelling to and from Birmingham which was the most convenient place for me to sit for the London Matric examination my mother and I had ample experience of what a disrupted train service can involve. The coal strike was still on, and it was when we got to Crewe, and had to change there that we really struck it—17 passengers in a non-corridor compartment! I have no idea of the type of engine that hauled us. In Birmingham we stayed at a small commercial hotel fairly near to New Street station, which was convenient for the tram route that ran out to the University, at Selly Oak, but which also gave me some opportunities for exploring the dark recesses of New Street station. The London expresses were hauled by 'George the Fifth' Class 4-4-0s, and at the north end I found a very resplendent 'Experiment', No 902 *Combermere*, well placed for photography. But my principal recollection of those early walks round New Street was of a Midland Class '2' superheater 4-4-0. It was a type with which I was familiar enough up in Yorkshire, but this one was oil fired. I chatted up the driver, and he was not amused. I remember with what apprehension he emphasised that oil firing was 'too explosive' for his liking. Of the hazards and delays on our return journey to Barrow the less said the better, except that the long wait at Crewe gave me an opportunity to see the up day Irish Mail come in, change engines, and leave for the south behind a very smart new unnamed 'Claughton', No 808. Five years later this engine, still bearing her original LNWR number was to earn special distinction by making one of the finest runs ever, from Stafford to Euston, by an engine of her class.

Back at school for the last month of the summer term the air of uncertainty only increased. Even if I had passed the London Matric two supplementary papers were required to gain me access to the City and Guilds College, namely in more advanced maths and geometrical drawing. The school curriculum provided for the first named, but for the second I had to work on my own. Bob Douglas could not have cared less, but fortunately I had every support from Ernest Grant and Philip Haswell, though neither of them could do much in the way of direct tuition for the future. Haswell's support, as senior science master was very encouraging. He used to call me 'The Professor', and several times said he thought I would do well in engineering. The term's end drew near with my still not knowing whether I should be returning in the autumn; and one day Grant asked, if I did go to London where would I live? It was strange, but neither my parents nor I seemed to have given any serious thought to this. Everything had been concentrated on passing the London Matric. Grant said at once: 'Go to Toc H'. He then gave me some literature outlining the aims and objects of that movement, which I took home with me at the end of the term; my father and mother swooped on to it, as providing the Heaven-sent answer to a problem that had been at the back of their minds, but until then subjugated to the prime objective of passing London Matric. My father wrote to Toc H headquarters for more information, and within days it became of immediate concern, when we learned that I had passed the vital examination.

I can appreciate my parents' concern at the prospect of their rather 'green' son, not yet 17, being pitchforked into the life of London; but residence at a Toc H 'Mark', however sheltered an existence it may have offered, involved certain obligations, and during the summer holidays I read of the wartime origin of Talbot House, and what its aims and objects were in peacetime. The war had ended less than three years earlier, and I was too young to appreciate the horrors of the Ypres Salient; but I was not too young to sense that in the Founder Padre, the utterly inimitable 'Tubby' Clayton, there was a personality that towered above any master that I had so far met in my school life. He was not only an outstanding cleric, and a great Christian gentleman, but he had a sense of humour that would capture the heart of any man, or woman, regardless of their estate. Who but Tubby would have put a notice on a wall in the original Talbot House, in Poperinghe reading: 'If you are accustomed to spitting on the carpet at home please spit here'!

But Tubby also was an accomplished writer, and before drafting this chapter I took down once again from one of my bookshelves *Tales of Talbot House*, which he wrote some years afterwards to help raise funds for the post-war Toc H movement. It is a little classic, in its charm, its pathos, in the simple beauty of the telling of how Talbot House came to be. Thus of Poperinghe, its birthplace, he wrote:

'Alone free for years among Belgian towns, close enough to the line to be directly accessible to the principal sufferers, and not so near as to be positively ruinous, it became metropolitan not by merit but by the logic of locality. In migrant and mobile times, its narrow and uneven streets filled and foamed with a tide-race of transport. Year in, year out, by night and by day, the fighting troops, with all the blunter forces behind that impel and sustain their operations, set east and west, with that rhythm of fluctuation that stationary war induces. Until the great switch road was opened, and the railway track was doubled, every man and every mule (whether on four legs or closely packed in a blue "bully beef" tin) came up by one pair of rails or one narrow street'.

I must not dwell upon my own first impressions and experience of life in Mark I. The men living there in the autumn of 1921 were a greatly assorted crowd. Some had not long previously been demobilised; others were students like myself; we were all of many different disciplines and of different ages. Although a brave attempt was made to sustain the spirit of service that had emulated Talbot House, it was not easy in peacetime, among men young and old who had their own affairs to shape, by some indeed who had to reconcile the restlessness and uncertainty of their life in the trenches to civilian standards, in a topsy-turvy world. The obligation that Toc H put upon its members to undertake some form of voluntary social service struck men in various ways, sometimes unwillingly, sometimes as how one could get by with a minimum. Most of us fit youngsters took up the challenge of helping in boy's clubs, some in very unsalubrious parts of the London slums. Not all of these were run with the efficiency and understanding of the Oxford and Bermondsey Club, and some of us had rather grilling experiences.

In 1921 Mark I was at 23 Queens Gate Gardens, less than ten minutes walk from Imperial College, and I was very interested to find among the hostellers, men in the 2nd, 3rd and 4th year at the City and Guilds, and all were old boys of Christ's Hospital, Horsham—known affectionately by every boy of that famous school as 'Housey'. Naturally we were drawn together, on my part as having a glimpse of what my own studies would involve as the years passed; but I was even more interested in the extent they had been prepared for an engineering degree course even *before* leaving school. At 'Housey', where I believe the classics were equally encouraged, there was a strong engineering branch, in which boys received sufficient technical training to enable them to take the Inter BSc at school, and start at the City and Guilds in the Second Year. I thought back rather wistfully to my old headmaster at Giggleswick, on the last Speech Day I attended, decrying publicly the folly of taking 'Matriculation for this, Matriculation for that'—as he sarcastically put it—when a classics degree at one of the older universities would give you an unparalleled start in any profession. Oh sweet simplicity! I began at the City and Guilds a year behind a boy of roughly my own age from Christ's Hospital.

Work in the first year did not involve much in the way of evening study, and between college closing time at 5 pm and evening meal at Mark I, I began to explore the London railway stations. Paddington was no more than a pleasant evening walk across the Park; but the Great Western engines were still in their plain wartime green, and the only train worth seeing in that period was an express for Birkenhead. The famous 'two-hour' Birmingham schedules had just been restored, on certain trains; but there was nothing much coming in on the up side. Marylebone was much more exciting. The Great Central was one of those few railways that maintained their pre-war livery throughout the war—not only so, but both passenger and freight engines continued to be superbly turned out. The 6.20 pm express to Bradford was always worked by an 'Atlantic', one of the most beautiful passenger classes ever to run in Great Britain. The train ran non-stop to Leicester, via High Wycombe, but it carried two separate slip portions. The first of these was detached at Finmere, and was then worked forward to provide an excellent evening service from London to Helmdon, and Culworth. The second was slipped at Woodford, and went on by the branch line to Stratford-on-Avon.

The Bradford express, which the Great Central handed over to the Lancashire and Yorkshire Railway at Sheffield, was followed by a semi-fast which was usually hauled by one of the very impressive four-cylinder 4-6-0 mixed traffic engines, then painted black, with smart red lining out. Then, before stepping it out smartly across the Park, to be in time for evening meal, there was just time to see the 2.15 pm from Manchester come in, at 6.38 pm. On this train the engine and its crew worked through from Manchester and it was always hauled by one of the later Robinson engines, either a 'Director' Class 4-4-0 or one of the big 4-6-0s. These latter were either of the inside-cylindered 'Sir Sam Fay' Class, or a four-cylinder engine of the 'Lord Faringdon' type. Opinions would naturally differ, but to my eye these big Great Central 4-6-0s were among the most impressive engines working into London in that autumn of 1921. A chance conversation with a fellow student at the Guilds one day revealed that he too was an ardent GCR enthusiast, and thus my lifelong friendship with Harry MacGregor Pearson began.

With my own aspirations unshakably set on a career in some form of railway engineering, I studied the prospectus of the fourth year in which I noted that Sir Philip Dawson was the special visiting lecturer on railway electrification. I was not particularly keen on this at the time, but Sir Philip was consulting engineer to the London Brighton and South Coast Railway, and it was not long before my evening walks took me to Victoria. From *The Railway Magazine* I was familiar with the Brighton steam locomotives, and I saw in the flesh many types that I knew only from photographs; but what impressed me more than anything else was the tremendous intensity of the service into and out of the station. Of course 5.30 pm was one of the busiest times of the day, but even so, it was terrific. And at the time really very little of it was electric! It was then only the South London line, through Peckham Rye to London Bridge that was electrified. The extensions to the Brighton 'elevated' system did not come until later. It was not until I reached the fourth year at the City and Guilds that I met Sir Philip Dawson himself, and listened to his lectures on electric traction. I fear that on looking over my old notes they were a strong advocacy of his own system of single-phase AC at 6,600 volts. The rivals were treated rather summarily!

Of eminent men, we, in Toc H, had many opportunities of hearing some of them on very intimate grounds. Each week during the winter months the Marks had a guest night. During the war years in Poperinghe, Tubby's magnetic personality brought many celebrities, who were on active service, into Talbot

London Brighton and South Coast Railway: one of the newly rebuilt 'B4X' superheater 4-4-0s, No 60, on a down express approaching Quarry Tunnel, south of Coulsdon, in 1922.

House. The famous slogan, 'Abandon rank all ye who enter here', had been true beyond all measure, and Privates and Generals mixed freely. The contacts then made were too precious to be lost in the materialism of post-war England, and through them, on occasions, famous men came to our guest nights, at 23 Queens Gate Gardens. G.K. Chesterton, Sir Owen Seaman (Editor of *Punch*), the Duke of Devonshire were some to whom a timid young man, still in his teens, listened with rapt attention. But we never seemed to get any railwaymen. The nearest we got to an engineer, and his outlook was then 'way out', as the modern saying goes, was Sir Oliver Lodge.

In later years when I met many men who were with the Railway Operating Division of the British Army I realised why they had not come into touch with Talbot House, and its famous 'Innkeeper'. The geography of the Ypres Salient explains it all. Poperinghe was the terminus of the supply line for the forces manning the battle line round the entire perimeter of that perilous salient. The key point from the viewpoint of railway operating was the junction of this branch with the lines of north-eastern France at Hazebrouck, about 10 miles to the south-west. All supply trains for the salient had to pass through Hazebrouck, and when the ROD was first established, in November 1915, only a week or so before Talbot House itself, it was there that headquarters was first set up. The 10-mile section of railway to Poperinghe was the first to be taken over entirely by the ROD. The locomotives at first used were Belgian 0-6-0s of the so-called 'Caledonian' type—the goods equivalent of the famous 'Dunalastairs'. It was with this modest equipment, that the great Cecil W. Paget began his celebrated command of the ROD. One can appreciate that he, and the many distinguished British railwaymen he gathered round him before the war was over, did not get into Poperinghe. When the trains got there the job was done. The critical business was getting them through the French junctions.

My spare time explorations round London were apt to be erratic. Toc H was due to play Emanuel School at rugger one December day, and a little group of us went down from South Kensington to Clapham Junction by bus. Just on the south side of Battersea Bridge I saw a side road named Kersley Street. It rang a series of bells violently. This was where the famous *Railway Magazine* photographer, F.E. Mackay, lived. After his spell on active service his photographs had once again been advertised, and through the post I had bought a few of them. On the first available occasion, greatly daring, I knocked at his door, and received a most friendly welcome. As a photographer myself I had not long previously graduated slightly upwards from a Box Brownie; but we did not talk about the technicalities of photography. He was ready to talk trains, and trains, and trains! I was sad to learn that when called up for military service he had disposed of a large number of his early negatives, glass plates, but equally astonished that when the South Eastern and Chatham changed its gay pre-war engine livery for something less ornate he had scrapped his earlier negatives, as being no longer up to date! In such ways did some earlier records of priceless value disappear. We found a great common interest, we both loved the London and North Western.

The long vacation of 1922 was momentous for me because it would be the last opportunity to see the northern railways before Grouping, due to take effect on January 1 1923. My father always took his annual leave in one go, a whole month away, and at that time of course the family had to go with him. For the year 1922 we decided upon Whitby, and in readiness for this I obtained lineside

South Eastern and Chatham Railway: Hastings express passing Chislehurst, hauled by 'L' Class 4-4-0, No 776, in 1922.

photographic permits for the coastal route, from Robin Hood's Bay to Staithes, and for the inland route towards Malton as far as Grosmont. My recollections of journeys to East Coast resorts in the years soon after the end of the First World War are rather daunting. In 1919, as told in Chapter 3, we had gone to Bridlington, and from Leeds on a very hot afternoon we travelled in a bumpy non-corridor carriage. As the recognised railways enthusiast of the family I was accorded the privilege of a window corner, facing the engine; but such was the crowd waiting for the train at Leeds that once seated one could not vacate it to go forward and see the engine. As a reader of *The Railway Magazine* I had visions of 'R' or 'R1' Class 4-4-0s, or perhaps even an 'Atlantic'. We started, and jogged along pretty briskly but looking out at the rather featureless countryside I succumbed to the heat of the afternoon, and to the great amusement of the female members of the family, fell asleep! When we eventually got to Bridlington, to my utter amazement, I saw that our engine had been a 2-4-0 'Tennant'.

Going to Whitby three years later was even more of an ordeal. Again we had non-corridor stock, but so crowded that passengers were sitting on suitcases between the seats. This time we had an 'F' Class 4-4-0, and such a load that from Malton, after which we left the Scarborough line and began our climb over the moors, we had an 0-4-4 tank engine as pilot. Even before we had started on that journey the North Eastern Railway had been brought vividly into the eye of a railway enthusiast, when, in its July issue, *The Railway Magazine* carried an article 'British Pacific Locomotives Compared'. Two months earlier the first illustrations had appeared of the first Gresley 'Pacifics', on the Great Northern Railway. They had come out when the ever-famous GNR 'Atlantics' were rising to positively Elysian heights of performance, and some devotees of the train timing art seriously wondered if such vastly enlarged locomotives were really necessary. Then it was made known that the North Eastern Railway was also building 'Pacific' engines at Darlington. There had always been friendly rivalry between the Great Northern and the North Eastern, partners though they were in working the East Coast Anglo-Scottish service; and Sir Vincent Raven

evidently thought that he could not let Gresley get away with all the 'Pacific' publicity. In time for the July issue of the *Railway Magazine* he released full dimensional details, and an outline drawing of his 'Pacific', although the first of the new engines was not completed until nearly six months later. Needless to say, the article in question also contained full details of the 14-year old 'Pacific' of the GWR, *The Great Bear*.

Another notable engine that came out in the summer of 1922 was Robert Whitelegg's massively impressive 4-6-4 tank on the Glasgow and South Western. This dynamic engineering personality had succeeded his father as Locomotive Superintendent of the London Tilbury and Southend Railway. It was a line that was vigorously and efficiently operated by a stud of non-superheated 4-4-2 tank engines; but, on taking over, Robert Whitelegg designed a huge 4-6-4 tank which, through an unfortunate misunderstanding, proved too heavy to work over that part of the line where the LT & S worked by running powers over the Great Eastern, into the city terminus of Fenchurch Street. So these great engines were never used for the job for which they were designed and, when the Midland Railway absorbed the Tilbury, in 1912, they were moved elsewhere. There is a magnificent model of one of them, in Tilbury colours, in the Science Museum at South Kensington. After the 'take-over' by the Midland, Whitelegg left railway service for a time, until he was appointed to succeed Peter Drummond on the Glasgow and South Western, in 1918. With provision to be made for the Clyde coast trains, Whitelegg returned to the 4-6-4 tank type, and it was these great engines that first took the road in 1922.

During the long vacation, in course of which I learned that I had passed the Inter BSc examination, my interests were mostly on the amateur side of railways, and photography; but returning to Toc H in October to begin the second year at the City and Guilds, I was reminded of the non-specialist nature of my own earlier education verily in letters of fire! Two new hostellers at Mark I were, like my older friends from 'Housey', entering straight into the second

year. They had won scholarships from the Dockyard School at Portsmouth, and although both had narrowly missed acceptance for training as Naval Constructors, both had a grounding in mathematics, thermodynamics, and all the basic disciplines of a mechanical engineering career that was far ahead of anything we ourselves had attained at the end of the first year. Apart from their technical status, I have the happiest recollections of Fred Crocombe and Tom Davies, both as staunch Toc H'ers and as fellow students. In the second year, as students, we met some of the more senior of the college staff, including the inimitable Professor E.F.D. Witchell, who lectured to us on applied mechanics. During the second year, at that time, all students followed the same syllabus. Specialisation into Civil, Electrical, or Mechanical Engineering did not begin until the third year.

In college itself, unless one entered into the social and sporting activities, which were then rather limited, one did not meet men from other years. The college was then entirely non-residential. In Toc H Mark I, however, we had one fourth-year 'mechanical', in T.C. Clinch, with whom I had already formed a number of common bonds of interest; and he, having surmounted the intense period of the third year and obtained his College Diploma and the University Degree, had a good deal more time for leisure pursuits in the rarefied atmosphere of the fourth year. He talked about the special visiting lecturers, and their subjects, one of whom was Captain B.H. Peter, General Manager and Chief Engineer of the Westinghouse Brake and Saxby Signal Co Ltd. As a student of railway operation I understood the principles on which the Westinghouse air brake worked. *The Railway Magazine*, the 'bible' for my extra-mural studies on railway engineering, had carried a very informative article on both forms of automatic continuous brakes in December 1918; but Captain Peter's subject at the City and Guilds was signalling, not brakes. I was most intrigued. I was still more interested when towards the end of the college year Clinch told me he had landed a job in the drawing office of the company, at Kings Cross. It was not until after the long vacation, when I returned to London for the rigours of the third year that I learned how he was getting on, and what the prospects were for a career.

Any interests in this direction were, for the time, no more than transitory, because all my efforts became concentrated on the all-out 'slog' of the third year at college. Many times since I have thought how fortunate it was that the 'mechanical' course leading up to the diploma examination was so varied—far more so than either the civil or the electrical counterparts. For in the mechanical course we did a considerable amount of surveying, and the electrical syllabus, though not so detailed or specialised, gave an excellent grounding in all the basic fundamentals we needed for electric traction on railways. The surveying course, under the delightful tutilage of Professor Hewson, was fascinating to me, because one of our projects was the survey for the route of a railway across Hyde Park. As well as plotting the route we had to settle the gradients so as to balance the material we needed for the embankments from what was excavated from the cuttings. The field work was amusing at times, when our taking of levels, and chaining the distances were apt to be interrupted by interested passers-by or the inevitable gapers. The Americans have a splendid phrase for those onlookers who always know how much better, or quicker they could do the job themselves; they call them 'side-walk superintendents'!

I am afraid that during that hectic third-year I had to beg partial release from my social work obligations to Toc H. The folks were very understanding, and I must say I made very frequent use of the 'quiet room', when I was writing up lab reports, and the results of our surveying in the Park. At the same time the leisure moments that I could spare were being increasingly devoted to the study of locomotive running. In this I was encouraged by the articles 'British Locomotive Practice and Performance' in *The Railway Magazine*, contributed each month by Cecil J. Allen; and although I have notes of occasional journeys before this, including one prized, but rather sketchy log of the 1 pm Scotch

Visits to Bournemouth: London bound express on the LSWR near New Milton in 1922, hauled by a Drummond 'D15' Class, 4-4-0, No 465, with one of the new 5-coach 'Tea Car' sets immediately behind the tender.

Veteran LNWR 2-4-0, engine No 2180, Perseverance. *On October 1 1923, piloting unnamed 'Claughton' 4-6-0, No 119, this engine hauled the up day Aberdeen express from Crewe to Euston in which the author travelled.*

'Corridor' express from Euston to Crewe made in 1920, it had not been until my return from Barrow to London in April 1923 that I began the systematic logging of all my journeys. At the time I certainly did not realise how the experience gained in doing this was going to lead me into so many extra-mural activities in later years. As it is something of a period piece a brief mention of that first-ever of my regular recordings may be recalled. I was travelling by the midday service from Barrow, which had a through carriage to Euston, and it was after this latter was attached to the express from Aberdeen, at Preston, that I began timing.

We had a load of 12 coaches, including a 12-wheeled dining car, about 400 tons all told, and hauled by engine No 155 of the 'Claughton' Class, named after the last General Manager of the old LNWR *Sir Thomas Williams*. It is an interesting reflection on the conditions of service on the old railways of Great Britain to recall that Sir Thomas had already served 43 years on the staff on the LNWR when he was appointed General Manager. He retired at the end of 1920, and served another *18 years* as a director of the LMS. The engine bearing his name did well to take this substantial train from Preston to Crewe (51 miles) in 64 minutes, seeing that two severe checks were experienced costing 5½ minutes between them. With a load reduced at Crewe by two coaches, now 350 tons, another 'Claughton', No 208, unnamed, covered the 75½ miles to Rugby in 83¼ minutes, and the final 82½ miles to Euston in 92 minutes, having eased down towards the finish to avoid arriving too far ahead of time.

When I returned to London in the autumn of 1923, to begin the hectic 'third year', I had a journey that was even more of a period piece. It was on the same train, but with extra traffic (from tourists returning after the autumn sporting activities in Scotland) the train was much heavier. The engines as before were 'Claughtons', both unnamed, but both required piloting. Those of us who travelled on the North Western at the time would have thought nothing of using little 2-4-0s, with dates on their nameplates going back to 1868 on these duties; but in recalling the general railway scene in Great Britain at the time, with the first Gresley 'Pacifics' running on the LNER, it now looks like an almost heroic gesture. On that journey of mine on October 1 1923, our pilots were No 1674 *Delhi* (date 1868) from Preston to Crewe, and 2180 *Perserverance* (date 1874)

Capped and hooded—1924!

from Crewe to Euston. The latter little engine participated in some fast running, with maximum speeds up to 77 mph. This was by no means the last time I travelled behind the little 2-4-0 'Jumbos', piloting main line expresses because, in March 1925, the 5 pm from Manchester to Glasgow, which took our through carriage for Barrow as between Preston and Carnforth, was headed by No 1194 *Miranda*, (date 1868) assisting a 'Prince of Wales' Class 4-6-0. I must add, however, that those dates of 1868, on *Delhi* and *Miranda* were a bit of a 'have', because both engines had been completely renewed about 1890. Nevertheless they were tiny little things—sister engines of the celebrated *Hardwicke*—in an era that already included the first Gresley 'Pacifics'.

So the fateful summer of 1924 rushed upon us all at the City and Guilds. At that time Imperial College was not recognised for granting degrees in the University of London, and having sat for the term-end examinations for the College Diploma, those of us who were registered for the BSc examination had to return about 10 days later, to take a second and quite independent series of papers. (Incidentally, on my first return home that summer, by the 1.30 pm 'Corridor', our engines were another 'Jumbo' 304 *Hector* (date 1870) and a 'Prince of Wales'.) My chief recollection of those examinations—I can't remember whether it was the first or the second—was of the heat wave that was prevailing, and of one paper that we attended on a sweltering Saturday afternoon above all times! The papers were not entirely consecutive, and I remember taking time off on one free day to visit the British Empire Exhibition at Wembley, again in blistering heat, and taking many photographs of the attractive oriental pavilions.

I returned to Barrow in mid-July, and remained in a state of suspended animation and apprehension for just over a month. I see from my log book that on July 18 I travelled by a train that left Euston at 11.35 am conveying through carriages for Barrow, and which made a non-stop run over the 111½ miles from Rugby to Wigan, in 127 minutes—or that was what the timetable said we should do! The driver did his best, but I am afraid we became very late. After changing engines the next stop was Lancaster, a curious train; I think the main part of it terminated at Windermere. A month went by, and then at last came the news that I could put the initials ACGI and BSc behind my name.

Chapter 5

Entry into Westinghouse

'Fourth Year' at the City and Guilds was a leisurely, almost dignified business compared to the rush and tear of the 'third', leading up to the climax of the degree examinations in July. For one thing, there were only ten of us taking the Railway Engineering course. Many more were not expected, because we were accommodated in a very elegant and secluded drawing office, under the supervision of a man, Kirkland by name, with the title of 'demonstrator', but who was actually a fully experienced mechanical engineer, who had trained in the Midland Railway works at Derby. He was a friendly soul, and with only ten of us under his wing took a keen interest in our progress and future prospects. It was different with the Professor of Mechanical Engineering, currently Dean of the College, Professor W.E. Dalby. He was a Vice-President of the Mechanicals, and had innumerable extra-mural activities in the form of technical committees and such like. Only once I remember his coming into the drawing office, and then for no more than a perfunctory look round. He was the author of a massive tome of 760 pages entitled *Steam Power*, which we were expected to study.

He was billed, in the college prospectus, to give a series of lectures to the fourth year on 'Problems in connection with the design of express and freight locomotives'; but it resolved into no more than relatively brief dissertations on his two particular hobby-horses—the design of valve gears, and balancing. But referring to that gigantic tome once again I find that most of his undoubtedly brilliant analysis of valve gears was concerned with statical and dynamical problems of the mechanism in general, rather than with the basic need for getting steam in and out of the cylinders. He was, nevertheless, considered to be one of the great experts of the day, and I am told that when Sir Nigel Gresley was designing his famous 'Pacific' engines, first for the Great Northern Railway, and later to become an LNER standard, he consulted Professor Dalby on the design. The fact that he had to alter it after about three years experience may, or may not have any significance. As one of the foremost theoretical authorities of the day on the balancing of engines he became a member of the celebrated 'Bridge Stress Committee', set up jointly by the railways and the Department of Scientific and Industrial Research; but at the time I was at college its proceedings had not advanced to the stage of publishing any results, and his references to it in his college lectures were largely of incidental happenings.

On railway electrification Sir Philip Dawson dashed in, read his lectures, from a typewritten script, in seemingly breathless haste—pausing occasionally to mop his perspiring brow!—and afterwards just could not get away fast enough. The lectures on signalling were, of course, the prelude to my professional life's work, and must be specially mentioned; but as *lectures*, by far the most interesting to me were those on bridge design and permanent way, given by H. Deans of the Great Western Railway. Deans then held the office of Chief Stores Superintendent, but it was a promotional channel for many professional railway engineers; and, as a lecturer, Deans not only had the facility of making his subject extremely interesting, but unlike all the other visiting lecturers he always made time to walk round the drawing office, talk to each of us individually, and comment on the way our design exercises were taking shape. I shall always remember an occasion when he pointed out that the size of a small abutment on my drawing was not the multiple of a standard brick dimension!

As the winter term progressed the question of getting a job at the end of the college session loomed increasingly large, and my father consulted what would now be called the personnel department of Barclays Bank about the prospects of getting an introduction to the railway industry. By an extraordinary piece of luck, or so I thought at the time, the bank official concerned was a personal friend of Sir Felix Pole, General Manager of the Great Western Railway, who intimated that he was prepared to grant me an interview. On the appointed day I went to Paddington with my hopes soaring sky high, only to have them dashed into the dust. Sir Felix was friendly enough, but explained that all their engineering departments were fully staffed with pupils; how could he help me otherwise? He gave me letters of introduction to Vickers, in Barrow as my home town; to Armstrong Whitworth & Co at Newcastle, who were then building 2-6-0 mixed traffic engines for the GWR, and to Westinghouse. The first two offered me nothing more than indentured apprenticeships, with no prospects thereafter; but then, just before the signalling lecture at college was due to begin, Kirkland called me into his office to meet Major L.H. Peter, the electrical engineer of Westinghouse.

I had not been very impressed with him so far, as a lecturer, because he had dealt with the finer points of individual apparatus, rather than the basics of signalling. From my railway interests built up over the years, however, I had a fair working knowledge of the fundamentals, and had an advantage over my fellow students in this respect. I am afraid at the outset they voted him almost as much a dead loss as Sir Philip Dawson! But here was Peter offering me a job, as a graduate trainee, at what was quite a reasonable weekly wage, explaining that for a few years I should be put through the various departments for me to gain experience, and for them to find out for what I was best fitted. He indicated that future prospects for more permanent employment probably lay on one or other of the overseas railways, with which the company was closely associated. I jumped at the offer, and it was agreed I should join the firm at the end of the College session—if I got my DIC (Diploma of Membership of Imperial College). Kirkland told me afterwards that he had never heard of a fourth year student *not* getting his DIC, so I felt that all was well.

Although few of my fellow students had any prospects of employment at the session-end they did not appear particularly enamoured of the berth I had landed, and were looking for more lucrative employment. Then one day Kirkland came into the drawing office and said that Westinghouse were looking for more trainees, and that one of their engineers was coming to the college to try and do some recruiting. As far as I remember we were into the last term before session end, and only three of the ten of us, beside myself, had definite prospects ahead of them. I, and the six of us who so far had no job to go to were ushered into the presence, and for the first time I met Arthur Greenwood Kershaw. He appeared to me as an extraordinarily insignificant little man, with a shock of greying hair, a shabby suit and overcoat, and a flabby handshake. I was glad I was not to be joining his staff! He wanted two draughtsmen for mechanical work, and explained that his opposite number on the power signal side wanted two also. Kershaw chose the two he fancied. A third was earmarked for electrical work, and that left three students for two vacancies in the power-signalling drawing office.

All expressed an interest in the job, so Kirkland decided the only way to settle things was to toss for it! It was ironic that the one who lost out on this 'spin of the coin' was my great friend, Max Hoather, who subsequently joined the firm in the brake department, and became a tower of technical strength, during his 40-odd years of service. The only other one who remained from this 1925 recruitment by Westinghouse was Jack Aldridge, who came from the electrical fourth year at the City and Guilds, and was not one of Kirkland's protégés. Jack was a most able and forceful personality; a great friend and colleague and, when he was appointed director, and eventually deputy managing director, the best boss I ever had. There is much to be told of him later in this book.

The duties allocated to me in my first months at Westinghouse were something of a surprise. For the most part I was dealing with the power signalling 'daily wants' of a variety of customers. They were not the potentially large contracts, but the odd stores orders, such as the LMS wanting half a dozen signal arm circuit breakers: the LNER wanting a few DC track relays, and so on. It was my job to find out if we had a standard design that would fill the bill, check with the drawing office, and if so prepare the information to enable the sales department to place the necessary order on the works. It was often tedious, involving next to no technical work, and there were times when I wondered why it should have been necessary to engage a man with an honours degree to do such a job. But Major Peter was not very forthcoming in explaining why, and it

The signal demonstration room at Westinghouse head office, York Way, Kings Cross, showing modern types of colour light signals and point operating equipment.

Great Southern Railways, Ireland: the signal box at Mallow, with, left centre, hand generator equipment for remote control of points and signals at Killarney Junction.

was only after I had been on the job for several months that I began to realise that I was gaining a very good knowledge of the standard products of the company. Occasionally there were items of electrical design needed, but for the most part my slide rule was having a holiday!

Although we did not deal with big signalling schemes—these being handled by a separate signal estimating department—there was one interesting activity that soon came my way. During the political disturbances that followed the establishment of the Irish Free State in 1922, much damage was done to railway installations, including the burning down of isolated signal boxes. The signal engineer, J.H. Nicholson, in collaboration with Walter S. Roberts, engineer of our subsidiary, The Railway Signal Company, in Liverpool, patented a method of remote control for isolated junctions, using electric point and signal machines, the power for which was furnished, only when required, by a hand operated generator in the nearest available signal box. It was an ingenious conception for a time some years before the introduction of national electricity grids, and when there were no local electricity supplies available; it avoided the need to build new signal boxes. An interesting example for which I had the job of designing the circuits, was the remote operation of Killarney Junction, on the main Dublin–Cork line from the signal box at Mallow, about ¾ mile away. For the period it was quite a novelty.

If orders came in for any equipment not covered by standard designs a request had to be made by memorandum to the head of the power signal section of the drawing office—that remarkable, and at first, to me, inexplicable character, Walter Allan Pearce. He was a very old servant of the company having been 'in' at the very beginning of power signalling in Great Britain. He was a batchelor, living with two elderly maiden sisters, and had a squeaky high-pitched voice that rose several tones as his temper shortened—which it did very frequently. Writing a request for new drawings from him was a hazardous business, usually leading to a row over some ambiguity that one's memo contained, in which his stolid, imperturbable leading draughtsman, Charles Wood, was always a silent spectator. If my own duties were at times very humdrum I came to pity the lot of the two fourth year men from the City and Guilds who had been allocated to Pearce, and who at times seemed to be used as little more than tracers.

In the late autumn of 1925 Westinghouse landed one of the largest orders for signalling that had so far been obtained in the history of the company—for the resignalling, with colour-lights, of the Charing Cross and Cannon Street termini of the Southern Railway. So far as we were concerned it was not an installation job, and no circuit design was involved, merely the supply of large quantities of material, which the railway company's staff would install. A large number of new drawings were required, particularly in the great variety of signal posts and gantries required, and for the two large miniature lever interlocking frames. Major Peter dealt directly with Pearce for the majority of the work, and we younger men were spared the task; but it had always been my job to check the test sheets for the various items of electrical equipment passing through the works, and in the early months of 1926, with the first deliveries of the Southern equipment beginning to come through, this part of my work became intense.

The General Strike, in May 1926, did not affect Westinghouse very seriously. While the London works, where the brake equipment was made, came out, at Chippenham the entire work-force remained loyal and carried on normally throughout the period of national emergency. Consequently while the services of some engineers were lent to the railways to man signal boxes, and from the brake side to act as locomotive drivers and firemen, some of us were retained to continue the flow of technical information to the Chippenham works, and so facilitate the steady continuance of production. Naturally I was sorry to be one of those retained 'inside', though the reasons for it were cogent enough.

Next month the second stage of my training began, with a transfer, for an intensive 'course' to Chippenham Works. I was fortunate in the timing of this trip, for it meant I was based in the beautiful Wiltshire countryside for the months of June, July and August. Naturally I took my old bicycle with me, and during the long summer evenings, and at weekends, I was able to do a lot of exploring. The course was intensive indeed, taking me through the foundry, pattern shop, smithy and machine shops in two months, leaving the more specialised business of electrical signalling and testing for the last month. It was looked at somewhat askance by some of the supervisory staff I had to work with, and considered inadequate to give a proper appreciation of the various crafts involved; but in after years, comparing notes and experiences with colleagues who had done a full three-year apprenticeship, I felt that the intensity of my own training, coupled with the varying experience of work in the different London departments, fitted me far better for the specialised work in signalling that was to follow later.

I must not dwell upon the many 'characters' I met in the works. It is the same in any old established factory where the working conditions are good, and long service with the company is traditional. I had some congenial lodgings in the home of one of the die-sinkers, himself a man of long service, from whom I was interested to learn that it was unusual for trainees to be given any experience in the smithy. Even though for no more than a week, to work as 'mate' to one of the blacksmiths was a most useful item in my training. The works were along-side the Brunellian main line of the Great Western Railway, and in the hot summer weather the end doors of some of the larger shops were kept open, and I could see some of the passing trains. In June, following so soon after the General Strike, with coal in short supply, a very attenuated service was being worked; but once supplies from the Continent were organised—while our own coal industry continued the strike—the train service was restored to near normality, except in respect of timekeeping.

In travelling to and from Paignton in the previous summer, for my last holiday before starting work at Westinghouse, I had recorded locomotive performances, from 'Star' Class engines of such exceptional merit as to shake my youthful allegiance to the North Western; but in 1926 it was very different. It is generally understood that the very high standard of engine performance on the Great Western was due to the availability of picked grades of first class Welsh coal. Certainly it seemed that the imported fuel in use in 1926 had taken all the sparkle out of the performance, and some of the then-brand new 'Castle' Class engines gave me runs that showed every evidence of poor steaming—a trait almost unheard of on the GWR in normal times. Engines that I noted running below standard were the 'Castles' *Berkeley, Donnington, Highclere* and *Kenilworth*. At the August bank holiday week-end I went up to Barrow, taking the west to north route from Bristol to Crewe, via the Severn Tunnel, without any particularly interesting performance. But on my return journey, from Carnforth to Crewe, we had one of the LNWR 'Prince of Wales' Class 4-6-0s that had been temporarily equipped for oil firing, and had an adequate, if not very exciting, run.

My last month in the works was by far the most interesting. I was able to do some fitting on one of the miniature-lever interlocking frames then being built for the Metropolitan Railway, and this experience was to be invaluable to me later. I helped to assemble, and then to test many of the latest types of signalling relays—in some ways reversing the process that I had become familiar with in London. There I had checked the test sheets to see that the equipment was doing what was required of it; at Chippenham I made a number of the tests myself, and sent the figures forward for approval. Much of the equipment for the large Southern Railway orders was still going through the shops, though the two large interlocking frames—107 levers for Charing Cross and 143 levers for Cannon Street—had already been despatched. I gathered that in response to the most imperious demands of the railway they had been built in something akin to shipwreck hurry, massing the maximum number of men that could be physically accommodated on the job.

On my return to London my next spell of training was to be in the drawing office, under W.A. Pearce, and recalling the jobs allocated to my friends from the City and Guilds a year earlier, I was not altogether surprised when my first tasks were humble in the extreme. The employment of university graduates in the power signal section of the office was looked upon with the utmost disdain by the older and well established draughtsmen. I discovered in due course that these men had little technical or workshop training, but had been astute enough to gather a good deal of experience from that remarkable chief, Pearce. In the first months I had to put up with much snide criticism in the 'what did they teach you at that college' vein, and so on. Pearce himself took little interest at first, and my work was allocated and supervised mainly by his assistant C. Wood. But my joining the Institution of Railway Signal Engineers kept me in

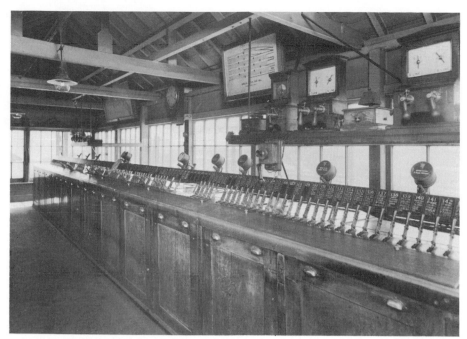

Above *The electro-pneumatic interlocking frame at Hull Paragon station, North Eastern Railway: one of W.A. Pearce's earlier designs.*

Below *Electro-pneumatic point operation on the London underground railways: a sharply curved layout on the Central line.*

touch with Major Peter and, in his often taciturn way he indicated that my training was going according to plan.

Just before Christmas 1926 a South American contract for electro-pneumatic signalling included provision of lower quadrant semaphore signals, but working through an angle of 45 degrees, instead of the 60 degrees standard on signals of this type used on the open-air sections of the Metropolitan District Railway since its first electrification some 20 years earlier. The arm needed re-balancing to suit the changed movement, and the senior draughtsmen for whom I was working was at something of a loss. I heard Pearce in that high squeaky voice of his say: 'Give it to Nock; he's a mathematical chap'. It was not a difficult job, but I was amused to find that among those so-called senior draughtsmen none of them would know how to start on it. My stock was rising—even if no more than slightly! In the next few months I was entrusted with more interesting jobs, particularly as an important contract for re-signalling in Manchester came our way. It was as a result of the merging of the LNWR and the Lancashire and Yorkshire in the LMS system, and the need to coordinate station and operating facilities in the former Victoria and Exchange stations, which were alongside.

Our contract provided for the use of the standard Style 'M2' electric point operating machine, but at Manchester the problem was that there were three different types of permanent way in use. There was the former London and North Western, the Lancashire and Yorkshire, and the new British Standard, and all had different fittings and switch drillings. It was my job, as a draughtsman, to try and devise a set of rod connections that could be fitted to all three. It looked pretty hopeless at first, but after a certain amount of fiddling with the drilled holes in each pair of switches I thought I had found a way. Permanent way being what it is the Chief Civil Engineer of the LMS had to be consulted. Alexander Newlands, the formidable Chief Engineer of the former Highland Railway, had recently succeeded E.F.C. Trench of the former LNWR in this high office, and with him at Euston an interview was sought. I went with Pearce, and H.M. Proud, the Chief Commercial Engineer of Westinghouse. Pearce began to explain our proposals, but immediately Newlands cut him short. There could be no question of drilling additional holes in the new standard switches. Pearce began to explain our difficulty, but was told roundly if your apparatus does not suit our track then you must re-design your apparatus!

Proud, by way of conversation began to describe how the 'M2' machine was used on the Southern, whereon Newlands rose from his chair and in icy tones said, 'Don't you think we are a large enough concern to decide for ourselves what we are going to do, without hearing what the Southern Railway are doing'. And in the word 'Southern' there was an indication of the utmost scorn! We were obviously going to get not the slightest help from Newlands, and we went back to Kings Cross to think the problem over again. Eventually we found a very awkward and expensive solution in solid forging a clip which fitted round the toe of the switch; it formed an anchor that avoided the drilling of one additional hole in the switch. It was an expensive job, involving precision machining of the slot, and then some fitting on site; because unless the clip fitted snugly round the toe it would be useless. The job that Newlands imposed upon us had an amusing sequel four years later, when we were resignalling St Enoch station in Glasgow, as will be told in Chapter Six.

The interlocking of points and signals at any station or junction, large or

Cannon Street, Southern Railway: the new layout completed in 1926, with colour light signalling and electric point operation.

small, can be as much an exercise in operational philosophy as in the basic protection of train movement that it provides. Cannon Street on the Southern, brought into service in 1926 was one of the most intensely locked frames Westinghouse had yet built; but after a year of service the traffic people came to the conclusion it was too restrictive. The long distance trains were then all steam hauled and, on arrival, the locomotives, detached from their trains and standing at the buffer stops, could not be released quickly enough and the platform cleared for the next incoming train. The traffic and signal engineers of the Southern got together, and worked out a revised method of providing the necessary movement-protection that they expected would save them an occasional minute at the busiest times. Yes, no more than a minute; but even a minute is worth having in the rush hours at Cannon Street. An order was placed with Westinghouse to design and install the altered locking mechanism required.

This order came in 1927 just after I had returned from my annual leave—a fortnight of splendid exploring and photographing on the Highland line of the LMS. On my return I was concerned to hear that Pearce had been taken seriously ill, and was not expected back for many weeks. The locking alteration at Cannon Street was a job that he would normally do personally, but it could not wait for his return. How I, a trainee of no more than two years experience, was chosen to make the drawings I shall never know; but it was probably at Major Peter's suggestion, knowing of my works experience in fitting up interlocking. A.G. Kershaw, who I had briefly met at the City and Guilds, took responsibility for the job. He, as a former chief engineer of Saxby and Farmer, was of course a past master in the job of interlocking, though all his previous work had been done on full-sized mechanical lever frames, rather than the miniature type in use at Cannon Street.

It really was one hell of a job. It is one thing to design the interlocking for a new frame, starting with a clean sheet, as it were; but here was a frame thick with locking, to which the alterations required were going to make it ever more complicated. I soon found Kershaw was a difficult man to work with. At times he was kind, and understanding, and at others just a plain bully. It was an experience of priceless value to me—to appreciate and absorb something of his skill in the art of interlocking design; to take the praise and the kicks that came with disconcerting alternation, but then, after three positively traumatic weeks, to realise, no more than dimly at the time, the magnitude of the operation into which I had been thrown at the deep end, as it were. It was not finished when the drawings were completed and sent to the works. When Pearce returned, after his long illness, I got the impression that he just did not want to know about the job, though in his reticent way I believe he was very upset that anyone else had altered his frame. It took a gang of our fitters from Chippenham a month of night working to make the actual alterations, because each night only a part of the new locking could be fitted. It then had to be dismantled and the old restored. Another section would be done the next night, and so on. Major Peter suggested to Pearce that it would be good experience for me to go down to Cannon Street from time to time, and have a night out helping with the fitting. It was indeed an experience.

My interest in overseas railways became stimulated considerably about this time, through working on large contracts for Capetown, South African Railways, and for Bombay. I recalled a colour plate in the first edition of the *Wonder Book of Railways* showing the Vice Regal train of the Great Indian Peninsula Railway, and remembered that the locomotive was chocolate brown. The re-signalling at Victoria Terminus Bombay, 'VT' as it was always known among railwaymen, was occasioned by electrification, not only of the suburban

On a huge South American installation: three position upper quadrant semaphores on the approach to Plaza Constitution, terminus of the Buenos Aires Great Southern Railway.

Semaphore signals in excelsis: the approach to Flinders Street station, Melbourne, Victorian Government Railways. This great installation was still in service when I went to Australia 45 years after I joined Westinghouse.

lines, but of the main line for some distance out of the city, and the work at 'VT' involved colour light signalling and electro-pneumatic point operation. The interlocking frame was to have been of one of Pearce's standard designs like the one with which I had become so very familiar recently at Cannon Street on the Southern; but the standard design had a very handsome polished teak casing, and the engineers of the GIPR assured us that these would not be acceptable in India. They would provide a tasty meal for the white ants that swarmed over the tracks. Pearce shrugged his shoulders, and gave the job of designing a steel case to me, another interesting job on a big locking frame. His suspicions, and eventual disgust were confirmed when shortly afterwards we received another large Indian contract for signalling at the nearby Bombay Central terminus of the Bombay, Baroda and Central India Railway. Apparently the white ants of Bombay were very selective in their depredations, because the BB & CIR engineers had no hestitation in accepting our standard teak casing for the big interlocking frame included in their contract!

I derived a great deal of interest and pleasure from studying the track plans of these large Imperial stations. Both for Capetown, and Bombay I had to design some quite large signal gantries, which brought back memories of my 'Theory of Structures' days at the City and Guilds. At both great stations we put in route indicators of the optical projector type, in which the figure or letter to be displayed was projected on to a ground glass screen, to show a character 12 inches high. This form of route indicator was an invention of Eric Challans, one of the Christ's Hospital boys who had been through the City and Guilds and joined Westinghouse a year before I did. He was also a staunch member of Toc H. He had recently been appointed personal assistant to Major Peter, and through our earlier association he frequently gave me items of 'inside' information. By the summer of 1929 I had been four years with the company, and although my time in the drawing office had been full of interest and good experience I was beginning to wonder what my next move would be. Quite casually I mentioned this to Challans one day, and he laughed, 'You're booked for the Chief Draughtsman!'. I was incredulous; but he persisted, 'It's God's truth. Pearce hasn't got very long to go'. It was obviously time for a word with Major Peter, and although not in so emphatic a strain he confirmed that he wanted me to stay in the drawing office because, he said, 'the chap who can originate design is bound to come to the top'. Then, as an afterthought he added, with a twinkle in his eye, 'For a start, go and ask Mr Pearce for a rise!'.

As it happened, however, things did not quite turn out that way. In February 1930 at a meeting of the Westinghouse Board, three very important new appointments were made. H.G. Brown, hitherto Managing Director and a tremendous power in the land, although no more than 55 years of age, moved upwards into semi-retirement, as Deputy Chairman, and his place as Managing Director went to Captain B.H. Peter, previously General Manager and Chief Engineer. He was the elder brother of Major Peter. But the appointment, the effect of which was soon to be felt from end to end of the company, was the promotion of the former Business Manager, W.H. Powell, to be General Manager, for to him, in future, all the senior executives of the firm reported. That he could be tough, near-ruthless, I had learned from the recollections of his spell as manager of Chippenham works that were passed on to me when I was there, under training; but for many Westinghouse men beside myself the year 1930 was a milestone.

Chapter 6

The Great Depression and after

My father was due for retirement at the end of 1930, and in readiness for this he had bought a large Victorian house at Bushey, Hertfordshire, where our family, dispersed since I went to Giggleswick in 1916, could be reunited. The next few years were to prove a time of much personal readjustment for us all. Quite apart from family affairs, however, the whole year of 1930 was to bring changes in almost every field with which I was associated. Although, as related in the previous chapter, my future role at Westinghouse, following the end of my period of training, had been clearly indicated to me by Major Peter, in 1930 the top level changes in the Company management, referred to at the end of the previous chapter, in less than a year altered the whole set-up so far as the power signal section of the drawing office was concerned and it dimmed my prospects considerably. This came at a very difficult time in the history of the National economy, because the Great Depression had us in its grip, and opportunities of alternative employment to Westinghouse were remote. But before this change in circumstances occurred the spring and summer of 1930 brought a crop of interesting new experiences.

It was in those last months that I worked directly under him that I came to realise how fortunate I had been to be associated with Walter Pearce. He never gave evidence outwardly of being a very scientific man, but the designs he evolved were so elegantly proportioned, and so essentially 'right', that they remained standard products of the Company for many years. When he began to entrust me with checking the drawings of more junior men, and I had to pilot them through his eagle-eyed scrutiny, one needed infinite patience to follow his often-irascible and roundabout cross-examination, which was his own way of ensuring that I had been equally diligent in my own checking. Recalling those last months, when he was in charge of the power signalling section of the drawing office, I have often thought how unlikely a figure he cut for a man holding such responsibility, and whose influence had been so great. A retiring, short tempered,insignificant looking little man, who never mixed with his fellow engineers, or indeed with his fellow officers of the Company, he could have been passed over as a 'nobody' but, to all who had to deal with him, he was a giant.

That summer of 1930, which was the last in which I was travelling to Barrow for the Bank Holiday weekends, brought some interesting experiences, because in addition to those eagerly anticipated holiday trips the Westinghouse contract for re-signalling at Glasgow St Enoch, gave me a week in Scotland, measuring

Holidays in the Highlands: southbound goods train on the viaduct across the main road at Crianlarich, Perthshire, hauled by 'J39' Class 0-6-0, No 2979. The mountain in the background is Ben More.

up on site preparing for the design of the point operating gear, and the new signals. At very short notice I had to travel up to Glasgow with H.M. Proud, the engineer responsible for carrying out the installation of the work; and we had to travel up from Euston on the 'Night Scot'. I was not then sufficiently senior in the Company to enjoy first class travel, and I remember Proud's concern as to whether I should get a good nights rest on the journey north. The train left Euston at 11.45 pm and a Pullman dining car was put on at Carlisle. All third class passengers requiring breakfast had to be up in time to take the first sitting, served before 7 am immediately after leaving Carlisle. The 'firsts' were not called until more than an hour later. Proud was expecting to see me at breakfast, not realising how the 'classes' were segregated on this train; but on hearing I had taken the first sitting he remarked rather ruefully: 'Sounds as though you didn't sleep very well!'. I didn't tell him that I had roused at first light to log the running of the train from Carnforth over Shap!

The night trains were not timed very fast at that period. The philosophy was to bring the 'Night Scot' into Glasgow at 9.35 am with its many sleeping car passengers, both first and third, handsomely breakfasted and ready for the business of the day. The overall time of 9 hours 50 minutes from Euston gave the not very exciting average speed of 40.8 mph. The train was a heavy one of 450 tons, hauled by a Royal Scot, No 6121 *H.L.I.* working through from Crewe to Glasgow. From the stop at Carnforth we took 51¾ minutes to climb the 31.4 miles up to Shap Summit but then ran fast down to Penrith, touching 74 mph to make the stop there in 65¼ minutes, for the 44.9 miles. We then ran smartly down the 17.9 miles to Carlisle in 20¼ minutes, maximum 76 mph. Then the addition of the Pullman dining car brought the load up to 495 tons, and our progress became really pedestrian, although keeping schedule time. Our start to stop runs were:

Carlisle–Lockerbie 25.8 miles 35 minutes

Lockerbie–Beattock 13.9 miles 19¾ minutes (stop for bank engine)

Beattock–Symington 27.2 miles 49½ minutes

We had taken 27 minutes to climb the 10 miles from Beattock to Summit, with a Caledonian 0-4-4 tank engine assisting in rear.

On meeting the railway engineers at St Enoch station, our first concern was that of the fittings for the electric point machines. Here we had to contend with switches of the former Glasgow and South Western Railway in addition to the new British standard. The man with whom we were immediately concerned was John Melville, the district engineer. He was a cheery soul, unlike his august father who, as Chief Engineer of the G & SWR was reputed to be something of a holy terror, and went by the homely nickname of 'Bloody Bill'. Out on the line I noticed some new standard switches in which additional holes had been drilled near the toe to attach a connection to an electrical detector. We told Melville of the trouble we had with Newlands at his Euston headquarters over drilling of the switches at Manchester, and how he had forbidden the drilling of *any* holes. Melville gave me an old fashioned look, and said, 'Well, Euston's a long way away!'. When I got back to London some wag in the office suggested that the name of the station should be changed to 'St O. Nock'!

In the autumn of 1930 the new top management of Westinghouse struck hard at the Drawing Office. Pearce was relieved of his responsibilities as head of the Power Signal section, and Arthur Kershaw, the former Chief Engineer of Saxby & Farmer Ltd, who had already taken charge of the Brake section, gathered in the 'power' section, putting him in control of the entire drawing office staff of the Company. The charge was distasteful on three counts: to Major Peter it ended the felicitous entente that had prevailed between the drawing office and the electrical engineering department, with cooperation at all staff levels; to Pearce himself it was like premature retiral, although that taciturn old character, never let slip much of his inner feelings; while to those of us who suddenly and unexpectedly got a new boss it meant that all contact with our colleagues in other departments would be made only by memoranda passing in both directions through Kershaw's personal hands. Gone for a while were the friendly discussions over the pros and cons of new projects. Requests for drawings had to be made in terms that admitted of no argument, or seeking of opinion. It all became stilted to an unpleasant degree.

It so happened also that the need for personal readjustment at Westinghouse came at exactly the same time as my father's retirement. In taking up residence at our new home at Bushey he and my mother had to re-adjust their standards to living on a considerably reduced income. As a provincial branch manager my father had not had a great deal of opportunity to build up capital in readiness for retirement at age 60. A good proportion of what was available went towards the purchase and refurbishing of our new home, and having lived previously in a rented house owned by the Bank there were new running expenses to be provided for. The fact that my sister, suffering from a nervous condition, could make no contribution did not help. The winter of 1930–1 was sadly unsettled for us all, not made any less uncertain by the deepening industrial depression, that was now flooding across Europe, after the catastrophic Wall Street Crash, in the USA. It soon became evident that Westinghouse was running sadly short of work. Major Peter, looking ahead hopefully to better times, obtained authority for drawings to be made of Anglicised versions of certain new American apparatus, which it was hoped that we might eventually sell, and for a time this provided a good deal of work in the drawing office. One project, for which I was given responsibility, was a new type of electric point machine.

The fact that all sections of the drawing office were now under a single control paid off for a time. The brake section was desperately short of work, and a number of its staff were allocated to me for the point machine job, and certain lesser projects. It was a tough experience to try and supervise the work of men considerably older than I was, and experts in their own field, in the making of drawings for apparatus that was alien to me also, at the start. They did not take kindly to it either, especially when I had to request alterations to their work. One way or another, however, it kept the drawing office as a whole going through that anxious summer of 1931, even though much of the work we did was quite apart from existing or near anticipated orders.

Then, in the late summer, the minority Labour Government, rent with internal dissentions, collapsed, and was replaced by a National Administration, still with Ramsay Macdonald as Prime Minister, but with strong Conservative and Liberal support. While most of us felt very relieved at this turn in the affairs of the country we in Westinghouse were soon to receive a stunning shock. One Friday afternoon we returned from lunch to find that 11 members of the drawing office staff had received notice that from the end of that very day their services were no longer required—roughly 10 per cent of the entire strength. The suddenness of the cut did nothing to relieve the uneasiness of those of us who remained. In one of his bursts of confidence Kershaw admitted to me that he

Signalling works for relief of unemployment in the 1930s: a gantry of searchlight type colour light signals on the Great Western Railway at Cardiff East. The new signal box, alongside the old one, can be seen at the right (Westinghouse Brake and Signal Co Ltd).

felt sure if other heads of departments did not make similar cuts it would be done for them. Actually, within a matter of months a cut of 10 per cent, was imposed upon all staff salaries, from top to bottom of the Company.

It was at this time and against so sombre a background that I began to do some pretty deep thinking as to where my future prospects lay. Until 1930 I was feeling assured of a career within Westinghouse. My outside railway interests in the direction of locomotive history and performance were rapidly widening, but so far entirely as a hobby. It was the same with photography, both of railway subjects and landscapes. But the depressing state of business in Westinghouse and the dead hand of Kershaw brooding over all our goings and coming in the drawing office made me think of diversification, and the turning of my spare time interests to some effect. I cannot remember now in what newspaper or magazine I saw the headline 'More Profit from Writing'; but it was a quietly worded advertisement for a school of journalism, teaching entirely by correspondence courses in a variety of subjects. As an avid reader of *The Railway Magazine* I had by this time appreciated that practically all the authors who contributed to it had other jobs, and wrote their articles in their spare time; but the prospectus of that school of journalism made me realise there were other subjects I might be able to write about, in addition to railways. I entered for the course, and had no cause to regret spending the modest fees involved.

Once students were enrolled the staff of that school did not pull their punches in criticising exercises that were submitted. Many of my earliest efforts gathered little except scathing comment but gradually I began to get the message. The course emphasised the openings there were for freelance contributions to the daily newspapers, and once those disastrous first efforts had been lived down the instructor who was dealing with my work hinted that he thought an occasional chatty article about railways might find its way into one of the London 'dailies'. Like many of the more dedicated railway enthusiasts of that time I am afraid I was inclined to regard railway items in the daily press with some scepticism, because they so often got things muddled up; but as an exercise in that correspondence course recalling my student days in surveying I wrote: 'Hyde Park's Ghost Trains'. To my surprise, and almost by return of post the instructor sent it back as 'most interesting' recommending I tried it at once on *The Evening News*. Still greater was my surprise a few days later when I saw it in print, thus:

'HYDE PARK'S GHOST TRAINS—It will probably come as a surprise and shock to most Londoners to know that for many years past a railway across Hyde Park has been planned, and, what is more, that the scheme is renewed each year.

'Since the origin of the idea, its course has varied slightly, but in general direction remains the same. It starts from a point on the Broad Walk near Palace Gate and runs to Marble Arch, two alternative routes being planned. The more direct route runs just south of the Round Pond, passes near the Physical Energy Statue and crosses the Long Water by a five-arch bridge. Thence it runs to the north of the Bird Sanctuary and heads straight for Marble Arch.

'The alternative route, starting from the same point on the Broad Walk, goes due east, passing just to the north of the Albert Memorial and, on a swinging S-curve, crosses the carriage road from Victoria to Alexandra Gate and then makes an almost right angled bend to the north on the ground once occupied by the great Exhibition of 1851.

Building the 'Princess Royal' Class Pacifics for the LMS at Crewe Works: engine No 6207, Princess Arthur of Connaught, *at an advanced stage in the erecting shop.*

'Then cutting right through the middle of the bathing station, it crosses the Serpentine by a five-arch viaduct and passes through the gap between the Bird Sanctuary and the Keepers' lodges to join the other route near Marble Arch.

'The re-surveying takes place regularly with much energy. Each year from October onward parties are at work with delicate theodolites taking levels and "chaining" the distances, whilst other parties can be seen at work on the site of the proposed Serpentine viaduct.

'Only on a closer investigation into their activities do you discover the comforting fact that these surveyors are engineering students and that the railway will never get beyond the drawing boards of South Kensington.

'Across deserts, in the Bush, through jungles, new railways are being pushed and on many such enterprises are engaged men who learnt their job in Hyde Park. Working maybe under a tropical sun, or in the jungle, their thoughts must often go back to the time when they surveyed the line for London's phantom railway.'

This was early in 1932, but so far as *The Evening News* was concerned it was only a flash in the pan. I did not sell any more articles to them. At that time, however, there was an assistant editor on *The Star* who appeared to be interested in railways, Wilson Midgley, by name. I never met him personally, though I had the occasional 'phone call. Between June 1932 and the beginning of 1934 I sold him a few light chatty articles of the kind I had been encouraged to write by that correspondence course, and among them was one about the coming introduction, in 1933, of the first 'Pacific' engines on the LMS. The two new engines *The Princess Royal* and *Princess Elizabeth* were put on to the London-Glasgow run and made locomotive history by being the first to work through daily between the two cities. Hitherto engines had been changed either at Crewe, or Carlisle. This innovation gave me an idea for another article in *The Star.*

I suppose it is the ambition of every steam locomotive enthusiast to have a ride on the footplate, and as a long shot I wrote to Midgley and asked if he would be interested in an article, if I could get permission to ride on one of these long runs. Without in any way committing himself he thought it might be worth a much longer article than my usual 'snippets'. The Easter weekend of 1934 seemed to give the best chance of good runs, when at Westinghouse we had the Tuesday off. So I wrote to the publicity department of the LMS, asking for permission to ride down on the Saturday and up on the Tuesday. Having seen the turns worked by the two engines I hoped that we might get 6201 going down and 6200 up on the Tuesday. To my delight, after a very few days I received a letter advising me that 'arrangements could be made . . .', but although authority was given to ride throughout between Euston and Glasgow in both directions they pointed out that as Easter was a busy time I was asked not to ride on the footplate for more than was necessary to obtain the data for my article.

I was too elated, and equally far too much of a novice to question why the prospect of an article in *The Star* had so readily brought me this privilege. In the weeks that remained before Easter, D.S. Barrie, who was then an assistant in the publicity department at Euston, got in touch with me. He was already well known to me, by name, from his contributions on a diversity of historic subjects, and his fine photographs, in *The Railway Magazine*; but now the foundations were laid for a lifelong friendship. From him I learned that the new engines had not been doing too well, and while they were only too anxious to give them some publicity he emphasised that my script must be submitted for approval before sending to any newspaper, in case I had inadvertently referred to incidents on the journey that they would wish to suppress. When Easter came although *Princess Elizabeth* was at Camden shed on the Saturday morning she was not on 'The Royal Scot', and I rode a 4-6-0 No 6137 *Vesta* instead. On my return trip we had *The Princess Royal*, and on the long run south, non-stop from Carlisle to Euston, I was not long in realising why Barrie had stressed that they might want to exercise some censorship! For most of the way we were short of steam, and had we not had a driver of the utmost enterprise and resource, in Laurie Earl, the result might have been very different.

Many years later, when the poor steaming and bad tender design of the two original 'Pacifics' had receded into the realms of history best forgotten, I revealed the full story of that epic journey*, but at the time, with an arrival in Euston four minutes early it was not difficult to conceal completely the struggle for steam we had on the way, nor the way the coal obstinately refused to trim forward in that tender. *The Star*, adding a few 'purple patches' of their own, splashed the article on their 'leader' page, under the banner headline *Four Mins Early* and everyone at Euston House was delighted. What I did not know until more than 30 years later was that a small, though strong anti-Stanier faction had grown up among the operating staff of the LMS. They were ready to blow up, disproportionately, any shortcomings, not only of the 'Pacifics' but of other new engines, and in the case of the two 'Princesses', the troubles had got to serious proportions. My article, in a London daily newspaper of wide circulation, gave a tremendous boost to the new engines.

I wrote several other articles about that run, and sent a full log of the journey to Cecil J. Allen for his use in the 'British Locomotive Practice and Performance' feature in *The Railway Magazine*. With this log, as agreed with Barrie, I

* *British Steam Locomotives at work.*

included details of the driving technique used on the engine, but made no reference to the steaming, and the low boiler pressures that we had to contend with. Allen worked my notes up into a most glowing account, concluding with this sentence: 'Performance grew steadily finer as London was neared, and culminated in the time of 65 min 33 sec, for the 72.9 miles from Welton to South Hampstead, an average of 66.7 mph which included the excellent time of 15 min 12 sec from Bletchley up to Tring'. Actually during this spell, for much of the distance the driver was in the tender getting coal forward, the fireman was shovelling for dear life, boiler pressure was at one time as low as 165 lb per square inch and I was looking out for any adverse signals, of which fortunately there was none. Barrie met us in at Euston, and there was little remaining to show him for our efforts—three very black faces, a tender practically empty of coal, and an arrival four minutes early! But the experience gave me the entrée to official circles on the LMS, and began the diversifications that came to form a very important part of my life.

The article 'Four Mins Early' was published in *The Star* on April 27 1934, and the fillip it gave me was soon eroded by an occurrence at Westinghouse. Since those sombre days of 1931–2 the business situation had somewhat improved. We secured contracts that included some interesting design work, and although Kershaw continued to deal individually with some of the more senior draughtsmen, jobs requiring new design came mostly my way, and I still hoped that one day I might attain the position of Chief Draughtsman in the power signalling section that Major Peter had outlined, before the drastic changes of 1930. Then, a few days before the Whitsun holiday of 1934, Kershaw told one or two of us in the drawing office that he was having his son, Norman, as his assistant. This *coup* was as much a bombshell to certain other senior executives of the company as it was to us. Hitherto it had been an understood rule that heads of departments could not have their own sons as members of their staff. Sons of senior members of the secretarial and accounts departments, for example, were apprenticed as engineers, at Chippenham. That Kershaw had 'got away with it' did not increase their sense of loyalty to the general manager, who had acquiesed in this move. For us in the drawing office it seemed as though all avenues of advancement were blocked.

It was therefore with very mixed feelings for the future that I set out with my great friend of City and Guilds days, Macgregor Pearson, to spend the Whitsun week-end in Paris. His parents were coming too, but on the strength of his railway employment, as a surveyor in the civil engineer's department of the Great Western, he had obtained permits for the two of us to visit the principal locomotive running sheds around Paris. So we two went on in advance, so as to get in a shed visit to the La Chapelle depot of the Northern Railway on the Saturday afternoon. Whitsunday was spent in conventional sightseeing, *en famille* Pearson, but on Monday Mac and I had a railway field day, doing La Villette (Eastern), Bercy (PLM) and Batignolles (State) sheds all in the one day. The weather was fine; the French *cheminots* most helpful, and we both took a lot of photographs. This was before the nationalisation of the French Railways and except at La Chapelle we saw none but indigenous classes. Electrification of the Orleans, however, was making a number of large main line steam locomotives of that company redundant and following some very strenuous trials between Paris and Calais in the winter of 1932–3 the Nord had purchased some of the magnificent Chapelon rebuilt 'Pacifics' of the Orleans. We were

Above *Early moves away from steam on the Great Western: a 3-car diesel mechanical unit entering Reading West station, from which I used to travel to Mortimer in my preparatory school days* (E.D. Bruton).

Below *Visit to France in 1934: a 3-cylinder 2-8-2 tank engine of the Eastern Railway, for high speed suburban service, photographed at La Villette depot.*

New signalling on the Southern: part of the 311-lever all-electric interlocking frame, with one of the four illuminated track diagrams at Waterloo (Westinghouse Brake and Signal Co Ltd).

able to see and photograph one, and have its footplate controls explained to us at La Chapelle. It was then resplendent in the chocolate brown livery of the Nord.

Back at Westinghouse there were the coming changes in the drawing office to be faced. Kershaw was at pains to impress upon some of us seniors that it would make no difference; and it was not until a few years later that I found out, quite accidentally, that in the strict chain of responsibility it had made none at all. Nevertheless the fact of having the boss's son delving into all activities could not fail to influence affairs, even though an attempt had been made initially to sugar the pill by giving some of us small increases in salary—'hush-money', as one of my colleagues sarcastically put it. The new order had, however, not been many months in action before one senior man, who had the reputation of being awkward at times, resisted what he considered an unwanted intrusion into his work by Norman Kershaw in somewhat forcible terms, and was sacked the very same day! Although, as I discovered later, I, and doubtless one or two others of my status were still officially responsible directly to his father, cooperation with his son seemed essential! I found no difficulties in that respect.

While the nation as a whole was climbing no more than slowly out of the great depression, the railways were full of enterprising developments by the summer of 1934. In Westinghouse we had some large orders for signalling undertaken on the strength of Government loans for the relief of unemployment, while on the brake side the securing of the £5 million contract for air brake equipment on the Polish State Railways, in the face of the most intense German competition, was signalised by the restoration in full of the salary cuts made nearly three years earlier. In design I was very much involved with signalling work at Leeds, Cardiff, and on the very busy approach lines to Waterloo. It was, officially, an entirely 'indoor' activity, though I took every opportunity of seeing the installation work in progress, entirely on spare-time visits. In a small, and very roundabout way the coordination between my work for Westinghouse and my freelance journalistic activities had begun.

Kershaw could be harsh and difficult enough as a boss. He could be equally awkward as a colleague and fellow officer of the company, and there were times when the heads of other departments sought unconventional ways of resolving the points at issue. A case occurred over some signal gantries for the Leeds contract. Some bracket structures with an overhang of about 15 feet were required. Kershaw's standard design, which was currently being used on the Southern Railway, was a functional, not very handsome affair. At that time the chief civil engineer of the North Eastern Area of the LNER, who was then responsible for signalling, was waging a strong campaign to tidy up and 'beautify' the line side, and in his drawing office at York a very neat and handsome bracket structure for those overhang signal locations was designed, and sent to us. Kershaw was furious, and stormed into Proud, saying 'the bloody things will fall down at the first puff of wind'—and much more to the same effect, and that he would take no responsibility for them. I was there at the time, and could see that Proud, as engineer responsible for execution of the contract, was in a cleft stick.

He could not very well go back to a man who was becoming a very good customer, and who, after all, was responsible for the structural work over a very large slice of railway, and tell him his design was no good; neither had he the status to override Kershaw. Nevertheless an order from a major customer was an order, and the York design had to be translated into production drawings for Chippenham. While my section of the office was engaged in this work I took the opportunity of roughing out some stress diagrams, and found, as I expected,

First Westinghouse developments in rail brakes for marshalling yard mechanisation: a demonstration at Chippenham. The photograph was taken from a wagon approaching the railbrake at speed, to be stopped clear of the obstruction ahead. In the left bottom corner of the photograph is Major L.H. Peter.

that they were thoroughly sound structurally. I met Proud in the corridor a few days later, and at his behest went into his office. He confided that he was worried about those structures, and I then told him about my own calculations. His reply, 'Thank you *very* much, Nock', could not have been more heartfelt, and I must admit that from then onwards there were an increasing number of back-stage contacts with him, and senior members of his staff, in circumventing the official awkwardnesses that arose from time to time! Incidentally those overhang bracket signals at Leeds stood four-square for 30 years, until a major station reconstruction necessitated their removal.

Reverting to locomotives, my article on the run of *The Princess Royal*, and several lesser ones that followed the big 'splash' in *The Star*, had scarcely appeared when news came of the first Gresley 2-8-2 express locomotive, *Cock o' the North*, on the LNER, and editors who had published the earlier articles began clamouring for more: how did the new engine compare with the LMS 'Pacific', and so on. There was scope for the spice of controversy, which every newspaper man enjoys and fosters. It was all very gratifying for me, but articles in that vein were just not on. From the Westinghouse offices at Kings Cross we had a grandstand view of the early comings and goings of the *Cock o' the North*; but with testing staff swarming around her, and dynamometer test runs in progress it was clearly no time for an outsider to ask for privileges. When the engine was running trials from Doncaster I managed to get a ride behind her, as an ordinary passenger, on the 4 pm down from Kings Cross, as far as Peterborough, and from observations in the train, and from conversation with some of the testing staff I was able to write a 'snippet' for *The Star*, and a piece on locomotive testing in more general terms for *The Times* Trade and Engineering Supplement.

While the engine was still in the south of England, prior to going to Edinburgh for work on the route to Aberdeen, for which it had been designed, there was a special test run, out of the ordinary routine series from Doncaster. The engine, plus the dynamometer car, was put on to the fast and heavy 1.20 pm Scotsman from Kings Cross. Gresley had been quite fulsome in his acknowledgement of his indebtedness to French practice for some features in the design of the engine, and its use on the 1.20 pm Scotsman, quite out of the ordinary link working of engines on the Anglo-Scottish expresses, was arranged for M. Lancrenon, the chief mechanical engineer of the Northern Railway, who rode on the footplate of the *Cock o' the North* and who was afterwards presented with the record of performance made in the dynamometer car. I have not seen any details of the actual run, but the train in question was allowed 114 minutes for the 105.5 miles from Kings Cross to Grantham, start to stop, and on the day in question they took a load of 16 coaches.

In the autumn of 1934 I made the acquaintance of E.G. Marsden, who then had the title of Information Agent of the LNER, a post that on other railways was usually known as publicity officer. It was a time of great and friendly rivalry between his company and the LMS, with one watching eagerly for any developments or innovations that the other might suddenly spring. The situation was the more interesting in that the following year, 1935, was the Silver Jubilee of the reign of King George V, and means of celebrating this were being discussed on every hand. It was not only the LMS and LNER, as railways, that were likely to be involved. The year 1935 was also the centenary of the Act of Incorporation of the Great Western Railway, and with them it seemed likely that they would be celebrating a double event. On the LNER the experimental running of the *Cock o' the North* between Doncaster and Kings Cross was followed by some trial trips of the second 2-8-2 engine, the *Earl Marischal*, and then in the late summer both engines went north to begin what was intended to be their regular work between Edinburgh and Aberdeen.

Then we learned, at first with some surprise, that *Cock o' the North* was being sent over to France for full-dress trials on the stationary locomotive testing plant at Vitry. While Gresley's personal friendship with some of the leading French locomotive engineers was well known, he had also, on numerous public occasions, regretted the absence of a modern locomotive testing plant in Great Britain—that owned by the Great Western at Swindon being of limited capacity, and in fact very rarely used. The persuading of the LNER directors to incur the expense of sending *Cock o' the North* to France was in certain quarters seen as a gesture of protest on Gresley's part that similar facilities were not available here. The second 2-8-2 engine, *Earl Marischal*, differed from the pioneer in having the standard arrangement of piston valves and conjugated gear for actuating the valves of the middle cylinder, as used on all the LNER 'Pacific' engines. *Cock o' the North* had poppet valve gear, and when working hard the very fierce blast led to much fire throwing. *Earl Marischal* was by far the better engine of the two, although *Cock o' the North* was remarkably free running.

The way in which I have jumped from one topic to another in this chapter in some way reflects the reactions of a young man, still not 30 years of age, to the confused and conflicting influences that were present in almost every walk of his life. Nor had the establishment of the family home at Bushey proved entirely successful. I was not altogether happy with my sudden success in the more popular branches of journalism; because I was, after all, an engineer, and would have preferred to have written about locomotives in the more serious and technical vein. But then Barrie had pointed out to me, in the purely railway and technical journals one is catering for the converted; they on the LMS wanted to present railway progress to the general public, and that, of course, meant the daily newspapers. It seemed evident that to obtain more facilities for riding on locomotives I had got to think up subjects of popular appeal.

Chapter 7

Pageantry—re-armament—war

The decade that began on New Years Day, 1935, saw the intensification and ultimate resolving of the confusions that had come to affect all my work. While it would nevertheless be a gross understatement to suggest that the terrible history of world conflict, from the lead-up through Abyssinia, Spain, Austria and Czechoslovakia to the war itself was anything more than a background to my own affairs, it was not until the very end of that decade that there was any sign of an appreciable change in my status at Westinghouse. Throughout the period I continued to report directly to Arthur Kershaw, working mostly through his son; but it was the increasing complexity of my outside interests, and the restraints put upon them that stoked the fires of discontent within me. This, however, is not primarily an autobiography. It is of events, rather than the degree of my own participation in them, that I write; and from the beginning of 1935, in the railway world, events did begin to crowd in upon the scene.

My friendship with Edward Marsden of the LNER quickly ripened to much more than points of day-to-day railway publicity, and I found that he, like Barrie on the LMS, was an out-and-out railway enthusiast, of very wide interests. We used to meet occasionally for a snack lunch in the quiet pleasance of the Georgian Tea Room at the head of No 10 platform at Kings Cross. From him I sensed that the LNER were a little envious of the publicity that the LMS had enjoyed with *The Princess Royal*. The moment was not yet opportune to attempt a similar 'splash' with the new 2-8-2 engines; but as a lead up to it, and ultimately it was hoped to show how much better the new engines were than the existing ones, arrangements were readily made for me to have some footplate trips between Edinburgh and Aberdeen. This would involve runs on the standard Gresley 'Pacifics', and hopefully some of the greatly cherished North British 'Atlantics'. In the meantime my friends at *The Star* wanted a fast and snappy article, and what better than the fastest train on the LNER, the Leeds 'Breakfast Flyer', which ran its last 105.5 miles from Grantham to Kings Cross in 100 minutes start to stop.

The run I made gave us all a surprise. The engine of the day, *Melton*, would not steam! The Gresley 'Pacifics' were generally considered to be exceptionally reliable in this respect; but after a good start, and keeping time as far as Peterborough the engine went steadily 'Off the boil' and we struggled finally over Potters Bar with no more than 115 lb per square inch on the gauge. We crept shamefacedly into Kings Cross 7¾ minutes late. The Running Superintendent of the Southern Area immediately offered me another trip, but my detailed report acted as a passport to many more privileges on the footplate in the spring and summer of 1935.

In the meantime Gresley and his staff were busy with preparations for the Silver Jubilee train. On March 5 we had been thrilled to learn of the high speed test runs between Kings Cross and Newcastle with the 'A3' Pacific *Papyrus*, on which a 6-coach train of 217 tons had been taken down over the 268.3 miles in 237 minutes despite a signal stop north of Doncaster, while on the return journey with a different engine crew, the run was made non-stop in 231¾ minutes with a maximum speed of 108 mph. But the test runs, which showed that the proposed 4-hour service between London and Newcastle could be made with a standard 'Pacific' engine and standard coaches also indicated, through the voluminous data recorded in the dynamometer car, that a considerably greater margin of power could be made available by modifications to the engine design, and by air-smoothing the coaching stock. That used on March 5 was of the well-known teak bodied type, developed from that of the former Great Northern Railway.

We were busy in Westinghouse that year on a variety of signalling jobs, and my annual leave was not to be taken until late in August. Furthermore, I had expeditions planned for the long Bank Holiday weekends at Easter and Whitsun that would take me far from LNER territory. At that time indeed the only spare time I had for journeys away from London were on the once-a-month free Saturdays; before the general introduction of the five-day week however railway travelling, except in the height of the summer, was little different from that on any other weekday. With the facilities that Marsden arranged for me I was able to make quite a comprehensive survey of LNER locomotive working. After a long term trial of Great Central engines, the ex-Great Northern 'Atlantics' had the Pullman trains to themselves, and I had an exciting and exhausting trip to

The Coronation Scot *of the LMS, safely back at Euston, after the exciting demonstration run to and from Crewe on June 29 1937.*

Leeds and back, on a day of sweltering heat, on No 4423 going down and 4456 coming back. The former engine gave me my first-ever maximum speed of 90 mph, which 4456 capped on the return journey by sustaining 93 mph near Essendine.

It was, however, my visits to Aberdeen that brought the richest rewards. Each time the Locomotive Running Superintendent, G.A. Musgrave, gave me a completely open pass to ride on what trains and locomotives I chose for the whole day; and on the Friday nights I went north from Kings Cross on the Aberdonian, ready to start work at 4.15 am next morning when we changed engines in Edinburgh and then set out non-stop for Dundee. I found the standard of performance on that route extremely and uniformly high. 'Atlantics', 'Pacifics' and the two giant 2-8-2s took their maximum loads with competence and economy, and although the 'Atlantics' had to be double-headed when the tare loads exceeded 340 tons southbound and 380 tons northbound, I had some grand runs with those splendid veteran engines when the loads were only a few tons below those maxima. It was, of course, the 2-8-2s that stole the show in the weight-hauling business, especially on the up Aberdonian, leaving at 7.35 pm when we had *Earl Marischal* as far as Dundee, and then *Cock o' the North* to Edinburgh. It was a long day's work, beginning at 4.15 am and finishing just before 11 pm with a return trip from Aberdeen to Dundee and back in between the through runs. But the recollections of that summer are rich with memories of those journeys.

Nor shall I forget the actual Jubilee day, May 6 1935, when King George V and Queen Mary drove through cheering crowds to the Thanksgiving Service in St Paul's Cathedral. It had, of course, been proclaimed a general holiday, and in the day-long pleasance of serene cloudless sunshine I remember sitting in the garden of my father's house at Bushey listening to the broadcast description of the scenes in London. This was long before the days of television. In the morning I had cycled down to the footpath beside the Bushey water troughs to photograph the down 'Royal Scot' express, which I hoped might be hauled by one of the 'Pacifics'. It came along, going strong, hauled by a 'Royal Scot' 4-6-0. I still have the photograph, but the image is not quite clear enough to me to establish the number. It looks like 6135, which at that time was named *Samson.*

1935 was also the year of two notable centenaries, the first of which, that of the newspaper *The Railway Gazette*, almost coincided with that of the Jubilee itself. Chiefly through its associated journal, *The Railway Magazine*, I had formed a close friendship with its Associate Editor, W.A. Willox, from whom I received much help and guidance in the early days of my more technical literary work. Willox, like his father, who was Engineer-in-Chief of the Metropolitan Railway, was a civil engineer by profession, and relinquished an appointment on the Southern Railway to take up his editorial work at Tothill Street; but he had wide interest and extensive knowledge of every aspect of railway engineering and management, and was a brilliant conversationalist. He was a bachelor with no fixed ideas about going home time. This was a good thing for me because, with closing time at Westinghouse 5.30 pm I could rarely get across to Westminster before 6 pm. He was always ready to make an appointment to see me at that time.

The second centenary to come in 1935 was, of course, that of the Great Western Railway. There is no doubt that in the eyes of many railway enthusiasts, this line was in process of being overtaken in the popularity stakes by both the

LMS and the LNER. No new locomotive type had appeared from Swindon since 1927; and although, in the summer of 1935, the Cheltenham Flyer still held the 'blue riband' of British railway speed, with its 71.3 mph start to stop run from Swindon to Paddington, its glamour had become somewhat diminished with the years. I had spent the Easter Bank Holiday weekend in Cornwall, and had some enjoyable runs to and from Penzance on the Cornish Riviera Express; but when the Centenary month occurred and the new 'Bristolian' express was put on, making the run between Paddington and Bristol in 1¾ hours, with a strictly limited load, I must admit I was no more than mildly interested.

My work with Westinghouse was taking me to Chippenham from time to time, and as we dawdled down on the 9.15 am from Paddington, with interminable station stops at Reading, Didcot and Swindon, I had ample time to reflect upon the great disparity in service provided by the very few crack trains, and the ordinary ones. For Chippenham we had three alternatives in the morning leaving Paddington at 7.30, 9.15 and 10.45 am, and over the 94 miles, the average speeds, inclusive of stops, were 47.8, 42.7, and a heroic 37.8 mph. When travelling by the 9.15 am, we stood for 10 minutes at Swindon to let the 'Bristolian' get ahead, the latter having left Paddington three quarters of an hour after we had. Cecil J. Allen, when he was inspecting materials in our works for the LNER, used to take the Westbury slip coach of the Cornish Riviera Express, and then reach Chippenham by the local train via Trowbridge and Melksham. It gave him a good fast run down from Paddington, with some interesting locomotive work, and an arrival at the works just after the workmen's lunch hour. In view of the immense popularity the GWR has attained since its demise, my earlier recollections of it are not inspiring.

On the other hand, the introduction of 'The Silver Jubilee' express by the LNER at the end of September 1935 created an absolute sensation. At that time the word streamline had become a catch phrase, and its sales value was reflected in the promiscuity with which it was applied to toothbrushes, domestic kettles, or even to signal boxes! One can well imagine how Gresley's *Silver Link* had a positively stunning effect, in comparison with the conventional 'apple-green' Pacifics which had preceded it. And when the streamlined train attained a maximum speed of 112½ mph on its very first run, its impact upon popular fancy was terrific. Nevertheless the connoisseurs of the graceful in locomotive lineaments were appalled, and regarded it as a rather feeble pandering to popular taste. Beneath its streamlined exterior, however, the 'A4' Pacific was a magnificent piece of locomotive engineering, and was the tool by which the journey time between London and Newcastle was cut by a full hour. In 1935 the 'Flying Scotsman' on its summer non-stop run to Edinburgh was booked to pass through Newcastle in exactly 5 hours from Kings Cross, and the 1.20 pm with stops at Grantham, York and Darlington took a few minutes longer. 'The Silver Jubilee', with a stop at Darlington, took exactly 4 hours. Like the show trains of the Great Western, however, it was very much a 'one-off' job.

For a dozen years prior to 1935 it had been traditional for *The Railway Magazine* to make its January issue a special Scottish number, and during Jubilee year Willox told me that he was proposing to make the May issue of 1936 a special Irish number. He told me he had a number of articles on railways in the Free State, but nothing for the North. Arrangements were made for me to go to Belfast at Whitsun 1935 to meet Major Malcolm Speir, the Manager and Secretary of the Northern Counties Committee section of the LMS to discuss the possibilities for a comprehensive article on the line, and this proved the prelude to a very enjoyable assignment. 'The Major', as he was everywhere known on the NCC, was a human dynamo, and as bursting with charm and warm humanity as he was with energy and expertise of the highest order in running the railway. I paid not one, but many visits, on my free Saturdays from Westinghouse, travelling from Euston by 'The Ulster Express' on Friday nights, crossing by the night boat from Heysham, and being in Belfast ready to call at the York Road offices immediately after breakfast, or to start on a trip down the line.

In all, I wrote four long articles for *The Railway Magazine*, two published in 1936, and two more dealing with the locomotive history in 1937. Visiting the NCC was always an exhilarating business. The system was small enough for a man like Major Speir to have his finger on every activity; but with him it was never a case of interfering with other officers. It was leadership of the highest order. In many places, that might be regarded as byways, men would display some gadget, or procedure and then with enthusiasm add: 'The Major suggested this'. He had the whole line working as a team. The Portrush expresses and the Larne boat trains were run in dashing style, and several of my stop-watching friends crossed the water to log the running. Then, of course, there was the charm of the narrow gauge sections, particularly the Ballycastle line worked by the 2-cylinder compound 2-4-2 tank engines.

Nevertheless, the innovation of a special Irish number did not go down well with all readers. I met a fellow enthusiast, a reverend gentleman, on Euston station not long after the appearance of the May 1936 issue, and he was most indignant about it. I saw Willox not long after this encounter, and on telling him he replied, with a rare touch of his pawky native Aberdeenshire humour: 'Oh well, we'll have to have a "Special English Number", all for him!'.

Until 1936 signalling matters in *The Railway Gazette* had been dealt with by H. Raynar Wilson, whose text books on both mechanical and power signalling, published some 30 years earlier, were classics of their kind, notably in the lavish inclusion of many large signalling plans. On the death of Raynar Wilson, T.S. Lascelles, engineer of the W.R. Sykes Interlocking Signal Co, and a subsidiary of Westinghouse, became signalling consultant to *The Railway Gazette.* Although acknowledged as probably the greatest expert in block working and a renowned historian on all signalling matters, he was one of the most modest and generous of men, and it was at his prompting that Willox asked me to write up, for *The Railway Gazette*, some of the notable new installations on which Westinghouse were engaged. It was then that my 'back-stage' contacts with H.M. Proud and his staff became invaluable, because they were able to arrange week-end visits for me to see work in progress. As usual in *The Railway Gazette* the resulting articles were to appear unsigned.

Westinghouse were always very strong advocates of the electro-pneumatic system, partly, of course, because we were the only contractors offering the system. So it was something of a novelty when the North Eastern Area of the LNER adopted it for the resignalling of Leeds 'New' station for the first time on a British main line railway for more than 15 years. It was followed by Hull Paragon, though in this latter case it was a modernisation of an earlier installation that had also been electro-pneumatic. Those engineers in the North Eastern Area of the LNER who had been foremost in putting forward graceful structures for the overhang bracket signals had perforce to stifle their

Marshalling yard mechanisation: a night shot of the Control Tower at Hull New Inwards Yard, brought into service in 1935.

sentiments when it came to Hull, because by then the great re-armament programme was gathering momentum, and steel was in short supply. It so happened that the pioneer electrified line of the North Eastern Railway, between Newport and Shildon, had outrun its usefulness and, needing extensive repair to the overhead line, was instead being scrapped. A good deal of steel girder material was still serviceable, and the civil engineer's department cut some of it up to make the overhang bracket structures for the new signals at Hull. The drawing office did its best, but the resulting fabrications were among the ugliest that ever carried colour light signals. Proud and his men were not backward in telling visitors to Hull that we had not made them! The articles I wrote for *The Railway Gazette*, which included two dealing with some important work on the Southern Railway, were afterwards reprinted as very handsome brochures by the publicity department of Westinghouse.

In Coronation year, 1937, many important railway events were staged. On Coronation Day itself, May 12, I listened to the broadcasts no more than intermittently, because only three days later I was to marry Olivia Ravenall, and there were many jobs to be done at our future home. Reflecting on the partnership that was consecrated at Bushey Parish Church, early on that Saturday morning, so early that we left our families to eat the 'wedding breakfast' on their own, and dashed up to London to catch 'The Flying Scotsman' for a brief honeymoon at Aberdour, I wonder if any man can have been more fortunate than I in the solid, sympathetic, if not always enthusiastic backing he has had, through thick and thin, in all the 44 years of our married

Above left *Our wedding was three days after the Coronation of King George VI and this is how Westinghouse dressed up my desk, and me (!) on the eve.*

Above right *Olivia, on a trip to Salisbury in 1936.*

Below *Christening party, July 1938, at Bushey. Seated left to right—Father, Mother, Olivia (with Jill), and Mac Pearson (Godfather); in front, my sister and me—not to mention the dogs, 'Pooh Bear' and 'Jock'.*

Our home station 1930-39, Bushey and Oxhey LMS. A down relief Anglo-Scottish express passes at 60 mph, hauled by Jubilee Class 3-cylinder 4-6-0.

life. Much that I was able to experience, and record in the later chapters of this book would have been quite unattainable without her constant support. History, and the work of great authors as portrayed in literature and on the stage and screen, are full of poignant sagas in which a marriage has foundered because a wife has found her husband's devotion to his work incompatible with family affairs; in my case, however, it was not only daily work but a spare time occupation taking an ever-increasing amount of attention that obtruded. In my case her support was steadfastness itself.

Her support was vital in so many ways. At the back of ones mind was the haunting spectre that another war with Germany was becoming ever more likely; and after delighting in the pageantry of the Coronation, and logging the brilliant performance of the LMS and LNER trains named after the event, the news reverted to Spain, and all the Nazi and Fascist propaganda associated with the civil war. With production of war weapons beginning in many a British engineering works, and consideration of air raid precautions filtering into railway operating philosophies, one did indeed wonder for how much longer the gracious life of Great Britain would prevail. On the north-going railways the high speed streamlined trains did not run on Saturdays, so there was little chance for me of riding on them; but a Westinghouse contract for resignalling on the LNER main line between Northallerton and Darlington involved some site visits, and I usually went from Kings Cross to Darlington on the Silver Jubilee.

Footplate passes for the high speed trains were not granted. At headquarters it was felt that the presence of a stranger could cause a momentary distraction of the driver's attention. It must be remembered that no audible cab signalling, nor automatic train control apparatus was in use on the main lines either of the LNER or of the LMS. But from my footplate work on the big 2-8-2 engines in

Diversifications: Beckton Gas Works, Gas Light & Coke Co, where Westinghouse installed signalling equipment. Here coke ovens are shown in action.

Scotland in 1935 I had been able to place major feature articles with *The Glasgow Herald*, and that newspaper commissioned further articles on Highland railway working in which I described runs between Perth and Inverness, on the West Highland line, and on the Callandar and Oban route. I was in Scotland at the time the Munich crisis blew up in the autumn of 1938 and hurriedly returned south by the Saturday 'Midday Scot'. Yet we ran in such a way as to dispel, for a couple of hours, the ominous thoughts that were in the minds of so many of us. For a 14-coach train we had one of the latest streamlined 'Pacifics', the *Duchess of Rutland*. We left Crewe 9 minutes late and, despite being twice pulled up dead by signals, reached Euston 7½ minutes early!

From that week-end there were just 50 weeks left before the lamps of Europe went out for the second time in my lifetime. Looking back through my travelling diaries I am surprised at the number and variety of the journeys I was able to fit in; except for the Whitsun bank holiday week-end it all had to be done on my free Saturdays, still only one every four weeks. I made two visits to Ireland, and one to Scotland, and elsewhere secured some remarkably good running with two new English 4-6-0 classes—the *British Legion* of the LMS, taper-boilered replacement of the ill-fated high pressure 4-6-0 *Fury*, and one of the 'Lord Nelson's' of the Southern, which Bulleid had improved almost out of recognition by the fitting of a multiple-jet blast pipe and new cylinders. I had also my finest-ever run with one of the original 'Royal Scots', on which No 6132, working the Edinburgh and Aberdeen portion of the train (355 tons) passed Stafford 9½ minutes late, because of signal checks, but was on time at Tring and 1¼ minutes early at Watford having covered the intervening 116.1 miles in 95½ minutes, an average speed of 73 mph. Looking back wistfully at no more than my own records of those 50 weeks, one cannot help wondering how British locomotive practice might have continued developing, had war not come.

Just before the war the first steps were taken towards the most important literary commission that had so far come my way. At this distance in time I cannot remember from whom the first suggestion was made that I should write a series of articles for *The Engineer*, on developments in railway signalling. But the pleasant and exceedingly erudite assistant editor, Dr T.W. Chalmers, was interested, and asked me to write a specimen piece. This request had barely come when war was declared, and I wondered if such a series would be advisable, on the grounds of security and, with all the immediate upsets of war conditions, the project lay fallow for a few weeks. Westinghouse had decided to move the engineering departments, with all the drawings and technical data to Chippenham and, amid all the expectations of heavy air attack, the first weeks of the war were occupied with preparations for the move, both in the office, and at home. For me, having had seven 'home' addresses in 35 years, a house-removal was nothing new; but to the majority of my colleagues in Westinghouse it was just 'the end'. Born and bred in London they had all the inherent disdain of country dwellers; and in the six weeks that elapsed between the outbreak of war and the actual move of the office, when there had been no bombing, many of them felt that the move was unnecessary, and that they would rather stay, and as one man put it 'risk his neck'.

In that six weeks, as can be well imagined, there was little ordinary work done. On the railways, too, it was a time of general upheaval, with all four of the main line companies moving their headquarter offices from London to country houses. It was not until the end of October that things began to assume a degree of normality, but with the public passenger services decelerated beyond belief. Maximum speeds everywhere were limited to 60 mph, and start to stop averages did not exceed 45 mph. The critics at once compared the situation to that prevailing during the first two years of the first world war, when it was not until January 1917 that deceleration of service began in earnest. But really there were no grounds for comparison. In 1914 there had been no conception as to how long the struggle would go on, and the general view was that every effort should be made to maintain a state of 'business as usual'; whereas in 1939, most of us were under no delusions as to what we were in for! It is true that the despatch of the British Expeditionary Force to France, with the number of mechanised road vehicles involved, put far less strain upon the railways than had been experienced in 1914, although many of the railway workshops had already been adapted to the production of war material before the end of 1939.

Domestically we were fortunate in our transition from Bushey to Chippenham. We secured a 2½ bedroom detached house on a new estate. It was unfinished when the office moved, and we had a rather miserable two-months in 'digs' with one of my works colleagues. He was a man with whom I had always got on extremely well; but at home, his wife's outlook was unbelievably bounded by even less than the parish limits, and Olivia frequently found things difficult—to put it mildly. There were times when it was inferred, not only by my colleague's wife but by others that the war was the Londoner's business, not theirs! In the evenings, behind the black-out screens, I was able once again to do some quiet thinking, and I wrote to Dr Chalmers about that suggested series of articles in *The Engineer*. He seemed just as enthusiastic, and said that as long as I did not specifically mention where such a development had taken place he could see no objection to the articles. I wrote a specimen piece; he approved, and I was given the 'rightaway'. It was a welcome relief from the tedium of evening in 'digs' in the black-out.

Behind Chalmers was that truly great editor, Loughnan St Lawrence Pendred, a past-President of the Institution of Mechanical Engineers. It was not until I had contributed a second and third series of articles, one on Automatic Train Control systems, and another on French Locomotive Performance, that I met Pendred himself. I had seen him at meetings of the Institution, but only when I was in a far too-junior capacity to talk to the President. From my earliest attempt at freelance journalism I had come to regard most editors as remote boffins notably adept at delivering rejection slips to would-be contributors; but Pendred was a delightful character. While it could be said that some eminent personalities age to become 'grand old men', he became a 'dear old boy', though still one of the keenest brains, who could be devastatingly critical, when not bubbling over with his native Irish wit. His approbation of my work and his constant encouragement was a solace to me when I needed it badly.

The war brought some interesting constructional jobs to Westinghouse, though little to exercise the specialist expertise in signalling and brakes that had been so assiduously developed over the years. There were other disturbing trends, quite apart from the desperate situations in the war itself, that certain of my colleagues in other departments felt, perhaps even more keenly than I did. Major Peter, with certain important Government assignments, remained in London, though his engineering staff was evacuated in 1939 at the same time as ourselves in the drawing office. It meant that A.G. Kershaw was by far the most senior of the London staff resident in Chippenham during the war, and we were coming to realise that instead of the 'father figure' he might have been he was becoming something of an embarrassment.

At the beginning of the war W.H. Powell, the General Manager, had taken up residence at Chippenham, and each morning he attended the daily conference held between the Works Manager and his senior staff, a gathering that was somewhat irreverently known as 'morning prayers'. It was perhaps symptomatic of his difficult nature, and dislike of meetings generally that Kershaw was never invited to attend, even though there must have been times when the presence of the Chief Mechanical Engineer of the company would have been advantageous. The most senior amongst us in the evacuated London staff, came to feel that there was a rift business-wise between us and the works, which increasing comradeship at lower levels, in the Home Guard and Civil Defence, did little to eradicate.

It was an unhappy situation to exist in the midst of such a war as we were waging, but it seemed to be fostered by the General Manager, in his cordiality towards one side, and frigid attitude to the other. At some times it showed rather obviously to senior officers which way his predilection lay. At midsummer 1942, following a serious illness, he retired, although retaining a seat on the Board of the company. In preparation for post-war development Major Peter was then appointed Chief Engineer, and although it did not make a great deal of difference to our immediate activities it was significant that Kershaw (as Chief Mechanical Engineer) in future reported to Major Peter, there being no appointment of General Manager in succession to Powell.

Civil Defence would not have been a British institution if it had not produced some hilarious moments in our rural community. I had it by day and night,

Our wartime home at Chippenham, before we took possession, at 20 Yewstock Crescent East.

because I was Chief Warden of the Hathaways Building of Westinghouse, where the evacuated London engineering staff were accommodated, and at night I was one of the District Controllers of the Chippenham area, under the Wiltshire County Council. When bombing started in 1940, sporadic though it was in our area, the country folks were quite fearless. One of the wardens, a farmer, rang the Control Centre to report a shower of incendiaries in one of his fields, and that he and one of his men had gone round with pails of cow manure. 'With what?', almost screamed the controller on duty. 'Oh yes, zur; it puts 'em out fine': effective, but not in the instruction book!

One night, when the enemy was not about, there was a heavy west wind blowing. Those of us on duty were enjoying a quiet rubber of bridge, when suddenly the 'phone rang. It was the Chief Warden of a village some four miles away. Taking a look round before he went to bed he saw 'a dark object, judged to be about 10,000 feet up with sparks coming out of it'. The Chief Controller of the area, who happened to be in the room at the time said, 'Sounds to me as if one of the Bristol barrage balloons has broken loose, and is on fire'. The village warden readily agreed with this diagnosis, and the next 10 to 15 minutes were spent in telephoning every authority likely to be affected if our suspicions were true: the RAF; fire brigades, County Control and everyone else we could think of. In a slight pause the phone rang sharply, and was just as sharply snatched up. It was the country warden who had first given the alarm. He said: 'I've just discovered what that thing is—its my own chimney on fire!'.

Early in 1942 I had learned, to my great regret, that W.A. Willox had relinquished his appointments as Associate Editor of *The Railway Gazette* and Editor of *The Railway Magazine*. No mention of his going was made in either journal, nor of any other editorial staff changes. I learned also that John Kay, the Manager and Editor-in-Chief, had made certain appointments that he regarded as little more than temporary. Willox's departure was due to serious internal differences of opinion on editorial policy. Just what those differences were I do not know, but I gathered that the situation eventually became very unpleasant, and doubly difficult in war conditions. Kay asked the veteran consultant and mechanical engineering contributor, Charles S. Lake, to become an Associate Editor, even though he was already 70 years of age; but within a year Lake died, and with the war situation building up to the climax of re-entry to the continent of Europe, plans for post-war development had to be made.

Early in December 1943 Kay wrote and asked when I would next be in London. At that time it was not easy to arrange, but eventually an appointment was fixed for late one afternoon, only a few days before Christmas. He then astonished me by asking me to join his staff as chief associate editor, of both the railway papers, and at a salary roughly double that I was currently receiving from Westinghouse. I spent that Christmas in something of a daze. The conflicting prospects crossed and re-crossed my mind. Olivia, as usual, was marvellous, and helped me at every turn. While the salary offered was highly attractive, joining the staff at Tothill Street would see the end of my contributions to other journals, notably *The Engineer*, and eventually after days of cogitation I went to see Major Peter. He said at once 'Take it'. He went on to tell me that in the post-war reconstruction he had got me booked for a fresh job, but at nothing like the salary that Kay had offered. Before finally agreeing to the appointment, which I made clear would have to wait until the war was sufficiently near its end for Westinghouse to release me, I asked Kay how certain senior members of the editorial staff would regard my appointment. I was thinking particularly of the man who was mainly responsible for the departure of Willox; but Kay was reassuring on that point, and I became sufficiently confident to tell Major Peter I should like to be released after the war.

Then the summer of 1944 brought not only D-Day, and the Flying Bombs, but disturbing news about happenings at Tothill Street. Tom Lascelles, as signalling consultant, had his ears very close to the ground on other matters as well, and he told me that the 'grape vine' regarding my forthcoming appointment had reached certain senior people, and that preparations were being made to give me a rough passage. This was disquieting, remembering what had happened to Willox; but what caused me to hesitate still more was a very attractive suggestion for an extensive series of articles from *The Engineer*, on locomotive working in wartime. What finally determined me to turn down John Kay's offer, however, was the news that at the end of the year Kershaw was being retired. The way would thus be clear for a continuance, under greatly improved conditions, of my professional life's work, but with the assurance that my literary work would be openly regarded as an asset to the firm. The cloak and dagger situation would be ended.

Chapter 8

Years of austerity and opportunity

The year 1945 began with the war still raging; and while in Europe the tide of battle on both eastern and western fronts was rolling heavily against Hitler, the German high command had nevertheless discerned a weak link in the west and in the majestic mountain country of the Ardennes gone over to the offensive with a success that for a few weeks was distinctly embarrassing to the American units affected. Even so, there could no longer be any doubt about the eventual military outcome, however complex and disturbing the developing political and international situations might appear. In Westinghouse, in the drawing offices, the prospects were brighter than for many a long day. In pre-war days Kenneth H. Leech had been chief draughtsman of the brake section, and while reporting to Kershaw like the rest of us, he was senior in status and on a higher level. Before the First World War he had been a pupil of Robert Whitelegg, locomotive superintendent of the London Tilbury and Southend Railway, before its absorption by the Midland, and subsequently he had served as a locomotive officer in the Railway Operating Division through the later years of the war. As from January 1945 he was appointed Design Engineer of Westinghouse, taking charge of all the drawing offices.

The prospect of having as my boss someone who was sympathetic to my extra-mural interests was, of course, more than welcome. Furthermore I received not only from him, but from higher authority, every encouragement to contribute to the technical press. In Westinghouse itself I received something of a jolt when I was asked to undertake the chief draughtsmanship of the *brake* section. From my interests in locomotives generally and from riding on the footplate I was familiar with the principles on which the air and the vacuum brake worked; but the finer points of design would be new ground for me, not to mention the 'uncharted area' of road brakes, in which the company had fulfilled very large contracts for military vehicles during the war. However, the 'old guard' of the brake drawing office gave a generous if slightly patronising welcome to the 'new boy', and relations became very cordial. I am not going to deny, however, that it involved me in some pretty intensive homework, for a few months!

Early in 1946 a brake job of an unusual kind came our way. A dispute between two unions at Swindon Works, which in retrospect seems to have been of the Tweedledum *versus* Tweedledee order, brought the construction of new carriages to a halt, from January, and this footling disagreement was not resolved until nine months later. In the meantime, with new carriages of the

Hawksworth bow-ended type urgently needed, orders were placed with the Gloucester Railway Carriage and Wagon Co Ltd, to the Great Western design. The contractors placed orders for the vacuum brake equipment on Westinghouse. This was to the GWR standard pattern and involved designs that were new, to us. Swindon supplied drawings readily enough, but we soon found that many details were apparently left to the imagination. I went to Swindon to try and clarify many points, but to my amusement found that the drawing office there were none the wiser. We had to go into the works to find out just how certain details had been made—apparently for the last 20 or 30 years!

At John Kay's suggestion, at the time when there was a likelihood of my joining his staff, I had joined the Institution of Civil Engineers, much to the amusement of Major Peter, who in backing my application thought it highly incongruous that anything electrical should be designated as 'civil' engineering. He was still unconvinced when I told him how the 'Civils' originated, to bring together all engineers who were not involved in military engineering, with Telford as the first President. It was in the Christmas holidays of 1945 that the 'Civils' determined that the traditional lectures for boys should be about railways, and with Cecil J. Allen and L.G.B. Rock of the Southern Railway I was one of the three engineers chosen to do the job. Peter was most enthusiastic, and asked me to look out for likely recruits for Westinghouse in the audience. To get the 'feel' of the occasion I went to the first one, given by Allen, and not long after he had started I was called outside to answer a telephone call. In the corridor I met the assistant secretary of the Institution splitting his sides with laughter. He told me he had just met a boy, arriving for the lecture who had said breathlessly he was sorry he was late: it was because he had come by train!

We repeated those lectures in Glasgow, in the 1946–7 Christmas holiday, and in Belfast in 1947–8. In the latter case the lead up to it was traumatic in that I had my lantern slides impounded by the customs! I had also received an invitation to lecture to the Royal Dublin Society on modern locomotive development, and by some adroit planning managed to get the two lectures on to successive days. The Dublin folks were most careful to point out that lantern slides were a dutiable commodity so far as the Irish customs were concerned, and impressed upon me how necessary it was to get them checked in, when I landed in the Free State at Dun Laoghaire—otherwise I should never get them out again. I followed the instructions, and had no difficulty, nor in passing them out at Dundalk next day. But nobody had warned about the United Kingdom customs, and that I should have had them checked out at Holyhead. At Goraghwood the Northern Ireland customs swooped, taking my suitcase as well! Fortunately in Belfast my host for the day was the Chief Engineer of the Port of Belfast Authority. He sent an assistant to the custom house, who played all hell. My slides (and my suitcase) rejoined me when I was a quarter of the way through the lecture!

While the change in the high management at Westinghouse had opened up for me greatly increased opportunities to develop my literary activities, the British General Election of 1945 in which Winston Churchill, to quote his own words, was 'dismissed by the British electorate' and the rest of the world was stunned into disbelief that such a leader could thus be discarded, caused a grievous decline in confidence in Britain, and plunged us into a period of severe financial austerity, while preparations began in Parliament for the Bill that would

Post-war Westinghouse signalling in the North-East: the new control panel at Newcastle Central.

nationalise the railways. That the new Minister of Transport, Alfred Barnes, had no previous experience of transport in any form was typical of the new era. In the meantime I had from Loughnan Pendred, of *The Engineer*, a literary assignment that was to take me far and wide, on the still privately-owned railways of Great Britain. It was a pleasant change to be able to do so, confident of the backing from Westinghouse, where my contacts with railway officers were coming to be regarded as good public relations work for the company.

Pendred wanted some first-hand accounts of how British locomotives were standing up to the conditions of wartime. When I pointed out that I would be able to go out and ride on the footplate only at week-ends he tossed my slight hesitancy to one side, remarking that it couldn't be better from his point of view, because I would see things at their worst. Authority to ride was readily forthcoming from all the four main line railways, and so, from November 1944, I set out stage by stage, upon an extraordinary saga. During the war, the little travelling I had done for Westinghouse had been enough to open up some of the difficulties that were met in getting accommodation, and food. It was perhaps even worse, in 1945 and 1946 when post-war austerity hit us in all its misery. I slept in some strange places during that footplate odessey; but all in all it was the experience of a life-time. The flying-bomb and 'V2' rocket attacks were still in progress when I began my field-work for this assignment, and at the start I made journeys that kept clear of London and the Home Counties.

To get the maximum mileage in the time I had available I travelled only by express passenger trains, and although the overall scheduled speeds were slow compared to what was required in pre-war days the loads were generally heavier, and demands upon locomotive power often quite severe. Having regard to the quality of the coal often provided, and that in many cases the locomotives were well beyond their normal mileages for shopping, the engine performance was, for the most part, remarkably good, though because of congestion on some of the lines the time-keeping was often pretty chaotic. During the war even the most important express passenger trains were not given priority, and at the time I made my journeys wartime conditions still prevailed. Even after the cessation of hostilities in Europe a large number of special trains were still needed, while at week-ends, when nearly all my journeys were made, many of the trains that I selected for observation were running in two, or more sections.

My first trips on the Great Western, made late in 1944, were not representative as far as engine condition was concerned. The West to North expresses worked as double-home turns by Shrewsbury and Newton Abbot engines and men on alternate days were treated as prestige jobs, even to the extent of keeping the engines themselves quite regally clean. On my northbound journey No 5032 *Usk Castle* was a positive apparition, in wartime, and her mechanical condition matched her outward appearance. But there was a relief portion running ahead of us from Newton Abbot as far as Bristol, and this picked up most of the traffic at intermediate stations, with appropriately long waits at stations like Exeter, Taunton and Weston-super-Mare, with the result that we were closely on her tail, and frequently sighting adverse signals. We were 21 minutes late on arrival at Bristol, and with the almost inevitable delays through the Severn Tunnel and through the congested areas of South Wales our lateness had nearly doubled by the time we left Pontypool Road, and could at last run, with a welcome succession of clear signals.

It was much the same on my southbound trip from Shrewsbury a month later, on one of the 'Castles' that had been renamed in honour of aircraft famed for their exploits in the Battle of Britain, No 5072 *Hurricane*. In the early days of the war, when travelling passenger on this same train I had noted an exceptionally fine run with this engine, when carrying her original name of *Compton Castle*, and the run of 1944 was little inferior to that of 1940.

On the first of the 'Kings' to have high degree superheating: No 6022, King Edward III, *giving us a splendid run on the up 'Cornish Riviera Express' approaching Reading West* (M.W. Earley).

Riding a 'Urie-Arthur' in 1945 on No 747, Elaine, *on the 11.30 am Waterloo to Bournemouth passing Battledown Junction* (M.W. Earley).

Despite war conditions the locomotive department of the LMS had begun the reboilering of the 'Royal Scot' Class 4-6-0s, using a tapered barrel, in the Stanier tradition, and the carefully shaped firebox that had served the Great Western so well from Churchward's day. By the spring of 1945 four of these rebuilt engines were stationed at Leeds, and primarily engaged on the double-home turns to Glasgow St Enoch, with the Midland route Anglo-Scottish expresses. H.G. Ivatt, who was then Principal Assistant (Locomotives) to the CME, then C.E. Fairburn, told me with pride of the good results they had obtained during trials with one of these engines. It was not practicable to use the dynamometer car, and all its staff and appurtenances in wartime, but they took indicator diagrams from engines working service trains. Mr Ivatt readily arranged for me to ride one of them from Leeds to Glasgow. The former Midland shed at Whitehall Junction, Leeds, had a reputation for keeping its express locomotives in excellent condition and, on the occasion of my trip, No 6117 *Welsh Guardsman*, although in plain wartime black, looked very smart.

The day 'Scotch Express' from St Pancras, was one of those wartime trains that had a bad timekeeping record, and there was a complication north of Hellifield. The express was due to leave there at 4.47 pm and it was followed, at 5.20 pm by an all-stations local to Carlisle. The express provided the only evening connection from the south to those intermediate stations, and its late running could be an embarrassment. It was undesirable to hold the local at Hellifield later than 5.50 pm because it had forward connections to make at Carlisle; so if the 'Scotch Express' was more than 60 minutes late the local was sent away from Hellifield on time, and the express doomed to stop at all stations beyond Hellifield for which it was carrying passengers—very nice and considerate for them, but disastrous for the further running of the express. On one occasion noted by Cecil J. Allen the train was 75 minutes late at Hellifield and, with six extra stops, reached Carlisle 105 minutes late. On the occasion when I travelled, however, fortune favoured us. We left Leeds no more than

16½ minutes late, and with a wonderfully clear road for wartime, were able to recover all the arrears and clock into Glasgow on time.

The taper-boilered 'Scot' was impressive in the apparent ease with which she did the work. Except between Horton and Blea Moor she did not appear to be opened out at all, with a heavy train of 450 tons. But although for the most part steam was being cut off in the cylinders very early in the piston stroke, indicating exceptional economy by comparison with other locomotives of comparable power, this was not borne out by the coal and water consumption, which was normal for the nature of the work performed. This was my first experience with one of the rebuilt engines. The opinion I formed after many subsequent runs was that they were no better, if as good, as the original 'Scots' in heavy traffic. Their merit lay in the reduced maintenance costs, which amply justified the rebuilding as the boilers of the original engines fell due for replacement.

I returned from Glasgow a few days later on the corresponding southbound train for St Pancras; but one of the new 'Scots' was not available, and we had instead a Stanier 3-cylinder 'Jubilee' Class 4-6-0, so indescribably dirty that a close look was needed to discover the name, *Victoria*. She also belonged to Leeds shed, and was mechanically in excellent condition. Some hard thrashing was needed to keep some of the fairly sharp intermediate timings; but, scruffy thing though she looked, she stood up to it magnificently, and turned in a superb performance. My authority to ride on the footplate extended only to Leeds; I was travelling through to London, but anticipating that there would be the usual tremendous wartime crowd waiting to board the train at Leeds itself, and that the chances of getting a seat from there were minimal, I decided to bring my footplate work to an end at Hellifield. The train was already very crowded but I expected there would be a big interchange at Leeds. Good thinking, but I didn't anticipate the difficulty of getting *any* entry to that packed train at Hellifield. The people jammed in the corridors were not unwilling, but were physically incapable of making room for a dirty fellow in overalls. How I did manage to board the train, and find my way to a lavatory for a clean up was an epic in itself. But the ploy worked. I got a *seat* at Leeds.

'VE' day had come and gone when I made my first trips on London and North Eastern locomotives. To get as great a variety of working as possible I rode the 6.45 am from Colchester to York, and thence continued by *The Flying Scotsman* to Edinburgh; and what a day it was! The first train was the wartime equivalent of the North Country Continental, but starting from Colchester instead of from Parkeston Quay, for the benefit of the many servicemen quartered thereabouts. On the first stage we had an ex-Great Eastern 4-6-0, rebuilt by Gresley with a larger boiler, and fitted with long travel valves. The engine was originally No 1556 of the GER, built in 1920, and it became 8556 in the LNER stock. By the time I rode it, in 1945, it had fallen a victim to the nonsensical renumbering of the entire locomotive stock initiated by Edward Thompson, after he had succeeded Sir Nigel Gresley as Chief Mechanical Engineer. The engine in question then became No 7470.

That renumbering and all its attendant paper work, carried out in the middle of the war, was just one of the ways in which the new chief turned the CME's department upside down, and at a most unpropitious time. It had some surprising repercussions. In pre-war days the spectacular performances of the Gresley 'Pacifics' had attracted a following, in the railway enthusiast world, stronger in its devotion to the products of the 'master engineer' than anything that has been worked up on behalf of the Great Western in post-war years. In fact such was the attention given to it that a sarcastic partisan of another railway suggested that the name of the Stephenson Locomotive Society should be changed to the Gresley Locomotive Society!

Thompson's first moves were watched with bated breath; but when he rebuilt one of the magnificent 'P2' 2-8-2s as an ugly ill-shaped 'Pacific', and followed this with a horrible mutilation of the pioneer Gresley 'Pacific', the *Great Northern*, the heather was ablaze! Enthusiasts of every estate and calling wrote not only to the hobbyist journals, but also to *The Railway Gazette* asking in plain terms just what the hell Thompson was thinking about. The neophytes tried in reply to justify him, and the battle was joined in earnest. Thompson read it all, and was apparently very upset; but it was not until I had run nearly 1,000 miles on LNER engines, in 1945, that I became embroiled in it personally. First of all, however, I must summarise the results of a remarkable sequence of journeys.

I could have wished that my run on the ex-GER 4-6-0 had been longer, because she was a real lady, hauling a 12-coach train with ease, although the schedule times were not exacting: 14 minutes for the 7.8 miles from Colchester to Manningtree, and 17 minutes for 9.2 miles on to Ipswich, in each case start to stop. Then at Ipswich we changed engines, and got instead one of Thompson's 'B1' 4-6-0s. She had been out of the shops, since construction, for 16 months, and looked appropriately scruffy. The 'B1' was undoubtedly Thomson's best design. It was a skilful synthesis of existing standard parts, taking the cylinders from the 'K2' Mogul, the boiler of the 'Sandringham' 4-6-0 and 6 foot 2 inch coupled wheels of the 'V2' 2-6-2. It was an entirely commendable job for wartime, involving no new tooling or pattern making. But no adjusting wedges were fitted in the coupled wheel axle-boxes and, as wear developed, the riding became unbelievably harsh. On turning up my scribbled notes made on the footplate at the time I had stigmatised the engine as 'a vicious, kicking little brute'. So we made our way round to March, stopping intermediately at Bury St Edmunds and Ely. We made no speed records on that trip. The schedule did not demand it, and the engine did the job easily and economically; but of cab-comfort there was none. The engine was named *Blackbuck*, and in sending me a photograph he took of us leaving Ely, in miserable weather, E.R. Wethersett capped the situation by saying 'It was a *blackbuck* of a day!'.

At March I was sorry to say farewell to the friendly Ipswich enginemen, but *not* sorry to part from their steed. I was beginning to feel my bruises already. I wondered also what was to follow when I saw a grimy travel-stained 'Green Arrow' 2-6-2 backing down on to the train. Amid all the sound and fury that had marked the Thompson controversy in the railway press the liability to failure of the conjugated gear for actuating the piston valves of the middle cylinder had loomed large, and the 'Green Arrows', as the intensively used heavy main line work-horses had, according to Gresley's detractors, suffered severely. So it was in some curiosity that I climbed aboard engine No 4838 at March, which in 1945 still retained its original number. As we gathered speed, slowly because of a tendency to slip on wet rails in the prevailing drizzle, I was interested to see the driver open out to absolutely full regulator, and wind back the reverser till the cut-off in the cylinders was as early as 10 per cent of the piston stroke; and this shabby, apparently uncared for engine revealed herself as a lady of ladies! Never before, or since, have I ridden an engine that was sweeter in her action, or more luxurious to ride. It is true that the schedule did not demand speeds of more than 60 mph between stops, but the line from March up to Doncaster, with stops at Spalding, Sleaford, Lincoln and Gainsborough, has never been one of the country's speedways.

At Doncaster we changed engines, and got another 'V2' No 4808, with Grantham men in charge, but I was interested to find we were taking the original route from Doncaster to York, via Knottingley, that was used by East Coast expresses from London to Edinburgh prior to the opening of the direct North Eastern line via Selby, in January 1871. It was used as a relief route to a considerable extent during the Second World War, to avoid congestion at Selby. We were heading north from Doncaster just ahead of what used to be called the '10 o'clock group' of expresses from Kings Cross, those preceeding and following *The Flying Scotsman* at close headway. During the war there was a heavy flow of traffic to and from Hull, much of which crossed the East Coast main line to Selby. The routing of some trains in the close procession from Doncaster via Knottingley (only 2¼ miles further) provided a few gaps through which west-east intersecting traffic could be passed at Selby. Line occupation in this area was as tight as that in 1945.

Engine No 4808 was also in excellent condition, continuing to belie the reputation accorded to the 'V2s' by the anti-Gresley faction but, with the 60 mph limit prevailing, we did no spectacular running. Two incidents on the journey remain vividly in mind. We had reduced speed to 30 mph to take the left-hand turnout at Shaftholme Junction, and were getting powerfully away again with our big load, now of 475 tons, when, at an occupation crossing not 200 yards ahead, a farmer nonchalantly drove two horses across the line in front of us, as we were bearing down upon them at 55 mph! It was one of those incidents that are over so quickly that there is hardly time to think. There were muttered exclamations on the footplate—we dare not whistle—and fists were shaken as we passed. But it was all to no purpose, for the farmer did not even deign to look round, even though he had got clear by no more than a few seconds!

At Church Fenton, where the line from Leeds to York came abreast, we continued on the eastern pair of tracks of the quadruple line northwards. But after having regained maximum speed on the fine level stretch that follows we were cautioned by signal approaching Chaloners Whin Junction and crossed over from the east to the west lines so that the 9.40 pm from Kings Cross, which had come via Selby, could approach York at the same time as ourselves. As we were threading our way through the crossover road she came round the curve from Naburn headed by another 'Green Arrow', and the two trains ran abreast of each other up the four-track section to York—an excellent example of traffic regulation. Though again we had made no speed records I climbed down from No 4808 convinced that whatever their detractors might say these 'V2s' were as good as any Gresley 3-cylinder engines I had ridden before the war. The train from Colchester terminated at York and the platforms were soon swarming with the many hundreds of passengers we had conveyed. Many piled into the 9.40 am from Kings Cross, alongside which we had run from Chaloners Whin Junction, while others waited for *The Flying Scotsman* itself. The 9.40 am left behind the same 'Green Arrow'. During the war through engine workings between Newcastle and Grantham were common, often with remanning at York.

No more than ten minutes later *The Flying Scotsman* came in, with a colossal load of 17 of the heaviest LNER coaches, packed to the guard's vans, and hauled by an 'A4' No 4482 *Golden Eagle.* The Grantham men handing her over were not enthusiastic; they just said: 'She won't steam'. But in 1945 this was nothing new to the cheery York driver and fireman who were taking over, and while the train stood at the platform they worked assiduously on the fire and had nearly 250 lb per square inch showing on the gauge before we left. The engine just 'lifted' that enormous train out of York, and by Tollerton, less than 10 miles out, was doing 68 mph on the level. But by that time pressure was dropping rapidly; it was no more than 175 lb per square inch, and the best the keen and hard working fireman could do thereafter was to give his driver 135 to 145 lb per square inch. The boiler was overdue for washout. Many of the tubes were blocked, but despite this we regained 6 minutes of the lateness on departure from York, taking 94 minutes for the 80.1 miles to Newcastle.

There No 4482 was exchanged for No 4483, *Kingfisher,* in first class mechanical condition, and steaming freely. By this time, however, the weather had become very bad, and with this heavy train the engine slipped repeatedly on each of the severe rising gradients, in particular when starting from up the continuous 1 in 190 gradient from Berwick-on-Tweed. On the favourable stretches we forgot about wartime speed restrictions and, 17-coach train or not,

Post-war footplating: on LNER 'A4' Pacific Golden Eagle, *from York to Newcastle with the 630-ton* Flying Scotsman, *when the engine would not steam!*

Waverley Station, Edinburgh, in 1948: an 'A4' Pacific No 19, Bittern, *on which I travelled south, alongside a 'Glen' Class 4-4-0.*

we went like the wind along the Northumberland coast, making an average speed of 71.7 mph over the 17.8 miles from Christon Bank to Goswick, including a maximum speed of 83½ mph. In view of the official limit of 60 mph over the entire LNER system at that time, I had to keep the details of this exhilarating spurt very much 'under my hat'. I can add that the engine rode magnificently, and after six years of war it was a joyous experience. It was not until seven years later that I was able to publish that exciting maximum speed.

I returned to London in somewhat spartan conditions on 'The Night Scotsman', but it was after my second trip to Scotland, when I made return trips on the footplate from Edinburgh to Carlisle and back, and to Aberdeen, that Edward Thompson invited me to visit him at Doncaster, and to stay as guest in his home. In a long evening session he went to great lengths to explain to me why he thought Gresley's policy had been wrong, and told me of an incident that took place immediately after he had received the appointment of Chief Mechanical Engineer from the Chairman, Sir Ronald Matthews. The Chairman, in words to this effect, said there was no need for any new types of locomotives in wartime. They had the best in the country; just carry on where Gresley left off. Thompson told me how he replied, 'My appointment is at your disposal, Chairman, but I cannot do this'. He went on to tell the astonished Sir Ronald what he considered was so seriously wrong, and asked for an independent examination of the 3-cylinder valve gear situation. After much hesitation the Chairman agreed. Thompson first of all asked Bulleid to do it, who refused. Eventually Stanier agreed, but the assistant he sent to Doncaster to investigate the records made his report in such a way that it could readily be interpreted equally as for or against Gresley. It was no more than natural that a mechanism including many pin joints would develop undue travel in certain directions if the wear in the pins was allowed to become excessive. It was, however, not until many years later that the basic cause of over-travel on the valves of the middle cylinder was diagnosed, and eradicated. But in Thompson's day, on the LNER, the report by Stanier's assistant was taken as enough to justify rebuilding the existing 3-cylinder engines.

I found Thompson a charming host, but in the short time of my personal contact with him, and in the Works next day, I saw several glimpses of the harsh and spiteful side of his character. At his express wish I wrote a booklet, which the LNER published, detailing the standardisation programme that he had initiated, and the policy in design that had lain behind it. An author writing of contemporary events, and particularly of engineering matters conducted against a background of such conflicting emotions, inevitably finds himself doing something of a tight-rope act. Certainly the prowess of the Thompson locomotives did not turn out quite in the way I predicted in that booklet, particularly with his 'Pacific' engines. Reading it again there are some passages where I would very much like to eat my words today! Even Thompson, with all his persuasive and eloquent advocacy, could not convince me that his drastic rebuilds of the beautiful Gresley 'P2' 2-8-2s, as 'Pacifics', and of *Great Northern* had produced better engines. It does not behove a privileged guest to

Riding one of the last of the Great Western 'Stars', No 4062, Malmesbury Abbey, *on the up 'Merchant Venturer' at Thingley Junction, near Chippenham* (Kenneth H. Leech).

speak ill of his host's work, and my criticisms had to wait until many years after he had passed on.

The last round of my footplate expeditions for *The Engineer* in 1944–5 were on the Southern and there, of course, the principal objects of interest were the Bulleid 'Pacifics'. By the end of the war the very controversial 'Merchant Navy' Class was being followed by the smaller and lighter 'West Country' Class and my first expedition took me to Ilfracombe, to gain some experience of both classes. My free time was still very limited, but on Sundays there was a good train up from Exeter, and I began with the 2.45 pm down from Salisbury on the Saturday afternoon, which I could catch by travelling from Chippenham, after business hours, via Westbury. So I was able to get in runs with three different 'Merchant Navy' Class, and two 'West Countries' between Exeter and Ilfracombe. However much those of us who were more conservatively, or traditionally minded as far as locomotive lineaments are concerned, may have looked askance at the Bulleid 'Pacifics' there is not a shadow of doubt that he had caught popular fancy in these engines. When we changed engines at Exeter on the down journey, and a brand new 'West Country'—startling in its malachite green and yellow stripes—backed on to take the train forward to Ilfracombe, a little crowd looked on with positive awe, and one man exclaimed: 'doesn't it give an impression of *power*'. How a tin casing could do that rather baffles me, but in the eyes of the public Bulleid had shown that the Southern was 'with it', in the post-war world.

I wonder what those awe-struck onlookers would have thought if any of them could have ridden back from Exeter to Salisbury with me on the following day, and experienced the almost indescribable racket that developed when one of the

The family in gala mood at a lineside picnic near Midsomer Norton, Somerset and Dorset line. Trevor was then about 10 years old.

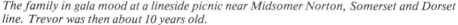

'Merchant Navys', somewhat run down and wildly off her beat, was taken all out down the Seaton bank? With a heavy train of 450 tons she was weak on the banks, and even on a wartime schedule was losing time uphill; but her driver and fireman were a resolute pair, and one can imagine their attitude: 'If she won't go uphill, then by thunder she'll go down'. Now Seaton bank is very steep and very straight, and once we had crawled through Honiton Tunnel the fun—if I can call it so!—started. It did not need much steam to assist gravity here, but the driver gave her as much as he'd got; and after scrambling over the summit away we went, pell mell, in a crescendo of noise, flying coal dust, and a sensation that the whole thing was going to rattle itself to pieces. When I add that we approached Seaton Junction at 85 mph one can imagine what it was like on the footplate. The one saving grace was that even in such a rough and run-down condition the engine was still quite steady.

This was just the beginning of the tempestuous Bulleid 'Pacific' saga, about which so many stories true and apocryphal have been told. Nevertheless although his work may be heavily criticised on engineering grounds, wittingly or unwittingly, he gave the Southern Railway a tremendous fillip in those drab days immediately after the end of the war when, having had to 'make do' and patch up throughout the war, the whole nation was yearning for a 'new look' to cheer us up. In the railway world Bulleid certainly gave it to us in the 'Merchant Navy' and 'West Country' Classes. I have much cause to be grateful to him personally. He wrote a most generous foreword to my very first book, *The Locomotives of Sir Nigel Gresley*; published in 1945, and he gave me much help with subsequent ones. I used to send him the draft of my articles, or chapters of books concerned with Southern Railway locomotives, and was amused when he

Memories of early post-war holidays: Shaldon, Devon, old houses around the bowling green.

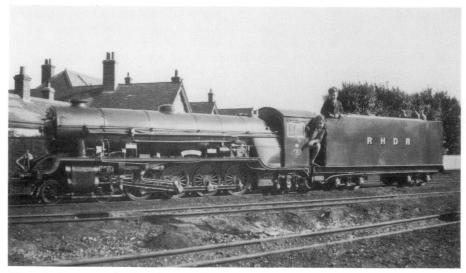

Jill and Trevor on the footplate of the 15-inch gauge, 4-8-2, Hercules *of the Romney Hythe and Dymchurch Railway, at Littlestone.*

sent one back annotated in his own writing. I had entitled it: 'Modern 4-6-0s of the Southern', and it came back with the first word deleted. In his letter he said that the Southern had no 'modern' 4-6-0s!

The commission that Loughnan Pendred had given me, and which his son urged me to continue long after the wartime conditions had largely disappeared, enabled me not only to gain a most comprehensive picture of locomotive working all over the country, but to meet most of the leading railway mechanical engineers of the day, and to be taken into their confidence. I never cease to be grateful for the opportunities that opened to me through that original commission of 1944.

Chapter 9

Upheavals on all hands

At the end of 1945 the British railway world was agog with the prospects of nationalisation. The huge majority accorded to the Labour Government made inevitable its major election pledge to nationalise transport. Those who held other political views had just got to swallow that pill. As the proposed legislation was presented to Parliament, however, it seemed clear at the very outset that an opportunity of centuries was going to be lost. To any *user* of the transport industry of Great Britain, as distinct from employees of one branch or another, or from contractors, the crying need was surely for a carefully built up coordination of road and rail facilities, and expertise, using each to the best advantage, to replace the ruinous competition that had developed in the inter-war years, and led the privately owned railway companies to embark upon the 'Square Deal' campaign. But in 1945 and afterwards political dogma rather than a true imaginative grasp of the transport needs of the country was uppermost.

In his very revealing book, *The Birth of British Rail*, Michael Bonavia has, in three sentences, laid bare the keynote of the whole business. He writes, 'Alfred Barnes, the Minister of Transport who piloted the 1947 nationalisation Act through the Commons, was an uninspiring character. His promotion to Cabinet rank had been a reward for years of service in the Co-operative movement. He had had no previous involvement in transport and merely stuck to the task laid down for him in the party manifesto and in the briefs written for him by his civil servants—treating the whole vast operation as a chore to be performed without complaint'. He will be remembered by the members of the original Railway Executive for his love of treacle pudding and his insistence upon having it every time he came to lunch with them. And 'treacle pudding' just about summarises much of the legislation incorporated in the 1947 Act!

While Barnes was plodding his way through the Parliamentary debates, in technical circles the call to modernise motive power was gathering strength. The Americans who had been with us in such numbers prior to D-Day had not seen the British railways at their best. They were surprised at the smallness of our locomotives and at the preponderance of the type they call 'Ten-wheelers'—otherwise 4-6-0s; and they had emphasised, perhaps then in a slightly exaggerated manner, how steam traction was being replaced by diesels. It was disconcerting to those of us who were concerned with the grass-roots of railway motive power how this unintentional propaganda began to spread, even to railway technical officers. On one of my visits to Swindon, in connection with the vacuum brake business referred to in the previous chapter, I was rather appalled to hear one quite senior engineer refer to steam locomotives generally as antiquated.

Two experiences of my own among the many footplate runs I had made in 1945 had displayed the extraordinary resilience of the steam locomotive in adversity, and how utterly indispensable a tool it could be in a time of the deepest austerity such as we had begun to experience since the result of the General Election of 1945 was known. I have referred briefly to the Bulleid 'Pacific' engine on which I rode from Exeter to Salisbury, which was named *Canadian Pacific*. So many things were loose, and rattling, and the motion was so much out of adjustment that the wonder was it would run at all. But this engine was nothing to a Gresley 'Green Arrow' 2-6-2 on which I rode from Aberdeen down to Edinburgh. I think it was the roughest thing I have ever known. Yet the driver and fireman flailed it along with a confidence that took one's breath away, and they ran the train dead on time! Like the Bulleid 'Pacific', because of the maladjustment of the valve-gear, it was a bit weak uphill, but no hesitation was shown in driving it fast downhill, and we frequently exceeded the 60 mph speed limit in force over the whole of the LNER. With such a termagant of an engine I feel constrained not to apply the traditional feminine gender. 'She' was no lady, not even a 'she'; only an 'it'!

The moral of these two experiences, however, is that no matter how rough and run down these engines were they would still go, and go fast and safely. The simplicity of the machinery and the robustness of its construction made that possible. In more recent times we have learned, only too often, how slight a defect can produce a total failure on a diesel. It is safe to say that if diesel-electric locomotives had been introduced in Great Britain, on any scale, immediately after the war, the result would have been catastrophic. Some of the manufacturers were anxious to see the building of new steam locomotives terminated; but the economics of the day, and the conditions in which locomotives were currently being maintained in this country, made it out of the question. This did not, of course, preclude the building of a few non-steam locomotives for experimental purposes; but nothing more was expedient at the time.

It was in these same eventful days that a crisis of personnel developed in Westinghouse. With the end of the war the former London staff, evacuated to Chippenham, looked forward to a return to their old homes and environment; and while it was appreciated that the serious damage suffered by the headquarters building in York Way, Kings Cross, would need considerably more attention than the patching repairs after the 'incident' of 1941, hopes of an early return stayed high. There was, therefore, every gratification when Donald F. Brown, son of the Managing Director of the 1920s, and now himself a director, came to Chippenham early in 1946, and urged all members of the London staff to start making arrangements for their personal return, because, as he emphasised it, the company did not want men to be troubled with family removals when the time came for the office to be transferred back.

Many of us at once began laying plans. Our own pre-war home had been rented, and was not available; but nearby was the old family home from 1930, which had been let, to various families during the war. My father and mother, both in their mid-70s, had no desire to resume occupation of so relatively large a house, and so arrangements were made to transfer the ownership to me. The sitting tenant was ready to vacate in the early autumn, and so we decided to sell the little house in Chippenham and for Olivia and the children (then aged 8 and 4) to take over in Bushey at the beginning of October. The hazards of the day take some believing now. It was a time when squatters could enter any unoccupied premises, and the legal proceedings to evict them could take much time. So we arranged our removal to take place the very next day after the tenant had gone. Even so, my father received a requisition order from the local Council on the very day the tenant moved out. Fortunately we were in, and the new tenancy established, before any action could be taken on the requisition order. But it was a frightening thought as to what could have happened had we delayed for only a few days!

In Westinghouse it was generally agreed that a considerably larger drawing office would be needed and that the build-up must begin at once. In view of the foreshadowed return to York Way it was logical that the new entrants should be men resident in the London area, and after week-ends spent in our post-war home in Bushey it became part of my duties to interview prospective new staff at Head Office on Monday mornings. We had, fortunately, two men of section-leader status released from their wartime duties who were able to take charge of a growing staff, and on my own weekly visits I was able to oversee the progress of work furnished by Chippenham. This arrangement enabled me to spend most week-ends at home at Bushey; but while this was congenial up to a point, the onset of exceptionally severe weather at the end of January, ushering in what was described as the worst winter since 1895, made my week-end journeys hazardous to a degree, but not to be remotely compared with railway conditions in the North, in South Wales, and some parts of Devon. We never knew when and how trains would be held up. During the week I lived at a small private hotel beside Chippenham station, and one morning awoke to see a down express standing there which had an unfamiliar look. It was the Penzance 'sleeper', which had left Paddington at 9.50 pm on the previous evening, and had just arrived in Chippenham (94 miles) 10 hours later!

There was much more to it than the late running of passenger trains during that fearful two months of February and March 1947. The transport of coal became woefully disorganised. Stocks had been allowed to get low and, with the collieries lying in some of the most snowbound areas, further supplies were badly held up. It was perhaps not surprising that the responsible minister of the Labour Government was rather slow in realising what was happening; but when factory after factory closed down for lack of coal, industry—trade unions and management alike—began to bombard the Government to take action. At first, of course, blame was showered upon the railways but, as overlord, the ex-Co-Op Minister of Transport had not a clue how to cope. The railway managements themselves cancelled many thousands of daily passenger trains to make available engines and crews for freight and mineral trains; because in certain areas food supplies were threatened, and the arrival of coal trains in the London area was at one time as much headline news in the press and on the radio as the safe arrival of wartime convoys in Malta! During this crisis in transport I was fortunately travelling no farther than my week-end journeys between London and Chippenham. My visit to Glasgow, for the Christmas lecture of the Institution of Civil Engineers, had been in early January when the weather was still mild.

We had scarcely begun to recover, after the sudden end of the great freeze in mid-March, when a *coup d'état* at Board level in Westinghouse struck a shattering blow at the London engineering staff. Awaiting an occasion when Captain Peter, the Managing Director, was away from London, a meeting of directors reversed the solemn promise made at the beginning of the war, and repeated several times subsequently, that as soon as practicable the staff would return to head office in London. This is no place to try to conjecture how executive directors, who were widely respected, were brought to acquiesce to such a volte face. Major Peter, younger brother of the Captain and Chief Engineer of the company, was as stunned as any of us. It came to be generally understood that Donald Brown was at the heart of it. Certain it is that, when Captain Peter returned a short time afterwards and promptly resigned from the Managing Directorship, it was not very long before Donald Brown was appointed to succeed him.

It was fortunate for the top management of Westinghouse that no trade union organisation then existed in the engineering departments, because feelings ran high for several weeks. There is no doubt that the more conciliatory members of the Board were deeply concerned at the reaction of the staff. A short time after his resignation as Managing Director Captain Peter was appointed Deputy Chairman, but he took little further interest in Westinghouse affairs, officially, and retired altogether later in the year. John Kay of *The Railway Gazette* asked me to prepare some biographical notes. On one of my Monday visits to head office, and going to see him, I found him as gracious and cheerful as ever. I wish I had had a tape with me to record the flow of reminiscence he poured out; and for a man who had every reason to feel bitter about the treatment he had received from the company he had served so brilliantly I could not detect the slightest trace of any rancour. For the record I append the text of the editorial article I wrote for *The Railway Gazette*.

'Captain B.H. Peter

'The approaching retirement of Captain B.H. Peter, CBE, from the Westinghouse Brake & Signal Co Ltd, announced in our issue of April 4, recalls some of the landmarks in power signalling. Captain Peter retires next September; he relinquished last month the Managing Directorship, and has become Deputy-Chairman. When he joined the Metropolitan District Railway in 1903 the planning of the signalling to be applied in connection with its electrification was commencing, and with it a most interesting period of signalling development in this country. He was responsible for bringing into service, on June 5 1905, the first illuminated track diagram to be installed anywhere in the world, at Mill Hill Park, as part of the first electro-pneumatic interlocking on any of the London Underground lines. Captain Peter was the inventor of the resonated impedance bond, and of the condenser-fed track circuit—both important factors for the improvement of track circuit performance under difficult conditions. Later, as Chief Engineer of the McKenzie, Holland & Westinghouse Power Signal Co Ltd, he was responsible for bringing into service the first installation of day colour light signals in this country, on the Liverpool Overhead Railway in 1921. In more recent times, his securing for Westinghouse of the famous £5¾ million contract for air brakes on the Polish State Railways was a triumph, not only for his company, but for British industry generally in the face of intense competition from Germany. This was succeeded by his introduction of the Westinghouse air brake to Lithuania.

Our first post-war home in the West Country: No 20 Sion Hill, Bath. The model railway as described in Chapter Eleven eventually ran across the full length of the top storey of the house.

'In the many years during which Captain Peter has been such a well-known and respected figure in our signalling and brake industry and its associates, he has travelled widely and done much to establish and enhance the high credit it enjoys in all parts of the world. His services to that industry as Chairman of its Export & Industrial Group have been of lasting benefit. During the recent war he also acted as South Western Regional Officer, Board of Trade, and he has served as a member of the Industrial Council, Board of Trade, of the Economic Advisory Committee, Colonial Office; and of the 1944 Patent Committee.'

It was thought by some that the virtual dismissal of Captain Peter—for that is really what it amounted to—would have a serious effect on his younger brother, for it was known that there was a very deep bond of affection between them. The Major was not popular with some members of the works management for his forthright attitude at times and I have heard it whispered that there was a hope that the departure of the elder brother might lead to the resignation of the younger. But Major Peter stood firm as a rock, even when he was apparently demoted and moved sideways to become Chief Development Engineer. He quickly made his new command one of the most vital in the engineering organisation of the company.

The immediate outcome of the reversal of policy in location of the head-quarters' engineering departments was that a number of us who had loyally fallen in with Donald Brown's exhortations of 1946 had, a year later, to face the upheaval of moving house and home back to the West Country again. To Olivia and me the prospect, apart from the finance and mechanics of the job, was not unwelcome. With two children coming up to secondary school age environment was important, and we finally decided to concentrate our attention on Bath, leaving me, of course with the prospect of commuting daily by train to Chippenham. With severe petrol rationing still in force there seemed no point at that stage in considering a car. In such of my spare time as I could devote to house hunting I soon found that there was little difference in price between a 'modern' house of immediate pre-war vintage, that was too small for a growing family, and the larger Georgian villas that no one seemed to want at that time. I found an imposing three-storey detached house of this character on Sion Hill.

The decoration was shabby but the structure was absolutely sound. By the time Olivia came to see it she was so disenchanted by the vicissitudes we had been through that she was ready to agree to anything. 'You do as you like, dear', was all she said. I don't blame her after having moved to Bushey, gone through that fearful winter virtually on her own, with heating that was totally inadequate for such conditions, and then having to move back again! But I am glad to think our decision was a good one, because she grew to love that big house on Sion Hill, and did a wonderful job in redecorating many of the rooms in true Regency style.

In the midst of the Westinghouse turmoil, and the unwelcome prospect that railway nationalisation would be an accomplished fact by New Years Day, 1948, John Kay asked me to do some special articles for *The Railway Magazine* that were to involve a good deal of field work. The first was to cover the network of travelling post office services centered upon the West Coast Postal Special, from Euston to Aberdeen. With Kay's sponsorship an interview was quickly arranged with F.G. Fielder, the Chief Superintendent, TPO Section of the London Postal Region, and a programme was worked out to cover journeys on a number of trains carrying TPO carriages, in addition to the renowned 'Special'. From my friends at Euston also I had learned that the 'Down Special' was the fastest train then running between Crewe and Carlisle, the arrangements were made for parts of my journeys to be made on the footplate of the locomotives. At that time the pre-war LMS regulations still held that only one person, in addition to the driver and fireman, was allowed on the footplate. There was, therefore, not the complication of having to arrange for motive power inspectors to accompany me, as became necessary everywhere on British Railways after nationalisation.

Kay was very anxious to have the articles profusely illustrated. Between them

The dynamometer car of the Great Western Railway in which I was privileged to travel on many important test runs.

the GPO and the LMS provided a splendid series of official pictures; but in 1947 'double summer time' was still in operation, and on a fine evening in June E.R. Wethersett was able to get a fine shot of the 'Down Special' picking up mails at Harrow, in the light of the setting sun, at about 8.50 pm. The engine was a characteristically filthy 'Pacific', No 6204 *Princess Louise*, though she appeared to be in good shape, with not a wisp of steam leaking from her front end. I made several trips on the 7.20 pm Midland TPO from Bristol to Birmingham, which I could catch by a local from Chippenham that left after Westinghouse working hours, though my truly marathon journeys, made on Friday nights—after a full day's work in the office!—took me through to Glasgow, and to Aberdeen. Except north of Stirling I covered the entire route **north** of Tamworth at different times both on the footplate and in the TPO carriages. I must admit I was usually feeling just a *little* jaded by the time I reached those northern destinations. Fielder sent a very enthusiastic travelling inspector named Martin with me on all these journeys, and he just packed me in with data.

During the war the travelling post office services had been suspended, but in readiness for the restoration of the West Coast 'Specials', in the autumn of 1945, the GPO and the LMS together produced a most comprehensive route guide, to assist the men in renewing their acquaintance with the line. Not a few of them would probably be taking up this branch of post-office work for the first time. Two pages from this guide are reproduced herewith, showing very full instructions for the men working 'the apparatus', as the gear for picking up and setting down bags at speed was always known. The right hand part of the guide refers to a section that involved the slickest operation I have seen in a TPO with two operations in rapid succession. My journey to Aberdeen on the 'Down Special' was made in high summer, and although because of 'double summer

Two pages from The Travelling Post Office Route Guide *showing the route and the accompanying abbreviations and symbols.*

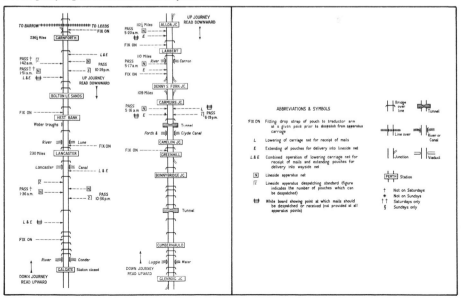

time' sunrise was an hour later than usual at that time of year, it was broad daylight by the time we reached this part of the line.

While we swept down Cumbernauld Glen, doing well over 60 mph another heavy dispatch was being prepared. At Carmuirs West the mail for Falkirk was set down, followed immediately afterwards by that for Larbert. At Carmuirs the postal net was just opposite the signal box, and the Larbert one was less than a mile further on, between Larbert Junction and the station. We came down the bank from Greenhill at nearly 70 mph with six pouches for Carmuirs ready fixed to the tranductors; the two Larbert pouches were on the van floor to be fixed the moment the Carmuirs ones had gone. At this speed there was only a matter of seconds in which to do the job. The short tunnel after Camelon Junction provided the first recognition mark; just after this the Carmuirs pouches were lowered and, at 62 mph, they were caught in the net. With lightning fingers the Larbert bags were made fast on the arms, and the operator had then comfortable time to look out and precisely note his mark for lowering the Larbert dispatch.

From Stirling northward I rode on the footplate. From Carstairs our engine had been a Midland compound, but when I showed the driver my pass, climbed aboard and was going to stow myself out of the way on the fireman's side, I was rather taken aback when the driver said, 'Och, if ye're on here ye're the dr-r-river!'. Fortunately I knew the road as far as the gradients and stations were concerned, and although I had never previously handled the regulator on a compound I was familiar with the necessary technique; and so I drove the 'Postal' from Stirling to Perth. Such a thrill was certainly not included in the privilege granted to me by the LMS, and it was not until many years later that I was able to reveal I had driven the engine myself. We got a delayed start, being stopped by signal at Bridge of Allan while a freight train ahead was clearing into the loop at Dunblane; but when the signal cleared, I was able to run the remaining 30 miles to Perth in 33¾ minutes, accelerating to 43 mph up the stiff bank past Dunblane, and sustaining 75 mph down hill from Gleneagles. I took notes of the times and speeds, and for the record I append a brief log herewith:

		Time		*Speeds*
		min	*sec*	*mph*
0.0	Bridge of Allan	0	00	—
2.0	Dunblane	4	30	38
4.7	Kinbuck	8	28	43
12.1	Blackford	16	00	65
14.3	Gleneagles	18	11	60
20.5	Dunning	23	32	75
26.2	Forgandemy	28	25	71
28.1	Hilton Junction	30	10	slow
30.1	Perth	33	50	—

For the final stage into Perth, not knowing exactly where a stop would be required at the long platform, I handed over to the regular driver. We parted in high humour.

In the articles I wrote for *The Railway Magazine* John Kay wanted the fullest details of all my journey, including times, speeds, engine numbers and all else, and I learned afterwards that Cecil J. Allen took the strongest exception to any details of the locomotive performance being published. As long established

Footplating on the Talyllyn Railway: on the Edward Thomas *fitted with a Giesl Ejector, at the Wharf station at Towyn* (Ivo Peters).

author of the monthly 'British Locomotive Practice and Performance' feature he took the view that no one beside himself should write anything about engine performance. Any details for publication should be sent to him, for use as he thought fit. Tom Lascelles, the signalling consultant of the Tothill Street journals used to attend the regular editorial conferences, under Kay's chairmanship, and he told me of the fuss Allen made. I gather, however, that Kay just laughed it off, saying that no one had exclusive rights to any subject. Nevertheless Allen had evidently worked hard on one of the assistant editors, B.W.C. Cooke, because when I was setting off to do the field work for the next big article, 'Twenty-four hours at York', and it became known at Tothill Street that I was going down from Kings Cross on the footplate, Cooke impressed upon me that they did not want any account of the journey in the articles I was to write. Such references would, of course, have been completely out of place, and I had no intention of including any. It was quite otherwise in 'Scottish Night Mails of the LMS'.

My journeys in the travelling post offices brought an added interest, in that from my boyhood I had been a keen stamp collector, and knew that on certain of the trains, letters posted in the boxes on the TPO carriages received special postmarks. In the course of my field work for *The Railway Magazine* articles I discovered that there were many more than I expected, and that on many of them the pre-grouping names of the routes concerned were retained. The 7.20 pm from Bristol to Newcastle, for example, carried the postmark 'Midland TPO Going North'. Other pre-grouping references of which I have examples are 'Caledonian TPO Day Up', 'Highland TPO', 'NE TPO Night Down' and, of course, the 'Great Western TPO' which, like the West Coast special, is a purely postal train. There are others indicating the route, such as 'Shrewsbury–York', 'Birmingham–Crewe' and so on and, above all, the king of them all, the West Coast special, which carried the postmark 'Down Special TPO' and 'Up Special TPO'.

One of the most interesting visits I was able to make in the last year before nationalisation was to the stationary locomotive testing plant of the Great Western, at Swindon. Although it had been built in the early 1900s its capacity

Shortly after Nationalisation: 'The Night Scot' climbing Beattock Bank, just after dawn, hauled by the 'Pacific' engine named after its designer, Sir William A. Stanier FRS. *The train is a very heavy one including many sleeping cars, and has a bank engine on this severe gradient* (W.J.V. Anderson).

for absorbing power was known to be limited, and until the mid-1930s it had been little used. At that time Sir Nigel Gresley was frequently referring to the lack of a modern locomotive testing plant in Great Britain and, as if to emphasise the deficiency, arranged for his great 2-8-2 engine, *Cock o' the North*, to be shipped over to France for testing on the Vitry plant. After Stanier had gone from the Great Western, to become Chief Mechanical Engineer of the LMS, he got together with Gresley on the project of a jointly sponsored stationary locomotive testing plant and Stanier, knowing the limited capacity of the Swindon plant, thought that the Great Western might like to come in and share the cost. But the 'grape-vine' worked very efficiently, and long before the joint LMS-LNER proposals had reached the stage of a formal approach, C.B. Collett knew all about it and, with characteristic insularity, determined to have nothing to do with it. Instead, work was immediately put in hand to modernise the Swindon plant, and when, in 1935, representatives of the two northern companies were courteously received at the works they saw one of the 'Saint' Class 4-6-0, the *Arlington Court*, going 'flat-out' on the stationary plant, developing around 1,200 indicated horse-power. And it was made clear to them that the plant as modernised could absorb around double that power, if need be. With the Southern motive power interests directed entirely to electrification—in the pre-Bulleid days—the LMS and LNER would have to go it alone.

By 1947 the practice of locomotive testing had been advanced to a very high degree at Swindon, first under Charles Roberts and then S.O. Ell, who was in charge when I had the privilege of seeing the plant in action in 1947. Hawksworth was actively breaking clean away from the medium superheat tradition inaugurated more than 40 years earlier by Churchward, simply because the quality of coal available in post-war years did not permit consistent rock-steady steaming at maximum boiler pressure. I saw on test the first of the 'Kings' to be fitted with a much larger superheater, the *King Edward III*. Anchored at the rear end 'she' was running at an equivalent road speed of 60 mph, hauling an equivalent of 20 coaches. It was a most impressive sight, but even more so was the exposition of the modern Great Western testing techniques made clear to me by Sam Ell, and so enthusiastically backed up by every member of his staff. After nationalisation the Swindon system was adopted as standard, after the closest investigation by the newly appointed chief officers of the British Railways.

In the autumn of 1947 after the passing of the Act, and the fixing of New Years Day, 1948, as vesting day, everyone interested in railways, whether of the railway staffs themselves, the press, railway contractors, or the railway enthusiast fraternity, watched with bated breath while the senior appointments in the new organisation were made, because these were going to affect every one of us in our several ways. The two-tier arrangement, with the British Transport Commission accommodated on the top floors of the Underground headquarters, at 55 Broadway, and the subservient Railway Executive in the former 'Hotel Great Central', 222 Marylebone Road, was awkward and unfriendly from the start. Sir James Milne, General Manager of the Great Western, was offered the Chairmanship of the Railway Executive, and promptly turned it down. This was the signal for every Great Western officer, save one, to refuse to join the new set-up. Milne realised, only too clearly, that the post would not be that of a chief executive, but a vaguely constituted coordinator. Sir Eustace Missenden of the Southern was the second choice.

With the other main line companies to be given participation, Allan Quartermaine, Chief Engineer of the Great Western, was first choice for the Member responsible for civil engineering, signalling and architecture; but he turned it down as promptly as Sir James Milne had done. J.C.L. (later Sir Landale) Train of the LNER was second choice, and he accepted. The LNER got a second representative in V.M. Barrington-Ward. He was a fairly obvious choice from his immense operating experience in two world wars, and a very tough character. Much to the disgust of his former colleagues at Paddington, David Blee, the former Chief Goods Manager of the GWR, took the job of commercial member on the Railway Executive. A few months after vesting date a senior officer at Paddington said to me: 'He's forgotten he ever was a Great Western man!'.

The appointment that was of the greatest moment to railway enthusiasts and contractors alike was that of the member for mechanical and electrical engineering and research, and this went to R.A. Riddles, a Vice-President of the LMS, and former Principal Assistant to the Chief Mechanical Engineer, in pre-war days. This seemed to presage a continuance of LMS policy in locomotive design, particularly when his two chief assistants, R.C. Bond as Chief Officer, Locomotive Works, and E.S. Cox, Executive Officer, Locomotive Design, were both LMS men. In retrospect, however, these were among the wisest and most forward looking of all the new appointments made in January 1948. On the other hand there was dismay among most of us in the signalling business at the appointment of another ex-LMS man, H.H. Dyer, as Executive Officer for Signals and Telecommunications, under J.C.L. Train, because Dyer was a pedestrian of pedestrians. Early in 1948 Riddles arranged for the large scale series of Locomotive Interchange Trials, which excited much interest and engendered a vast amount of comment at the time—a good deal of it remarkably ill-informed. When the official report was published some months afterwards, the results appeared to be generally inconclusive. They are discussed later in the light of the constructional policy decided upon by the Railway Executive.

In the summer of 1949 one of the outstanding personalities of the railway world, John Ayton Kay, died at the relatively early age of 67. It would be no exaggeration to say that he was the friend, adviser, and confidant of everyone in the railway industry. As Editor of *The Railway Gazette* from the year 1910 he built up a towering reputation, but he was no less a railway enthusiast and delighted in all aspects of what could be termed the amateur side of railways. I shall always remember the first time I was introduced to him, in the Tothill Street offices, and his first words to me were: 'Have you been to the Model Railway Exhibition yet?'. I have told earlier in this book how he invited me to join the staff. When negotiations had proceeded a little he invited me to lunch, at 'The Ivy', in Soho. An epicure himself he always expected his guests to have discerning tastes in food and drink, and of this I have a story to tell against myself. My father was an agent for the Scottish Temperance and General Assurance Company, and arranged a life insurance policy for me at a reduced rate as a total abstainer—which until the war I was. It so happened, however, that one day I had to see the London manager of the company, a close friend of our family, on an occasion when I had been to lunch with Kay at 'The Ivy'. He had lunched me very well indeed, and I thought the time had come to confess to that kindly insurance manager that I did, now, occasionally have a drink! He made no change in the premium I was required to pay.

B.W.C. Cooke, who succeeded Kay as Editor of *The Railway Gazette* and *The Railway Magazine*, was a good friend to me in later years, but the immediate effect of Kay's death was to close the doors of Tothill Street against me for a time. But the autumn of 1949 was very important to me in another respect. As from November 1, I was appointed Chief Draughtsman of the company, taking charge of the signal and rectifier drawing offices in addition to my existing responsibilities on brakes. It was the beginning of one of the most exciting periods of my life. In every discipline the business was expanding, and I had the job of building up the staff accordingly; but the situation in 1949–50 was nothing to that which developed in the mid-1950s when the British Railways Modernisation Plan was launched, and the drawing office staff had to be more than *doubled*. To meet the fluctuating demands of the three principal activities, not to mention the growing involvement with pneumatic decking equipment for collieries, we found it convenient to have a pool of juniors, members of which could be switched from one section to another as the pressure varied. We took a number of men and women direct from Government training centres, and I shall always remember an amusing conversation with a business associate in Birmingham. I had been telling him how we were taking on, virtually, anyone who could make marks on paper, and he exclaimed: 'Marks on paper! Up here, if a chap can sharpen a pencil he's in!'.

Chapter 10

Railway modernisation—at the vortex

The decade that began at the mid-point of the 20th century may well be set down as the most bizarre in all British railway history. At midsummer 1949 The Railway Executive circulated to the press the report of the Locomotive Testing Committee on the Interchange Trials carried out in the spring and summer of the previous year. It was a remarkable document in itself: 131 pages entirely in typescript, and I had the job of preparing an extract from it, and a review for *The Engineer*. Ben Pendred, who had then succeeded his father as editor, was anxious to be first with the news, and I shall always remember the hectic week-end I spent extracting what I considered the more significant figures. The three tables that I prepared relating to the various aspects of fuel consumption included no fewer than 1,122 entries and, for once, with a weighty supplement

The last steam locomotive built for British Railways, the '9F' 2-10-0, No 92220, Evening Star, *allocated to the Somerset and Dorset line, and here seen emerging from the twin-bore Chilcompton Tunnel on the heavy climb to the crest of the Mendip Hills* (Ivo Peters).

and records of horsepower, it was not exactly a labour of love. The weekend was one of the most gloriously sustained sunshine, and there were jobs in the garden that would have been a delight. To make the most I could of the balmy atmosphere of the day I remember working up on the first floor of our Sion Hill house, in the huge Regency-style drawing room, with the windows wide open; and then when I had gone almost cross-eyed amid the mass of figures, there still remained a leading article to be written. The latter opened thus:

'Few recent events in the railway world have created more interest than the Locomotive Exchanges of 1948. From the very first announcement of the scheme rather more than a year ago, the workings were keenly followed equally by locomotive men and by the host of enthusiasts, engineers and laymen alike, over whom the steam locomotive continues to cast its spell. Runs were timed in great detail and accuracy by outside observers travelling as passengers in the trains on which dynamometer car trials were conducted—indeed one such observer, a retired railwayman, travelled thus over 10,000 miles behind locomotives on test. After the trials were completed items of information other than mere running times began to circulate, and some of these formed the basis of controversy in our own correspondence columns. All this testifies to the eagerness with which full results were awaited . . . .'

Reading that report again today, more than 30 years later, and admittedly with the advantage of hindsight, one must be pardoned for wondering if the whole exercise was not a colossal waste of time and money! Technically it revealed nothing that was not known in the headquarters drawing offices of the former main line railway companies; and although much was made of the supposed difficulties on Great Western locomotives in using hard Yorkshire coal, instead of soft Welsh, no one pointed out that some of the finest locomotive work done on the GWR in pre-war days was by the Wolverhampton links using Staffordshire coal. Putting some of the reliable unofficial observations alongside data in the official report did, however, reveal that far greater variations in coal consumption arose from the disparities in the handling techniques used by individual enginemen than from the underlying features of design, or coal. Discarding the obvious excesses in either direction, arising from there being no standardised code of driving practice imposed upon the participating engine crews, the result was as near to a quadri-partite dead heat as could possibly have been expected, in the diverse conditions prevailing on the various routes.

There was another side to it, however, that no statistics of performance, official or otherwise, touched upon. Whether it was an aspect that the organisers had additionally in mind at the outset I had no idea; but in retrospect it was about the only lasting benefit to emerge. None of the Chief Mechanical Engineers of the old railway companies had any taste for nationalisation; they took little interest in the Interchange Trials, especially when men of the status of F.W. Hawksworth and H.G. Ivatt had to obtain permission from the Railway Executive to ride in their own dynamometer cars. Somewhat naturally they did not bother! On one occasion, when the former Great Western car was in use on the 'Atlantic Coast Express', Bulleid fancied a ride from Waterloo to Exeter; but he had no permit, and was refused entry. Whatever the former CMEs thought about it the younger men had to do the job, and it brought engineers of marked and proven ability together in a way that nothing else could have done. After all the privations of wartime and the drab years that followed it was a

Building and testing railbrakes at Chippenham. The test ramp was built to provide wagons with the speeds needed for test purposes.

joyous exercise, in which some who might have had pronounced partisan views were knit in a team having a common object. It was they who would be leaders in the new age, when 'BR' policy would replace the GW, Southern, LMS and LNER viewpoints.

Having said that, however, what was to be the new policy? It already seemed clear that in most things, traction particularly, The Railway Executive was going it alone, without any reference to the supposedly parent body, The British Transport Commission. It is true that the 'five wise men' appointed by Alfred Barnes were an oddly assorted lot, and the Chairman, Lord Hurcomb, with a long and distinguished record in the Civil Service behind him, was more at home in implementing directives from Ministers than formulating policies of his own, and taking executive responsibility for seeing them through. Apparently, without any consultation with the BTC, Riddles took a decision on future traction policy that seemed based on a short-term view of national economics, but had a much longer-term view of railway requirements. I was at a meeting at the Institution of Mechanical Engineers when he said that they were going to have the form of traction that gave the highest tractive effort per pound sterling. Put in such terms it was an overwhelming case for steam—at that moment; but for how long were those straitened economic conditions going to last?

New locomotives were certainly needed to make up for the arrears in replacement of life-expired units during the war; but one would question the wisdom of adding no fewer than 110 steam 0-6-0 tank engines, ostensibly for shunting, when the LMS diesels had proved so effective. Furthermore, when the Southern already had 89 'Pacifics', of the 'West Country' and 'Battle of Britain' series, was there any justification in authorising another 15 of the wretched things in 1949? It is true that they had done some of the most brilliant work in the 1948 Interchange Trials, admittedly on an inordinately high coal consumption; but already the multiplication of the class was proving something of an embarrassment to the running department, who found themselves reduced to using them, in some areas, on 3-coach locals. The inconclusive results from the 1948 Interchange Trials, and the view that steam traction would have to be retained as the principal form of motive power in the foreseeable future, between them led The Railway Executive to a decision the validity of which will be questioned as long as there are railway historians—to introduce an entirely new range of 'standard' locomotives.

It seems to have been a decision made as much on psychological grounds as any other. Because no one group of regional designs had shown itself superior to the rest it was determined that the new standards should be a synthesis of all the best features of the existing ones; not only this, but that the work of designing the new engines should be shared by the headquarters drawing offices of four regions, between them representing design staffs of the four pre-nationalisation railway companies. The process of sharing the work was carried a great deal further; for while in design the new standard types were shared out between the four drawing offices, they each undertook design of components on behalf of the whole series. For example, Doncaster did cylinders, slide bars, crossheads, coupling and connecting rods and valves for all the new engines. It was a gigantic corporate task, presided over by E.S. Cox, the Executive Officer, Design, of the Railway Executive.

But was it all really necessary? This tremendous task which the mechanical engineering section of The Railway Executive had undertaken was begun without any consultation with the BTC. From the latter little, if any, coordinated guidance on policy was forthcoming, yet to transport men on every hand it seemed that, despite the prevailing economic conditions affecting the price of oil, the days of the steam locomotive, as a principal source of power on British Railways, must surely be numbered. Past experience had shown that the economic life of a steam locomotive in Great Britain was at least 20, and probably nearer to 30 years. The new engines already on the drawing boards at Brighton, Derby, Doncaster and Swindon could not be expected to have shorter lives; and although some of them bore a remarkable resemblance, in capacity, to existing designs, the changes in detail involved new tooling and processing at all the main works that would eventually be concerned. This, in addition to those at

The pneumatically operated railbrakes at the foot of the test track at Chippenham. Beyond the wagon can be seen the steeply inclined ramp built to arrest any runaways, in case of a misjudgment in application of the brake.

which the drawing offices were situated, included Crewe, Darlington and Norwich.

Of the 12 'standard' designs decided upon by Riddles and his team, six could have been met by building to existing LMS designs; two, the Class '6' 'Pacific' ('Clan' Class), and the Class '4' 4-6-0 appeared quite unnecessary, equally so the Class '3' 2-6-0. Only one example of the Class '8' 'Pacific' was built, and the only one of the series for which there would have seemed to be a real justification was the Class '7' 'Pacific', 'Britannia' Class, to provide for the improvement of service in East Anglia. The Class '9' 2-10-0 freight engine, although the finest of the whole range, was something of a curiosity, as a locomotive, related to the motive power situation of British Railways as a whole. In view of the launching of the Modernisation Plan in 1954 the building of no less than 150 more of these large and expensive locomotives in 1956–8 would seem inexplicable. They were remarkably versatile machines in passenger as well as freight service; but again one would ask, in relation to prevailing traffic commitments, were they really necessary?

For the enthusiasts, as distinct from the professionals in the railway business, 1951–4 were vintage years. A veteran photographer, whose name was once a household word among locomotive 'fans', was rubbing his hands with delight at the appearance of new designs while, of course, the number-spotters equally revelled in it. There were also more serious grounds for pleasure in the introduction of new names for many express trains, in connection with the Festival of Britain staged in 1951, and acceleration of services. The stationary testing plant at Rugby was also commissioned in 1951, and a healthy rivalry between it, and the rejuvenated Great Western plant at Swindon began to grow up. It was in 1953 that the latter plant registered its most spectacular results. K.W.C. Grand, the General Manager of the Western Region, was anxious to restore full pre-war speed. That included *The Bristolian*, making a non-stop run to Temple Meads in no more than 1¾ hours, and taking the Cornish Riviera Express to Plymouth in 4 hours. Gilbert Matthews, Superintendent of the line, was convinced that no existing Western Region locomotive was in a condition to do either job, on post-war coal.

Alfred Smeddle, who had come to Swindon from the Eastern Region, and who did not know the word 'can't', set the testing staff, under the inimitable Sam Ell, to work on 'hotting up' the 'Kings'. How they succeeded in increasing the maximum steaming capacity of those famous engines by *30 per cent* is a heart warming story. In the spring of 1953 I was invited to Swindon to see engine No 6001, *King Edward VII*, running at 75 mph on the stationary plant, and then to ride in the dynamometer car, on a day when they were taking a test load of 25 coaches from Reading to Stoke Gifford sidings, site of the present Bristol Parkway station. With this enormous train the 74.2 miles of the outward journey were covered in 80 minutes, while on the return the slightly shorter distance of 73.5 miles to a stop at Scours Lane Junction took 77 minutes. With a load nearly double that of the heaviest trains on the South Wales service this was a marvellous performance. Even Gilbert Matthews was convinced that, with engines of this calibre, *The Bristolian* could be accelerated back to its pre-war schedule.

Then, on October 1 1953, under the Transport Act passed by Parliament earlier that year, The Railway Executive was abolished, and the British Transport Commission was charged with the task of re-organising the railways

An impressive aerial view of the two large mechanised mashalling yards beside the River Tees, near Middlesbrough, in the equipment of which the 'Westardair' railbrakes played a vital part (BR).

of this country. On the day the Executive was abolished Riddles retired from railway service, and headquarters entered upon a phase of internal conflict that was by no means resolved when General Sir Brian Robertson succeeded Lord Hurcomb as Chairman, and the 1955 Statutory Re-organisation scheme came into effect. This is no place to try and describe, even in outline, the in-fighting that took place at railway headquarters and in its relations with the regions. For those who would want to know something of how it affected the engineering departments I would recommend the book, *A Lifetime with Locomotives*, written by my great friend Roland C. Bond, who eventually became Chief Mechanical Engineer of the BTC. The thing that concerned us all at Westinghouse was the launching of the great Modernisation Plan, at the beginning of 1955.

From being starved of capital, British Railways were suddenly let loose on a gigantic spending spree. So far as new design work was concerned our immediate concern was with signalling, and simultaneously, with large contracts in all regions except the Western. At railway headquarters J.H. Fraser of the North Eastern had succeeded Dyer as Chief Officer; but although he had long been associated with panel interlockings, including such large installations as York and Newcastle, he had no time to initiate any form of co-ordination in panel design. The new plants were required in such a hurry that the various regions were more or less obliged to take what the contractors could supply in the time available. That is not to suggest that a large amount of drawing office work was not necessary. We received, more or less simultaneously, contracts in connection with the Kent Coast electrification of the Southern; for the Great Eastern outer suburban lines; for the Manchester–Crewe line of the London Midland; for the Newcastle–Berwick line of the North Eastern, and for the Cathcart Circle in the Glasgow suburban area.

While the equipment to be fitted to the new consoles and their associated panel diagrams was to be of standard type it soon became apparent that an enormous amount of work would be involved in drawing the track diagrams, work that would have to run concurrently to meet the delivery requirements of *five* regions. We had a very expert senior draughtsman who had done little else but this class of work for the past 25 years; but unfortunately he was something of a 'loner', with little aptitude for expanding his activities, and taking responsibility for supervising a large staff. Furthermore, as individual orders began to come in, it was evident that the sheer physical space required for laying out so many track diagrams was not available at Chippenham. We had already begun to use contract drawing offices in Bath and Bristol for self-contained individual jobs, but track diagrams involved specialised knowledge of railway working that could not be assimilated quickly by outsiders. It was then that a stroke of luck came our way.

In 1955 Westinghouse purchased the firm of Douglas (Kingswood) Ltd, well known as the manufacturers of Douglas motor cycles, and more recently of the Vespa scooters. The firm had a good deal of spare capacity, which it was hoped could be utilised for taking some of the road brake work from Chippenham, and making additional capacity available for railway brakes. The main point so far as we were concerned, however, was that in Kingswood there was a great deal of office space, which could be readily converted to a drawing office. J.S. McCormack, the Managing Director of Douglas was very helpful, though I know he was disappointed that we did not take on his leading draughtsman to

One of the first London Midland Region power signal boxes to be commissioned under the Modernisation Plan: Sandbach, on the Manchester–Crewe line, using the OCS type of control panel.

manage the new office. Kenneth Leech and I paid several visits to Kingswood during the period of gestation, and we decided that a more dynamic personality was needed to manage an office which would consist mainly of new recruits, and from which the closest liaison would have to be maintained with the associated sections of the drawing office in Chipenham.

A few months earlier we had been able to recruit a senior draughtsman, Cyril Oliver, who had recently returned from Australia. Having mainly electrical experience he had been placed in the Rectifier section of the drawing office at Chippenham and, at a time when that section was hard pressed, he had quickly shown himself a glutton for work. In setting up the reinforcing office at Kingswood, Leech and I had agreed from the outset that it should be established as a 'back-up' for all three divisions, and that it would be advantageous to have someone in charge having no particular allegiance to any one discipline. Oliver's massive presence and vigorous personality seemed to commend him for the job. Furthermore, there was always at the back of my mind the uneasy thought that the extraordinary boom we were enjoying in all three divisions was not likely to be sustained at its current level, and that a man with relatively short service in the company would react more readily to future changes than some of the veteran seniors at Chippenham, were one of them to be appointed to Kingswood only to be uprooted in a few years time.

So Oliver was appointed, and with him a man of medium section leader status from each of the Signal, Colliery, Brake and Rectifier sections at Chippenham. There were some mild instances of friction at the start, while the new arrangements settled into their stride; but Cyril Oliver proved himself a diplomat as well as a manager. Much of his time was at first spent in recruiting, almost entirely from the local Government training centres and, in view of the lack of specialist experience, much discretion had to be shown in the class of work allocated to

Kingswood. Arrangements had to be made for the section chief draughtsmen at Chippenham, or their deputies, to visit periodically and it was fortunate that petrol rationing had by that time ceased, and that the journey of 18 miles between the two offices could be made by road. From the outset the conveyance of all drawings and documents was made by private car, and as the work increased we had a company car, and a driver to maintain a regular scheduled service, morning and afternoon, by which visiting personnel from Chippenham were conveyed.

In May 1957 Kenneth Leech was due to retire and among the more senior of his staff a general air of anxious expectancy began to develop from the beginning of the year. Since the summary dismissal of Donald Brown from the Managing Directorship in July 1953, following a time of bitter acrimony with some of his fellow directors, Westinghouse had enjoyed a period of tranquility in management under Mervyn Shorter—a time likened by one of my colleagues to 'Baldwin Government'—in which the managers of the three Sales and Engineering Divisions, in London, had gradually assumed an increasing degree of autonomy. They had made representations to Shorter that the sections of the drawing office dealing with their branches of the business should be split off and brought under their control. As Chief Draughtsman of the company, under Leech, I served them all; and so, incidentally, did Cyril Oliver at Kingswood. Leslie Thompson, the Rectifier Divisional Manager, made a bid for my services, but from the associations and experience of my first 20 years of service with the company I was glad enough when Jack Aldridge asked me to join 'Signal and Colliery'. At first I retained my original title of Chief Draughtsman, but later, after some readjustments within the division, I was proud when he conferred upon me the title of Chief Mechanical Engineer. The eight years that I served directly under him, from 1957 to 1965, were the most exciting, productive, and happiest of all my time at Westinghouse.

The change came at a time when a notable extension of my literary activity was opening out. While Kenneth Leech had always taken care to keep his own erudite brand of railway enthusiasm strictly *sub-rosa*, so far as the higher management of Westinghouse was concerned, my own, inevitably, could not remain so. I was therefore always very careful to tell Leech of any new project I had been asked to undertake, and he in turn nearly always mentioned it to Mervyn Shorter, from whom wholehearted approval never failed to be forthcoming. This was very important, because there were some who imagined that I could only possibly sustain my current output either by doing a great deal of it in Westinghouse time, or by employing a team of ghost writers. Leech knew it was far otherwise. So did my own senior staff. There was a very amusing moment at Chippenham one day when the Institution of Locomotive Engineers was paying an official visit to the works. The tour was over and one or two of us were having tea with some members of the Council, when the President, E.S. Cox, remarked that we had not been shown the room where I retired in seclusion, to write my books. Amid the hilarity that greeted this, there was one of my staff who did not laugh. He said: 'I wish there *was* somewhere we could lock the old Governor away sometimes!'. From Jack Aldridge, recently appointed a Director of the company, I was assured from the outset that all my contacts with railway officers in connection with my literary work were regarded as beneficial, and I was encouraged to widen them wherever possible.

Two years earlier, in 1955, following the launching of the Modernisation

Electric traction extending to the Channel Coast: live rails for the Southern system of electrification laid in through the Folkestone Warren, through which a steam hauled express for Dover and Deal is passing, hauled by a 'Schools' Class 4-4-0, No 30926, Repton. *The tunnel is the 'Martello', so named from one of the defence towers on the shore in the vicinity* (Derek Cross).

Plan, John Scholes, Curator of Historical Relics of the British Transport Commission, asked me to act as adviser to a valedictory exhibition he was setting up, at Euston, to pay tribute to some of the great men of the age of steam, and to a tradition of excellence in design that would be a challenge to British locomotive builders in the years to come. We agreed that it would be symbolised by the work of eight men, using photographs, drawings and models. Before he became Curator of the BTC, Scholes had established himself as an absolute master in the art of museum presentation by his exquisite rendering of the mediaeval street in the Castle Museum at York; but we had much discussion as to who the 'eight men' should be. The recommendations were mine, though most searchingly questioned by Scholes and his two senior assistants. They were Robert Stephenson, John Ramsbottom, Edward Fletcher, Patrick Stirling, S.W. Johnson, Dugald Drummond, G.J. Churchward and Sir Nigel Gresley. We felt it advisable not to extend the story to engineers still living, however eminent they might be. I wrote a 40 page brochure which was on sale at the exhibition, and it was this that brought some very important results for me.

The exhibition was scarcely over before I received a letter from Philip Unwin, a director of the famous publishing house of George Allen and Unwin, asking if I would expand the booklet to a full-length book covering the work of not only eight, but of *all* the great British locomotive engineers. This proved the beginning of a very happy and continuing association with the firm, and including, some years later, my first book on railways outside the British Isles. The ink was barely dry on the contract for *Steam Locomotive*, when a letter came from an even older publishing house, that of Adam and Charles Black. Their Chairman, A.A.G. Black, wrote, saying that he had been to the exhibition at Euston, and would I call on him when I was next in London. I was greatly intrigued. For many years I had delighted in the magnificent 'colour books' that his firm had published, lavishly illustrated from the paintings of celebrated landscape artists; and, together with many of the same series that I had inherited from my father, I then had a collection of some 70 sumptuous volumes. When I met Archie Black I found that he was also a railway enthusiast, and that he wanted me to do precisely what I had so very recently agreed to do for Philip Unwin. He laughed off the fact that the other firm had beaten him to it, and immediately fell to scheming out how we could produce a variation on the same theme. The result was *Historical Steam Locomotives*, describing the ancestry of some of the more famous locomotives that were then preserved. This, however, was no more than a modest beginning, and today I look back a little wistfully to that yellow-backed, shilling brochure published by the British Transport Commission in 1955 that was the catalyst to activities that took Olivia and me right round the world.

All that, however, was still ten years ahead, and at Westinghouse, now reporting to a director, I was immediately involved with some major problems in mechanical engineering design—the equipment of the many new freight marshalling yards that were to be fully mechanised. It proved to be an interim stage in the evolution of the modern philosophy of freight traffic operation. It was still a time of single-wagon consignments before the great majority of the smaller goods depots had been closed. At that time great economies in operation could be effected by concentrating the marshalling in large areas in one or two major yards, instead of the many then existing. Tees-side, Newcastle, Carlisle and Edinburgh were areas on which attention was to be focused at first. Competition in this field was intense, and experience with yards in East London, and at Perth, showed that the existing Westinghouse design of rail-brake, based upon contemporary American practice, was just not competitive. We lost the contract for the large yard at Thornton, in East Fife, but, although we secured that for the smaller one at Perth, the portends were ominous. The rail brakes were by far the largest individual items of equipment and Jack Aldridge set up, and personally chaired, a small committee to investigate the design. I brought to those sessions a young designer-draughtsman, Eric Harris by name, who had shown great promise, vigour and enterprise.

The main difficulty lay in the very extensive use of steel castings in the existing design. From the viewpoint of pure design, cast steel was undoubtedly the ideal material for the great beams, and the actuating levers. The proportions could be tailored precisely to the distribution of stresses, but the cost was sky-rocketing. Furthermore, there was only one manufacturer who was prepared to cast these large members, and their delivery promises were getting longer and longer. We quickly decided that a change must be made to fabricated steel plate for the levers, and a rolled section, like a very much enlarged rail for the beams. The levers, large though they were, could be fabricated at Chippenham, and our first estimates of cost showed that they would be no more than half the cost of cast steel. But when we came to a first estimate of the size of those beams they looked like being around *three times* as heavy as the heaviest rails that had ever been used on the permanent way. Would any of the major rolling mills in the north of England be able to produce such sections for us?

While Eric Harris and his colleagues at Chippenham sought to bring the proportions of these rails to finalty I did some shopping around in the North-East. Several firms were no more than mildly interested; but then I went across to the West Coast, and contacted the Workington Iron and Steel Company. They were not only interested, but dead keen. If it was a major railway job, then they wanted to be in on it. The limiting factor was the size of their rolls. The section of the Chippenham design had to be adjusted somewhat, though in the meantime the commercial aspect had to be faced. Although there were quite a few new marshalling yards on the British Railways agenda, even if we swept the board and secured all the contracts, our total requirements would be a mere drop in the ocean compared to the regular output of a plant like Workington. But they assured me of a good competitive price if we ordered enough to give them one shift every three months. A shift represented 250 tons of steel and our immediate prospects did not amount to so much. From Workington I rang Jack Aldridge, and got an immediate and characteristic reply: 'You get the steel, I'll sell it!'. And so away we went, like a bomb.

With the cost of the rail-brakes, or retarders, so drastically reduced by the change in design, we did indeed secure all the immediate contracts for marshalling yards in Great Britain. There were two each at Millerhill, near Edinburgh; at Carlisle; on Tees-side; at Lamesley, south of Newcastle; and at Tinsley, near Wakefield. Later, it was a great thrill to be at Workington, and see the first beam come white-hot through the rolls, but no less a pleasure later still to take a party from that works to see the finished retarders in railway service, in one of the great marshalling yards north of Carlisle. How we came to export many more retarders of the same basic design must be told in a later chapter.

Designing and building retarders was, however, only one highly specialised facet of our work for railway modernisation. I was travelling more than ever before and, as usual, not solely on Westinghouse business. It was nevertheless fortunate that one of my visits to Workington coincided with an exhibition in Carlisle station in June 1958 wherein *Coppernob, Cornwall, Hardwicke* the Caledonian 4-2-2, No 123, and the Midland 'Spinner', were displayed in a breathtaking line in one of the bay platforms of the Citadel station. This was an easily attained bonus in no more than an hour's wait between connecting trains; but time for purely 'enthusiast' activities had been growing less and less, and in 1956 I had relinquished the authorship of the monthly feature, 'Locomotive Causerie', in the magazine then known as *Railway World*. When G.H. Lake, the founder-editor, had launched the magazine under the name *Railways*, late in 1939, it was generally thought to be a rather venturesome project; but, apart from a break in the autumn of 1940, while some re-organisation of the business basis of the magazine took place, it carried on with monthly publication, and at the time I gave up, in January 1956, I had contributed 185 articles in the one series. As I wrote at the time: 'I had hoped to bring the total of my own contributions to the level two hundred, but rather than let 'Locomotive Causerie' become 'just another job' written, perhaps, against time instead of as a welcome piece of recreation, I have decided to stop short with my present article'.

Little did I think when I wrote those lines that in less than three years time I would be invited to take over the authorship of another monthly feature, none other than 'British Locomotive Practice and Performance' in *The Railway Magazine*. Busy as I was, and having every regard for the reasons that had led me to relinquish 'Locomotive Causerie', it was an invitation I just could not resist. Because if there was one factor more than any other that had stimulated and nourished my early interest in railways, it was the monthly article contributed by Cecil J. Allen, a central feature in *The Railway Magazine* for as long as I could remember—back to the days well before the First World War when my father used occasionally to bring home a copy, to the Bank House in

The new signal box at Euston, showing the large control panel on the 'Entrance-Exit' principle built at Chippenham (Westinghouse Brake and Signal Co Ltd).

Reading. Allen had, indeed, contributed no less than 535 articles to the series. I was taking over at an anxious and critical time. The pessimists were predicting an early end to the cult of railway enthusiasm from those outside the profession. Snide remarks like: 'Who could enthuse about a lot of tin boxes', were being bandied about. The death-knell of steam had certainly been rung and in my third contribution I was discussing performance of the Class '4' English Electric diesels on the East Coast route.

Those last years of the 1950s were also the end of an epoch for me personally. My father died in 1955 and like him my mother lived to a great age, being in her 89th year when she died three years later. My surviving sister, still a spinster, had for some time tended to become more and more of a loner and, after my mother's death, she retired into virtual seclusion, resisting all attempts to bring her into my own family circle. Although in good health physically her desire to live seemed to be ebbing away, and little more than a year after my mother died, in the middle of the night, we received a telephone call from the police at Clevedon, where she lived, to say that she was critically ill and unconscious. I left Sion Hill, by car, at daybreak, and arrived to find she was dead, having taken her own life. It was a sad end; but as I write of it, 22 years later, I like to recall the happy times we spent together, as teenage children. In our joint beginnings in photography, and music, we had some good fun—she later became an LRAM—and there was much joint participation in amateur theatricals. But her first appointment as music mistress in a girls school at Gorleston-on-Sea was a disaster, and it broke every shred of confidence she had in herself. I do not think she ever recovered from that experience. With her death the last link with the family life of my boyhood was severed, but I cannot ever recall it without a profound sense of gratitude to my father and mother for the splendid education they gave me, and which gave me the start to the multifarious activities of the life that has followed. This seems a good point to pause in these recollections of professional and literary activities, and spend a chapter gossiping about hobbies.

*The Stirling 2-4-0, No 814, in actuality (**above**) and the 'O' gauge model of it acquired in 1940 (**below**).*

Chapter 11

Relaxation with models

At the beginning of the war a batchelor acquaintance in the Stephenson Locomotive Society, called up for military service, was disposing of a collection of very fine 0-gauge model locomotives. They were all vintage 2-4-0s and, so far as I know, had never been run. They were just collectors' pieces, hand made and in fine scale. When I heard about this disposal they had all gone except for the Great Northern Stirling, No 814, one of a class of 56 built at the Doncaster Plant between 1888 and 1895. I secured this little gem for the merest song, though I had no means of running it. Then in clearing space in one of the Westinghouse Works stores for war production some demonstration models of signalling apparatus, long disused, were to be scrapped. I found among these three well-nigh priceless historical pieces; two were exquisitely made one-eighth full-size models of McKenzie & Holland type locking frames, with 10 and 11 levers respectively, entirely in brass, though incredibly dusty and uncared for, while the third was a remarkable quarter-size 20-lever frame. I bought the three at far less than scrap metal price though, of course, there was never any question of their being incorporated in any working layout.

The seed of model railway building that had been quiescent in me ever since the oft-regretted sale of the Gauge 1 Great Western 4-4-0, *Sydney*, did not, however, begin to germinate again until after the war when I met Ivo Peters, and was invited to his beautiful home in the village of Corston for 'a game of trains', as he modestly put it. He was—and still is!—a devoted enthusiast for the Somerset and Dorset Joint Railway, and his finely equipped 0-gauge electric line included mostly LMS stock, but also a beautiful SDJR 2-8-0 freight engine. The growth of the germ within me had nevertheless to be severely restrained. When I first went to Corston my home was still at Bushey, and all resources had to be husbanded in readiness for the cost of equipping our new home at Sion Hill, Bath. It was some time before we had fully weathered the upheaval of the move, and taken the measure of a large house so unlike anything we had lived in before; but there were rooms to spare on the top floor, and ostensibly as a Christmas present for our 7-year-old son, Trevor, a circuit of 0-gauge tinplate Hornby track, an 0-4-0 tank engine and rolling stock, was assembled in secrecy in one of the top-floor rooms, ready for the 'opening' of the new railway on Christmas morning.

I do not know which of us enjoyed that opening the most. The Hornby equipment, though crude compared to the exquisite little Stirling 2-4-0 that stood on the mantelpiece in what we called the 'garden room', was well made,

General view of Broad Oaks Junction, showing the Midland compound No 2631, far left, just coming off the shed, and estuarine scenery on the wall between the windows.

and worked with unfailing reliability, and Trevor could soon run the trains without any help from Father. We added an 0-4-0 tender engine and much additional track, including points and crossings, and then one day, when I was in London, the seed within me suddenly burst into flower. In Southampton Row, near the point where Theobald's Road intersected, there used to be a model shop, and there I saw, second-hand, at little more than a give-away price, a clockwork Hornby 4-4-0 of the LNER 'D49' Class, No 201, *The Bramham Moor.* Although tailored to suit mass-production in tinplate it was a remarkably good likeness to the 'Hunt' series of engines and, assured that it would run satisfactorily on our tinplate track and sharp curves, I bought it on the spot. It quickly performed up to every expectation on the nursery floor line at Sion Hill. Our two original engines were also painted in LNER colours, so that the growing stud was also entirely in accordance with Olivia's sentiments. She, as always, did everything to encourage family enterprises, but the nursery floor line received its *congé* from her, when a year or so later I arrived home from London with a Bassett-Lowke 4-6-2 *Flying Scotsman*, which I had bought from that same shop in Southampton Row for a five-pound note!

The huge engine, which was in remarkably good condition, would *just* negotiate those sharp curves of ours, and then one day Olivia said: 'Don't you think it would be better to put the line up on trestles?'. I forget the exact date that those winged words were spoken, but we agreed to transfer railway activities to the larger bedroom in the front of the house. With clockwork locomotives it was essential to have a perfectly level track, and I arranged with a carpenter, who had done some excellent work for us, to build trestling that would carry a double-track circuit. Trevor by this time was at boarding school,

Monkton Combe, and the transformation was organised so that the new layout should be a surprise when he came home for the Christmas holidays. The curves were now 4 foot radius, instead of 3 foot, and a double track was intended throughout the circuit. But although I had managed to obtain, second hand, a certain amount of semi-scale permanent way—enough for the curves—some of the plain line on the straight had still be be laid in tinplate, Hornby type, and I burned a considerable amount of midnight oil getting the double-track circuit ready for its grand opening on Christmas day.

At that time we had four locomotives—the two 'toy' Hornby 0-4-0s, *The Bramham Moor*, and *The Flying Scotsman*. Soon after the line on trestles was opened I had the offer, from an amateur enthusiast in Hayle, Cornwall, of an 0-gauge clockwork model he had himself made of a Great Western 4-6-0, No 4933, *Himley Hall*. It was extremely cheap, even for those days, and was a very faithful *portrait* of the engine, including a wealth of fine detail; but the clockwork motor fitted in the engine was not very strong and he had put a second motor in the tender. The two together, when they worked properly, made quite a strong locomotive; but, although the engine as it was made a picturesque addition to our line, inexperience in locomotive building revealed itself in frequent running troubles, and her availability record showed up poorly against the expertly engineered Hornby No 201 and Bassett Lowke No 4472. Still, it was very nice to have a Great Western engine in the stud.

This chapter now begins to step completely out of the chronological sequence of the book itself, and carries the saga of the Nock model railways far ahead of the narrative as a whole. I will not dwell on those halcyon days when we added a Bassett Lowke *King George V* and a Hornby *County of Bedford* to our motive power stud, but, before then, I was getting more ambitious. The establishment of the line on trestles imparted a degree of permanence to the layout, and I judged that it was time to start building up a scenic background. I bought a copy of John H. Ahern's splendid book *Miniature Landscape Modelling*, and spent many hours studying his methods. As far as the ground itself was concerned the photograph on the dust jacket of his book gave me the clue to the whole operation. At the very outset I decided that the landscape should be 'north country'; not only would the creation of it bring back happy nostalgic memories of my time at Giggleswick, but dry-point stone walls could be realistically modelled far more effectively than hedges. At about the same time Edward Beal sent me a copy of his delightful book, *Modelling the Old-time Railways*, in which he had used some drawings of mine showing signals of the pre-grouping era; and between the two my ambitions were well and truly fired. The foundation for the 'ground' was pure Ahern—a light timber framework, covered with crumpled cardboard and coated with Polyfilla. To save a great deal of painting afterwards I mixed powder paint with the Polyfilla before use to provide a basic neutral green when it had set; local features of the ground could then be produced by subsequent tinting.

One of the most delicate tasks, that needed much experimenting before a satisfactory method was found, lay in blending the landscape where the three-dimensional cardboard formation met its two-dimensional continuation up the walls of the room. For we had decided that the railway should be *really* permanent in that erstwhile front bedroom, and that the scenic effect should be carried upwards to the picture rail. The aim was to disguise completely the join between the fabricated 'ground' and the wall. It was only in the room corners that there was a difficulty that I never surmounted at Sion Hill. To avoid the impression that the main line was nothing more than a plain oval, with 4 foot radius curves at each end, we introduced scenic features, including a short tunnel, an overbridge carrying a country road, and later a branch line that curved steeply away, and crossed the main line on a plate-girder bridge.

In building up the scenery the principles of 'work study' had to be followed, because as the 'ground' was extended outward from the walls the innermost areas became virtually inaccessible. I learned this to my cost one year when we were on holiday. The house was an old one, built around 1820, and massive in its construction. The slated roof was its most vulnerable part, and it never seemed to have fully recovered from a shake-up it received during the Bath 'blitz' in 1941. There always seemed to be one or two weak spots that we had to watch after heavy rain storms. In this particular summer, while we were away, there was a violent thunderstorm with torrential rain, and the neighbour with whom we had left a key, checked up afterwards and found a leak with water dripping—yes—into the railway room! She quickly put dust sheets over that part of the scenery that was affected, but trickles of water had come down one of the walls and though it dried off quickly enough it left streaks down the two-dimensional backdrop and further down. It was in the most inaccessible area, and was the very devil of a job to put right.

One of our attempts to secure realism had an amusing side-kick. As the scenery was gradually built up it seemed essential that the track should be ballasted and, in conversation with certain friends, it was suggested that chicken-grit would give a realistic appearance. I went to a seed shop in Bath, and was looking around when a friendly assistant asked if he could help. I explained that I wanted some chicken grit, and he asked for what breed of chickens it was required. I wish I could have recorded for posterity the look on his face when I told him it was for ballasting a model railway! It looked fine on the track, but I found that after a while the vibration from the passage of trains caused it to shake out sideways and, to keep it nicely packed up to sleeper-top level, a narrow edging of Polyfilla was necessary.

While the scenery was being built up, the locomotive and carriage stock was increasing and, like the preserved standard gauge steam railways of today, we soon had far more equipment than was needed to work the traffic. This again is carrying the story of the model railway ahead of the chronological sequence of the main part of the book, because I have not yet referred, in other chapters, to activities after my appointment as Chief Mechanical Engineer at Westinghouse. In connection with some experimental work I made contact with a small private firm in Keynsham, and quickly realised that I was dealing with craftsmen of outstanding ability, father and son alike. Business dealings developed into personal friendship and I found that the son, Kenneth Payne, was also a railway and model railway, enthusiast. One evening he took me down to Burnham-on Sea to meet a friend who was an expert model maker and had a finely equipped model railway of his own. Discreet enquiries revealed that he was prepared to build 0-gauge models to order and so, with Laurie Pickard, there opened up a new development on the Sion Hill Railway.

Pickard's locomotives, though of modern types, were all little masterpieces and, after tentative discussions on cost, I conceived the idea of having models of some of my favourite designs built to order. All my existing locomotives, with the exception of *Himley Hall*, were of commercial build, and had 'coarse scale' wheels. The line had been laid with track to suit. So that while Pickard would undoubtedly build to 'fine scale' standards above the running plate, the wheels would necessarily have to be coarse scale, to suit my track. Within those parameters he built me some beautiful locomotives. The first was one of my all-time favourites, a London and North Western 'Claughton' Class 4-6-0, and this was followed by a North Eastern 'Atlantic' of Class 'Z'.

It was in 1953 also that I first met another very expert model maker. Alan Pegler had just begun organising the annual summer outings, from Retford, of the Northern Rubber Company, of which he was Vice-Chairman. A railway enthusiast himself the trips were arranged to include some railway travel of an unusual kind. I was then writing the monthly feature 'Locomotive Causerie' in *The Railway World*, and in that year of 1953 he invited me to join the party, which was to run from Retford to Windsor, and then have a steamer trip on the Thames. The particular attraction for a locomotive enthusiast was that the train would be hauled by an ex-Great Central 4-4-0 of the 'Director' Class.

I wrote up the trip, praising enthusiastically the performance of the engine *Zeebrugge* in the August 1953 issue of *The Railway World* but the most important outcome, so far as I personally was concerned, was that one of the invited guests was a member of the Gainsborough Model Railway Club, a young schoolmaster from Sturton-by-Stow, George Hinchcliff by name. He already had a towering reputation locally as a model-maker of the highest class; and as the engineering mainspring of the Gainsborough club, he was the man who ensured immaculate performance of the intense and complicated operating schedules of that intricate model railway. He has since achieved fame first as engineer to the American tour of the *Flying Scotsman*, which unhappily ended in financial embarrassment for Alan Pegler, and now as the well-known General Manager of Carnforth Steamtown, that provides the power for so many greatly-enjoyed steam-hauled trips in the North of England. But before he became so deeply and successfully involved with 4 foot 8½ inch gauge he made some beautiful 1¼ inch gauge jobs for the Sion Hill Railway, including one of the very first Midland Compounds, in Johnson condition, numbered 2631 and having a double-bogie tender.

The Sion Hill Railway eventually ran through three rooms at the top of the house; but the Western loop line involved some major problems in construction. First of all we had to cut through the outside wall of the original house, the form of which can be clearly seen from the photograph on page 113. Those outside walls, in solid Bath stone, were tremendously thick and, even when we had got through, our problems would not have been ended. The first floor rooms in the western extension did not have the majestic loftiness of the great drawing room, which extended over the entire frontage of the original house; and, as can be appreciated from the photograph, the second floor rooms above were at a lower floor level than those in the original house. The trestles carrying the railway on the western loop had therefore to be much taller, in order to maintain a level track.

This was not all. The second floor rooms in the extension part of the house were entirely isolated from those in the original house and were reached by a separate staircase at the extreme western end. This meant that when the purely railway tunnel through the wall had been cut, for an operator to pass from the main room to that containing the loop line he or she would have to descend two flights of stairs, walk about 30 feet of corridor, and then ascend two more

The new shed in the third room at Sion Hill, with the backdrop painted in, but only the frame work of the roundhouse. The engines that can be seen are the 'Baby Scot', No 5538, Giggleswick, *as yet unpainted; the Bassett-Lowke 4472,* Flying Scotsman *and behind it the 'Claughton'.*

flights of stairs. As there would be many times when I was operating the railway alone this would be quite unacceptable, and to make running the railway a practicable proposition it was essential for the hole in the wall between the two rooms to be large enough for a man or woman to get through. Because of the difference in floor levels in the two rooms this access space was provided beneath the trestles carrying the tracks. There was some complicated track work *inside the tunnel*, but as finalised it worked out well. When displaying the railway to visitors it was always very satisfying to have a train waiting on the loop line, produce it through the tunnel to make a circuit of the main line, and then to disappear again.

The second extension, into the small adjoining room that had once been my daughter's 'den' gave access to the roundhouse. This was not finished by the time we decided to sell 20, Sion Hill and take a smaller property. The round-house itself was based upon that of the Highland Railway at Inverness, and had 18 berths for locomotives. After I had schemed out the design, and made the drawings, several people co-operated in its manufacture. The turntable, large enough to take a 'Pacific' with the Gresley 8-wheeled tender, was made as Inverness originally was, with the pit completely covered in by a timber platform at sleeper level. The section between the perimeter of the table and the pits needed for fire cleaning and maintenance jobs, and involving some intricate track work, was made as a single brass fabrication by Ken Payne's father. For the framework of the roundhouse building itself, made in two sections accommodating nine locomotive berths in each, I placed an order on Westinghouse for them to be made as an exercise by the apprentice carpenters. I had put none of the 'clothing' on those frameworks by the time we left Sion Hill.

Our move to 'Silver Cedars', in High Bannerdown, in the late summer of 1963 entailed the complete dismantling of the railway; but our new property, with its spacious garden, had plenty of room for extensions, and we decided to build an entirely separate 'summer house' in the garden, specially to take the railway. We were advised that no difficulty would be experienced in obtaining planning permission, because we were told, I quote: 'You can put anything you like in a summer house'. It had to be, however, of dwelling-house standard, built in the beautiful Cotswold stone to match the main house. The size 1 decided should be 50 feet by 20 feet to permit 6 foot radius curves on the main line. The larger engines did not really like the 4 foot radius curves at Sion Hill and, before we left there, a Hinchcliff-built 'A4' Pacific, *Silver Link* had been added to the stud.

With all the experience of working in rather constrained physical conditions I was now able to start again, on a much larger 'clean sheet'; and the new 'railway house' was designed to include a small entrance hall wherein my collection of railway coats of arms could be displayed, together with a number of paintings of locomotives and trains for which there was no room in the dwelling house itself. 'Silver Cedars' was a lovely Cotswold style villa, superbly built, and dating from 1938; but compared to Sion Hill it was small, and we had to dispose of much of our furniture, and some of the landscape paintings I had inherited from my father and my Uncle Fred. Over the porch of the 'Railway House' we mounted the whistle of *Silver Link*, Olivia's favourite locomotive, which was presented to her by T.C.B. Miller, when the engine itself was scrapped. Some members of my testing staff at Chippenham came down at week-ends and fitted up an old compressor and the necessary piping so that the whistle could be sounded by compressed air.

The new line at 'Silver Cedars': the Midland compound with the M & NB train in the fell country.

Above *'Silver Cedars': the unfinished running shed and carriage sidings. Engines on shed include HR 4-6-0, No 73,* River Findhorn; *LNER* Silver Link; *CR 4-4-0, No 766,* Dunalastair II; *GWR 4-4-0, No 3433,* City of Bath.

Below *A close-up of the shed, showing in addition the GWR 4-6-0 No 4933,* Himley Hall. *The tracks and formation in the foreground are unfinished.*

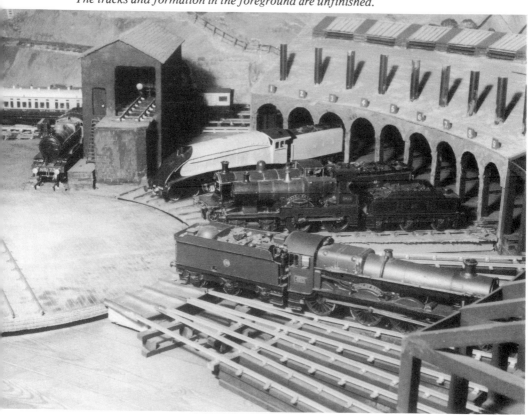

The new railway was considerably more elaborate than the old one. Although the special building was relatively large the garden also was extensive—more than three quarters of an acre. There were some beautiful trees, including the three silver cedars that gave the house its name, two very fine silver birches, and a copse of miscellaneous forest trees at the far end of the garden. I spent some time surveying before finally deciding on the site for the Railway House, and eventually I was able to fit it in, unseen from the road, and indeed from the entrance drive, without removing any of the trees. The neighbours were naturally very curious as to what was going on when building started so, as soon as the house was finished, the trestles erected and a single circuit of track laid, we invited them all in for a demonstration run. There was no scenery by then, and they all watched, ladies and gentlemen alike, goggle-eyed, while *King George V* and *The Flying Scotsman* tore around the circuit.

As finally developed the line was much more extensive than at Sion Hill. At the peak we had 21 locomotives*, plus two that were never run in ordinary traffic. One of these latter was the electric 2-4-0 Stirling No 814 of the Great Northern. I took her down to Burnham-on-Sea one evening, and she ran very sweetly on Laurie Pickard's line, but I was never tempted to change over to electric traction myself. The overriding consideration was the very intermittent utilisation of the line. With all my other commitments, very often a month or more would pass without a wheel being turned; and with electric traction this would be fatal. All the regulars were clockwork. I did, however, have one live steamer. Enthusiasts who have files of *The Model Engineer* going back to 1941 may recall an article by that master builder of miniature steam locomotives, 'L.B.S.C.', in the issue for September 4 entitled 'The Little "County" departs', or 'A Bat that went Great Western!'. It described an 0-gauge model of a 'County' Class 4-4-0 that was *coal fired*. At what seemed little better than a jumble sale of models in Birmingham, many years later, this very engine was one of the items for disposal and I snapped it up at a very cheap price.

Judging by the condition of the paint work the *County of Rutland* had been little used. With her I bought a large bag full of charcoal, and one evening two of my friends from Westinghouse, and their wives, arrived for a game of trains. We coupled up a hair dryer to the electricity supply to act as a blower, and quickly raised steam. She was put on the straight shed road, abreast of the water tower and, when I opened the regulator, she dashed away and stopped at the far end of the main passenger station with the fire dead out! We lit up, and tried again, but although we started each time with what looked like a healthy bright fire, the blower in the smokebox must have been choked, because we never got further than the end of the station. She was put back in the shed to await the time when I could really take her in hand; but alas the time never came. I did survey the route for an outdoor extension of the line for her to run as 'L.B.S.C.' said she did on her acceptance trials in 1941. More time-consuming matters intruded, however, and neither the outdoor extension, nor the engine that was to run it, were brought to fruition.

In the sale at which I bought the little 'County' I bought three other clockwork 0-gauge locomotives. One of them, a North Eastern 'J' Class 4-2-2, in its original condition as a 2-cylinder compound, was clearly a hand-made job,

---

* Complete list at end of chapter.

on which the paint looked as if it had been applied with a garden trowel! But the proportions of the model were good, and she proved an excellent runner. She is still waiting for a repaint however! The two Scottish 4-4-0s, Caledonian No 766, *Dunalastair II*, and Highland No 127, *Loch Garry*, gave the impression of being commercial models, robustly built and excellent runners, but they both include quite an amount of good detail work, and both are hand painted. *Dunalastair II* is painted in the dark blue that was the true Caledonian colour before the practice arose at certain shops of mixing white with it, to make it go further. The rather crude swivling coupling hooks on both the buffer beam and the back of the tender savour of Bassett-Lowke, though I have never seen an engine of this class advertised. Apart from these slightly incongruous fitments it is a very accurate model. The Highland 'Loch' in the plain green of the later Drummond days is in some respects even better, though on the left-hand side of the cab it lacks the apparatus for mechanical exchange of tablets. This, however, could be regarded as true to the original, because the 'Lochs', built by Sharp Stewart & Co, were delivered to the Highland Railway minus this fitment. This model has three-link chain couplings, front and rear.

Still on Scottish matters, when I went to Inverness in November 1961 I saw that the three special TPO vans, for so long used on the mail trains between Perth and Helmsdale, had been taken out of service and were lying derelict in the yard. Fortunately Mr Iain R. Smith had measured them up and made an excellent drawing, and I got those excellent model carriage builders, George and Doris Stokes, of Lower Dowdeswell, to make me a model. Those vans were of great historic interest. They were built at Lochgorm Works, Inverness, in 1916, for dealing with the enormous volume of mail passing over the Highland Railway for the men of the Grand Fleet, at Scapa Flow. When I saw the mail trains first in 1927 the vans were working through between Perth and Helmsdale, the only passenger train vehicles to continue north or south through Inverness. Naturally I had my TPO van in Highland colours, in the characteristic dark green, and with the scarlet ends of Postal stock on the Highland Railway.

To emphasise the Highland character of the 'Silver Cedars' roundhouse, George and Doris Stokes made me a beautiful scale model of the elaborate Inverness water-tower, though I must add that the coaling stage was pure Midland. I was favoured, by Scottish Region, with a set of the original drawings of the roundhouse; but having noted that as early as 1902, with the introduction of Peter Drummond's 'Castle' Class 4-6-0, those engines and their 8-wheeled tenders were too long to go completely into the shed, and were parked with part of their tenders extending out into the open, I made my shed deep enough for the LNER 'Pacifics' *Flying Scotsman* and *Silver Link* to go completely inside. In its later days the Inverness roundhouse had the smoke chimneys removed, no doubt because most of the 'inhabitants' were parked with their noses inwards. I never considered having the folding doors to each bay that were originally fitted. They were removed soon after the arrival of the 'Castle' Class 4-6-0s.

It will be realised by this time that any suggestion of a unity of association and period had been thrown to the winds in my growing collection of locomotives. *Loch Garry* was the only really legitimate inhabitant of 'Inverness' shed. I had another splendid Highland engine, in one of the 'River' Class 4-6-0s; but I had her painted as she was intended to be, in the lighter shade of Lochgorm green,

Sion Hill: the Highland 4-4-0 Loch Garry *bringing the local down the branch from 'Wanstrow'.*

No 73, *River Findhorn.* The 'Rivers' did not come to Inverness till 1928, and then they were in Midland 'red'. I do not know if the rejuvenated *City of Truro* ever got to Inverness during her sojourn in Scotland. At that time she was in the magnificent Dean style of painting, with red wheels and underframes; and I had my *City of Bath* repainted thus, from the shabby plain green thing that she was when I bought her. In Chapter 1 of this book I have told how my father bought me a Gauge 1 model of the GWR 'Atbara' Class 4-4-0, No 3410, *Sydney*, and I have always felt that my gorgeously arrayed *City of Bath* was recompense for the disposal of *Sydney.* Just at the time I was drafting this chapter I learned that a 2 inch gauge model of *Sydney* was to be auctioned at Christie's. She was, however, described as 'City' Class. While ten of the 'Atbaras' bearing names in that category were rebuilt as 'Cities', between 1902 and 1909, *Sydney* was not one of these. She remained an 'Atbara' until the time of her final withdrawal in October 1927.

Providing the power for vintage clockwork locomotives had its problems. Having acquired the North Eastern 'compound' 4-2-2 I was anxious to have one of my greatest favourites among 19th century classes—a Midland 'Spinner'. I obtained a copy of the original Derby drawing of the '115' Class from the London Midland Region, and then the question arose, how could we get a standard Bassett-Lowke mechanism beneath that very small boiler? I was out in the Railway House one day and my eye lighted upon the tender of *Himley Hall*, and the thought came, why not put the mechanism in the tender, and let the tender propel the engine? Too big again! Then the unkind idea came of cannibalising one of the Hornby 0-4-0s. They had very strong mechanisms, and could be fitted into the tender, disguised by covering with a good heap of coal.

She ran beautifully thus, and looked lovely piloting the Johnson compound, when the load exceeded seven Bain and Clayton coaches.

It was, of course, to be expected that locomotives powered with the same type of clockwork mechanism would show different traction characteristics. The North British 'Atlantic', *Liddesdale*, for example, would not take more than six of the M & NB stock, while the compound could manage seven. Neither of the LNER 'Pacifics' was as strong as the 4-6-0s, *King George V, Cardean, Giggleswick* and *Sir Gilbert Claughton*, though the Highland *River Findhorn* was the weakest of them all. When she had anything of a load we had to put *Loch Garry* on as pilot. But perhaps the most extraordinary difference was that between the two Hornby 4-4-0s, *The Bramham Moor* and *County of Bedford*. The former was a steady, sedate machine that would take four bogies smoothly round, and her action reminded me of the 'Hunt' Class engines on which I had ridden on the footplate. *County of Bedford*, on the other hand, was a wild thing that used to tear round, with a vicious, vibrating motion that made one pity anyone who was on *her* footplate. I shall always remember one of the senior Western Region running inspectors coming to Sion Hill, en route for an engagement in Bath. We ran some trains for him, including *County of Bedford*. He watched her go round and then said: 'Rough as the devil; just as she used to be!'.

It was at 'Silver Cedars' that I did the more ambitious scenic work. On the curve at the opposite end of the room to the running shed, against a background reminiscent of the Yorkshire fells on the Settle and Carlisle line, I built a model based upon Arten Gill Viaduct, but with a few less arches than the prototype. It was a fascinating job. Of course the arches did not carry any of the load. I had arranged for the trestling to be built so that there were uprights inside the two piers that were more massive than the rest, and trains were running over the 'viaduct' before there were any arches, or background scenery. The line in the Railway House at 'Silver Cedars' was never finished. There was much scenic work to be done around the main station, together with all the ballasting of the track in the station area, while only half the roundhouse was finished.

Regarding the priorities in completing the work I must tell a story against myself. The signals were positioned according to the best British railways practice, in fact one fairly large gantry was made specially; but, right down to the time when the line was closed, none of them worked. I had plans worked out for the two interlockings in the station area, and a ground frame was installed for working the points leading into the roundhouse yard, but nothing was coupled up. I had not gone to the extent of putting temporary crosses on the semaphores to show that they were not yet in use, and our few trains ran past signals at danger with joyous abandon. Then one day the Westinghouse Model Railway Club asked me to give a lantern lecture describing my railway. When it came to question time one of my own staff, who doubtless thought he was asking the 'right' question, enquired about my signalling. It was before I had even positioned any of the posts; and when I replied that I hadn't got any, there was, momentarily, a horrified hush, and then a gathering crescendo of uncontrolled laughter, at the idea of a Chief Mechanical Engineer of Westinghouse having a railway where they ran express trains without any signals!

Express trains—yes; the reader will probably have realised by now that I have spoken of naught save express passenger locomotives. I had no others—no goods engines, no suburban tanks, no shunters. Milk vans and horse boxes were attached to passenger trains, and the little four and six-wheeled GWR coaches that worked up that steeply graded, and sharply curved, branch line were hauled by 4-4-0s, usually the Hornby Midland compound No 1108, which would readily negotiate small radius curves. The 'County' was much too wild to be trusted anywhere but on the main line! The railway was never intended to be a true operational model. I enjoyed having well-made scale models of many of my favourite locomotives and coaching stock, and I derived as much enjoyment from scheming out the scenery and building the landscape as I did from running the trains. It was a happy and creative relaxation from my daily duties, and from the increasing complexity of my literary work.

The 'Silver Cedars' railway—locomotives

GWR 4-6-0 No 4933, *Himley Hall*,	(Anon)
GWR 4-4-0 No 3821, *County of Bedford*,	(Hornby)
GWR 4-6-0 No 6000, *King George V*,	(Bassett Lowke)
GWR 4-4-0 No 3433, *City of Bath*,	(Anon)
Southern 2-6-0 'N' Class	(Bassett Lowke)
LMS 4-6-0 No 5538, *Giggleswick*,	(Hinchcliff)
LNWR 4-6-0 No 2222, *Sir Gilbert Claughton*,	(Pickard)
Midland 4-4-0 No 2631 (compound)	(Hinchcliff)
LMS 4-4-0 No 1108 (compound)	(Hornby)
Midland 4-2-2 No 117 (Spinner)	(Pickard)
Caledonian 4-4-0 No 935 (Pickersgill)	(Anon)
Caledonian 4-6-0 No 903, *Cardean*,	(Pickard)
Caledonian 4-4-0 No 766, *Dunalastair II*,	(Anon)
Highland 4-6-0 No 73, *River Findhorn*,	(Pickard)
Highland 4-4-0 No 127, *Loch Garry*,	(Anon)
GNR 2-4-0 No 814 (electric)	(Anon)
NER 4-4-2 No 735 Class 'Z'	(Pickard)
NER 4-2-2 No 1522 (compound)	(Anon)
NBR 4-4-2 No 877, *Liddesdale*,	(Pickard)
LNER 4-6-2 No 4472, *Flying Scotsman*,	(Bassett Lowke)
LNER 4-4-0 No 201, *Bramham Moor*,	(Hornby)
LNER 4-6-2 No 2509, *Silver Link*,	(Hinchcliff)
GWR 4-4-0 No 3474, *County of Rutland*, (live steam)	(LBSC)

Chapter 12

Towards a climax and retirement from Westinghouse

At the conclusion of the preceeding chapter I referred to the increasing complexity of my literary work; only once, however, did it become anything but a pleasure. Then it was with what is commonly known as a 'pot-boiler'. The publisher concerned emphasised that I could just sit down and dash it off; it would need no research. That was just the point. It was the very negation of all that I enjoyed in book writing, no need to seek out new things, no field work to be done. But the times were hard, and when he flung down a bundle of treasury notes, and more or less ordered me to get on with it, I could not resist any longer! While all the rest of my books bring back pleasant memories in varying respects there are bound to be some that are special favourites; and just at that milestone in my professional engineering life there were three of which I have particularly happy memories—*Railway Race to the North; Main Lines Across the Border*, and *British Steam Railways*.

The first of the three came from a suggestion of Mr Ian Allan's. At the outset little more was envisaged than an expanded version of the Rev W.J. Scott's pamphlet, *Kinnaber*, including some of the subsequent writings of Charles Rous-Marten, and Norman Doran Macdonald. But I had still got no further than cogitating on the subject when I met once again my great friend, the late E.G. Marsden, who, as Information Agent of the LNER in 1938, had conceived the wonderful ideal of getting the old Stirling 8 foot 4-2-2 No 1 out of York Railway Museum and running it again on the 50th anniversary of the first 'Race to the North'. He immediately made available to me, from his own collection, an invaluable series of documents relating to the second 'Race', including copies of telegrams between the East Coast General Managers in the concluding stages. He also made the suggestion of putting letters in the railway press, asking for reminiscences, and such like. The response to this latter was remarkable, and writing the book became a truly thrilling task. Ian Allan commissioned a notable railway painter, the late Jack Hill, to produce six pictures illustrating incidents in the races; and, although we could not afford to publish more than one of them in full colour, the other five looked dramatic enough in monochrome.

I was responsible for providing the data on which he based his pictures, and I must now confess to a 'bloomer' that no one seems to have spotted, until now. One of the pictures showed the changing of engines in the middle of the night, at York, with the Stirling 8-footer No 775 coupling off, and the big North Eastern 4-4-0 No 1621 waiting on the centre road. The ensemble was based on a very fine modern photograph by Kenneth Field, showing the engine-change on a Bristol–Newcastle express, in which the principal actors were an ex-LMS 'Jubilee' No 45602, *British Honduras*, and a Peppercorn 4-6-2, *Herringbone*. Jack Hill skilfully substituted night for day, and put the clock back more than 60 years so attractively that, when the BBC produced their recent feature film on the 'Race to the North' in 1978, to which I was consultant, they used the picture for the basis of one of the scenes. The only trouble, that I have only just discovered, was that the platform depicted did not exist in 1895! It was only a few weeks before I wrote this present chapter that I had occasion to refer to *The Railway Magazine* for December 1897, and an interview given to the Editor by Mr (later Sir) George Gibb. Regarding York station he said: 'The fact that the main platform is one sided is a great drawback, from some points of view. Although the station was only opened in 1877, the traffic has already outgrown the accommodation and we are now contemplating an enlargement. It is to be made into a double-sided station'.

An artist's impression in Scott's pamphlet *Kinnaber*, shows the 8 pm from Kings Cross at the correct platform. I was aware of this picture at the time I briefed Jack Hill, but took it as a piece of artist's licence. Actually, it was that artist who was right, and I was wrong!

Main Lines Across the Border was a dreamchild of Eric Treacy's and my own; though when the suggestion was put to him no one could have been more enthusiastic than our publisher, Ronnie Nelson. Eric was one of the most charming and remarkable characters I have ever known. I met him first in the late 1920s, long before he was ordained, when we were fellow members of Toc H, with a joint interest and participation in Rugby football. It says much for our attention to the job in hand that although our home ground was at Folly

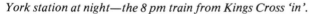

York station at night—the 8 pm train from Kings Cross 'in'.

Main Lines across the Border: The Thames Clyde Express *nearing Ribblehead, hauled by a 'Converted Royal Scot', 4-6-0, No 46112,* Sherwood Forester. *The mountain in the left background is Pen-y-Ghent* (Ian S. Pearsall).

Farm, New Barnet, flanked on the western side by the LNER main line, neither of us then discovered the other's passion for railways! *Main Lines Across the Border* was six years in gestation. While I rode all sorts and conditions of locomotives and got some very black faces in the process, Eric, in securing the photographs was, to quote his own words: '. . . exploring some of the loveliest and most peaceful country in the British Isles'.

'And so, every year for the past six years', he went on, 'I have spent part of my annual holidays in the Border Country. I have roamed from the savage coast of Northumberland to the peaceful shores of Solway Firth. I have followed the railway from Carlisle over Whitrope Summit along the glen of the Slitrig burn to Hawick; from Hawick, by the banks of the Gala Water, through the lovely villages and towns of the Scott country, via the coalfields of Midlothian, to that queen of cities, Edinburgh.

'I have stood in pouring rain on Shap Fell listening to the cry of the curlew, and watched terrified sheep bleating at the great monsters which belched their exhaust high in the air as they panted up the hill.

'I have waded through the heathery bogs of Blea Moor. I have been lashed by hail whipping over the shoulders of Wild Boar Fell as I perched myself on a wall at Aisgill. I have slithered on my backside down muddy embankments in the Valley of the Nith; I have been stung by Scottish wasps, chased by Yorkshire heifers; waited for trains that didn't come, and missed trains that did . . .', all to build up his share of a 'book and lyrics' collaboration that was one of the happiest in which I ever participated.

Main Lines Across the Border was published at a time when the Modernisation Plan of British Railways was getting into its stride, and we were able to include pictures of diesels hauling the West Coast expresses over Shap and Beattock. But the 'stride' was wobbling a little, as finance brought a temporary halt to the electrification of the Euston–Liverpool–Manchester lines, and the scrap-steam fanatics at BR Headquarters urged an ever-increasing acceleration of the pace. At Westinghouse we were dragged through the ghastly fiasco of the contract for 295,000 vacuum brake cylinders, signed in February 1958, and providing for an initial output of 1,000 cylinders a week, gradually to be stepped up to 2,000. A fine new works had been built near Manchester specially for the job, and output was already topping 1,500, when suddenly there came an SOS from British Railways: 'For God's sake stop—we've nowhere to put them!'. It was a classic case of management bungling, for in working towards the stipulated output we had far outdistanced the production of new freight wagons for which the brake cylinders were required. By April 1959 we were requested to restrict deliveries to 750 a week, revised again in June to no more than 400. Being then concerned only with the signalling and colliery business, I was not immediately affected; but with the new factory near Manchester, designed for an output of 2,000 cylinders a week, cut back to 400, the whole programme of brake production was thrown into disarray, and its repercussions were felt throughout the company.

This appalling situation, which was to change dramatically to something infinitely worse in little more than two years time, was having an increasingly adverse effect on the cash-flow position in the company as a whole; and although my own department was busy enough on contracts that we had no reason to believe would be anything but profitable, I was now near enough to the centre of affairs to realise how steadily we were moving towards a point of crisis. It so happened that in June 1961 Olivia and I were to spend our first-ever holiday outside Great Britain. We had been abroad together several times on the Summer Conventions of the Institution of Railway Signal Engineers; but a convention was not like a real holiday and, in the prevailing climate at Westinghouse, when we set out for Rapallo on the Mediterranean coast we felt like a couple of children briefly let out of school. Two weeks of blissful escape! I was not unmindful however of my literary commitments, particularly Philip Unwin's request for a book about continental railways, and it can be said that *Continental Main Lines* was almost completely schemed out on some lazy leisured afternoons on the balcony of that delightful hotel where we stayed on the hillside overlooking Rapallo, with the calm blue waters of the Mediterranean spread out below us.

We had travelled from Calais by train spending nights in Paris and Nice on the way. South of Dijon it was all fresh ground for me. We were travelling by the 9.15 am *rapide* from Paris and, on that train, lunch lasted for most of the 122 miles from Dijon to Lyons. Even so, with a CC7100 Class electric locomotive at the head end that distance was due to be covered in no more than 106 minutes, and after all what is a mere 1¾ hours for a meal in France! From many previous journeys between Paris and the Channel Ports I had become familiar with the little pantomime enacted before dining car service in France, where meals are a serious business. There is no nipping into the car half an hour before meal time, to get an extra aperitif, and the best seats. The connecting door is bolted and barred until *Monsieur le Chef de Brigade* is ready, and then,

Above Continental Main Lines: *The northbound 'Flèche d'Or'—Paris to Calais—crossing the Lamorlaye viaduct near Chantilly, hauled by a 25 kV electric locomotive* (G.F. Fenino).

Below *One of the grandly impressive 4-cylinder compound 4-8-2s of the 241P class, in 1961 used south of Avignon on the fast trains to the Cote d'Azur* (P. Ransome-Wallis).

with the pomp and circumstance of his calling, he parades the corridors of the train, tinkling his little bell. Once in the car you are there to eat and nothing else, and the idea of anyone wanting to secure a window corner to see the kilometre posts and do some stop watching between courses would be regarded as lunatic behaviour.

In 1961 electric haulage finished at Avignon, and out on the platform I was thrilled to see one of the huge 'P' Class 4-8-2s come backing down, to take over from the one electric locomotive that had brought our 18-coach train, 735 tons, over the entire 460 miles from Paris. Though among the mightiest of steam locomotives, French compounds were equally the most deceptive. Pacifics and 4-8-2s alike, they used to creep away from stations in almost complete silence, and always a complete surprise to British enthusiasts who were familiar with the cannonades of Gresley 'Pacifics' starting out of Kings Cross, or of 'Scots' and 'Lizzies' hammering their way up Camden bank. And, true to reputation, this great 4-8-2 was soon wheeling this lengthy train of ours in great style across the level of the Rhône delta from Arles, where the line is flanked on each side with a thick barricade of cypress trees to protect trains from the fury of the mistral. I know only too well how a strong side wind can affect the speed of an express passenger train and, however much they may block one's sight of the passing scene, these 'defence works' are amply justified. On this particular day all was calm and we swept along at 73 to 74 mph. It would have been interesting to see how we should have fared with such a load when the mistral was blowing its hardest.

Beyond Marseilles along the Côte d'Azur the American built 2-8-2s of the '141 R' Class had the line to themselves before the days of electrification. On our first run into this region, at the end of a long day of sightseeing and note-taking, my first impressions of these massive, very *un-French* locomotives were no more than superficial; and, on the continuation of the journey next morning from Nice to Ventimiglia, our attention was taken up far more with the magnificent scenery than with locomotive performance. Appreciation of these splendid workhorses came a few years later when we spent a week at Menton, and saw them working the huge international express trains over that switchback of a line beneath the range of high mountains that rises so steeply from the coast. There was nothing quiet about *their* going; they *roared*, but although so different from the indigenous types, the French *Cheminots* loved them.

We had not long returned from that delightful holiday when there was some shattering news in Westinghouse. On September 7 1961 British Railways terminated entirely the contract for vacuum brake cylinders after no more than 119,000, out of 295,000 originally ordered had been supplied. It was not only the premature ending of one of the largest single contracts the company had ever received, but the throwing into virtual idleness of a factory that had been built specially for the job. After urgent consultations, that extended over several months, a writ was issued in May 1962 against British Railways claiming damages for breach of contract. It can well be imagined that such a step as challenging one's best customer in the Courts was not a step to be lightly undertaken, but the feeling that we had been let down went very deep. While the cancellation of the contract supported the poor view that was being taken in many quarters of the progress of the Modernisation Plan, the increasing financial weakness revealed by the loss of roughly £1¼ million on the year ending September 28 1963 made Westinghouse ripe for a takeover bid.

In the meantime my involvement with the Institution of Railway Signal Engineers was increasing. On Christmas Day 1961, H.C. Towers, who had been Honorary Editor of the Proceedings for several years, died suddenly. He had not many years previously retired after a distinguished career in signalling in India, and was an author of some reputation on signalling matters. My great friend and close colleague in Westinghouse, George Hathaway, was then President of the Institution, and in the emergency he asked me to take on the Editorship. Furthermore, 1962 was the Golden Jubilee year of the Institution, and the Council had already been discussing the possibility of a special publication to mark the event. As Editor I was immediately involved, and how this initially modest project developed into a full-length book was a long, though rapidly-evolving story. After the lapse in time I cannot recall the exact date on which the Council gave me the go-ahead to write the book, and get it published; but I do remember, when negotiating the arrangements for trade distribution with Ian Allan Ltd, how one of their directors assured me there was 'not a hope in hell' of having finished copies by the time of the Golden Jubilee Dinner and Dance on October 26!

Prior to receiving the go-ahead, however, Olivia and I had sounded some family friends who had a small, but very efficient printing works in Bradford-on-Avon. They were most enthusiastic, and even before I was ready they were raring to go. The thing that worried me, however, was that the Council of the Institution wanted to see the script of the book before it was printed. This was reasonable enough; but in view of the extreme shortage of time I wrung a concession from them that they would see each chapter as it was written, instead of waiting until all was finished. The manuscript was typed on 'flimsies' so that the dozen or so copies required for simultaneous issue to the members of the Council committee could be run off in the Westinghouse print room. Bill Dotesio, our printer, gave the job overriding priority in his works, and no time was wasted in communications. Copy from Bradford-on-Avon was delivered by messenger to me at Chippenham, and as he lived in a lovely house at Middle Hill, overlooking the Western Region main line, at Box, I was able to call on him early in the morning to deliver manuscripts or corrected proofs on my way to the office. When we got really into our stride the earlier chapters had reached page-proof stage, while intermediate ones were going the rounds and while some of the latter ones were not even written. And despite the gloomy prognostications of that Ian Allan director we finished comfortably ahead of time.

When I wrote my book, *British Railways in Transition*, for Ronnie Nelson, which was published in the following year I made no mention of the crisis over vacuum brake cylinders in which they were embroiled with Westinghouse. Although it was, almost literally, a case of life or death for our company, the equipment of nearly 300,000 freight vehicles with the vacuum brake was one of the least glamorous features of the Modernisation Plan. It was a problem having not the slightest interest to the general reader. But, before *British Railways in Transition* appeared, the country had endured one of the most severe winters in living memory. Unlike the earlier one of 1947, which did not strike in all its intensity until January was nearly out, the blizzards in the West Country began at Christmas, and before February was out we had become quite expert in driving on roads that became packed solid with ice. But that spell of intense cold brought Olivia and me to one very definite conclusion: we no longer

Our new home: 'Silver Cedars', with one of our favourite cars 'Sam' in the drive.

needed that big Regency house on Sion Hill. Our children were away for most of the time and, without central heating, it was difficult to keep the few rooms we used warm in that Arctic weather. It was nevertheless with great regret that we came to that decision. Olivia had done some beautiful work in redecorating many of the rooms, and we had grown to love the Georgian style of architecture. There was also the small matter of the model railway, by that time extending through three rooms.

If there was one year that could be singled out as the most critically important in the latter part of my business life it would undoubtedly be 1963. The frustration of house moving was only one of those things that helped to make it so. There had been a prelude to this eventful year in the late autumn of 1962, when, because of a severe cut-back in British Railways modernisation, we no longer needed such a large drawing office, and the branch establishment at Kingswood was closed. Soon after Christmas, however, Jack Aldridge suggested to me that I ought to put up for Council in the Institution of Railway Signal Engineers. He was anxious to maintain the succession of Westinghouse Presidents, and if I were elected to the Council in 1963 there was a good chance of my attaining the Presidency in the year previous to my retirement from the company, in 1969. He felt that my sponsors should be members outside Westinghouse. Only two were needed at that time, and for me he secured the backing of Charles Darbyshire, Assistant Signal Engineer of the London Midland, whom I knew well, and Douglas Kidd, Managing Director of the Railway Signal Company, an old friend and close colleague. So, at the Annual General Meeting, in April 1963 I became a Member of Council.

Nine years almost to the week before the time about which I am now writing I received a little packet postmarked Teignmouth. It contained a little book entitled *Selected Poems*, by Gilbert Thomas, who I knew to be an essayist and literary critic, but particularly as author of a charming little book, *Paddingtom to Seagood: The story of a Model Railway*. In a happily worded letter

accompanying the gift he told me that he had reviewed one or two of my own books. When early in 1963 I received a letter from a publishing house of which I had not previously heard, David & Charles, based at Dawlish, inviting me to act as General Editor for a new series of books they were contemplating— monographs dealing with famous locomotive classes—I did not connect the two, even though the writer of that letter of invitation was named Thomas. It was only when matters had progressed to the stage of detailed discussion, and Olivia and I entertained him to lunch at that delightful country hotel 'The Bell House', at Sutton Benger, that we discovered he was the son of Gilbert Thomas, and indeed the little boy in some of the pictures in *Paddington to Seagood*.

It was the beginning of another happy and continuing literary association. David St John Thomas has published many of my books since our first meeting in 1963; but I shall never cease to be grateful to him for a rescue operation in which he participated in 1965. It happened thus-wise. Some two months after that meeting at Sutton Benger, Jack Aldridge instructed me to attend a meeting at the Charing Cross Hotel called by the United Kingdom Railway Advisory Service (UKRAS), under the auspices of the Ministry of Transport. The United Nations Organisation had as one of its activities an Economic Commission for Asia and the Far East (ECAFE) charged with assisting the developing countries of the region in a diversity of ways; and one of these had led to the setting up of a Railway Sub-Committee. This latter was a typically vast affair, that met every two years, and in 1962 the meeting had been in Melbourne. At that meeting the British delegation, led by my great friend, the late Roland Bond, together with the French, had promised to produce a text book on the management and operation of single line railways, and how the through-put of traffic could be increased. Many months had elapsed since the meeting in Melbourne and, since the French showed no signs of wanting to collaborate, the Ministry of Transport told UKRAS to go in alone. Time was slipping by. The next meeting of the Railway Sub-Committee of ECAFE would be held in the early autumn of 1964, and the syllabus of the proposed book was extensive. The people invited to that meeting at the Charing Cross Hotel on May 30 1963 represented a positive galaxy of expertise in their various fields, and they had previously been charged with the task of making contributions; and it was apparently taken for granted that I would be the editor! It was a rather frightening, if challenging assignment, particularly as it was all expected to be done in addition to my duties as Chief Mechanical Engineer.

This is no place to tell of the intervening stages—of how that diversity of erudite contributions was brought together and how it was piloted through that huge international Railway Sub-Committee, at Bangkok in October 1964; the fun began late in November, when the amended script was ready and I took it up to London to meet the publisher, and hand it over. Yes, the publisher! UKRAS had contracted with a man in South-East London of whom I had not previously heard. He was a strange character whose facile optimism I found slightly disconcerting, especially when it transpired that he had no staff to speak of, and worked on the packaged-deal principle from his own home. Well, to cut a long story short, when the printers he employed received our manuscript from him they promptly impounded it as a surety against his debts. The illustrations, so carefully collected from so many overseas countries, did not even reach the printer. They had been torn up by the publisher's wife in the course of a family row! So here was a pretty kettle of fish. The UKRAS people were in despair, and seemingly quite ready to call the whole thing off; but it needed no more than a moment's reflection to appreciate what a catastrophic loss of prestige the United Kingdom delegation would suffer when next the Railway Sub-Committee met, and I sought permission to try to find another publisher. It was then that David St John Thomas became interested; and after a new script had been prepared, and a fresh set of photographs collected, a contract was drawn up between his firm and the Ministry of Transport. The rescue operation was completed. The book, entitled simply *Single Line Railways*, and a meaty work of 358 pages, was published in 1966; but not many, even among those responsible for the original text were aware of the horrific interlude between the return of our four-man delegation from Bangkok and the signing of the contract with David & Charles Ltd.

Above left *Railway sub-committee of ECAFE, Bangkok, October 1964: the British delegation in serious mood! My colleagues, to left and right, are Herbert Howard, then of English Electric, and Donald Bartlett, of the British Railways Board.*

Right *The dust jacket of the handbook that resulted, including part of a timetable diagram of the Royal State Railways of Thailand.*

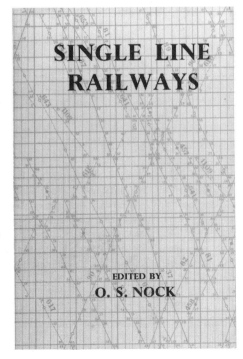

SINGLE LINE RAILWAYS

EDITED BY
O. S. NOCK

Reverting now to the year 1963—at home British Railways, having cast aside the recommendations of their professional advisers, and embarked in a shipwreck hurry on the replacement of steam, by diesel traction, were reaping the whirlwind with a vengeance. The regions were being flooded with new diesel electric main line locomotives before the depots had adequate facilities for their maintenance, and the failure rate was astronomical. At one major depot on the Midland line no fewer than 50 per cent of a large fleet of diesels were out of action at one time. It was a terrible time for the running men, all of them brought up on steam and loyally anxious to do their very best with the new power. Between the neophytes who continued to chorus their 'scrap steam' refrains, and the hard-line 'old guard' who manifested a positively unholy joy in any failures of the diesels, there was the great body of men toiling day and night to keep the trains running, and at times I felt very sorry for them. I liked the story of the senior officer who was presiding at a conference of manufacturers' experts to investigate failures of diesels, who got rather tired of the talk of technicalities, and said: 'Gentlemen, you know we've been having to take these locomotives off after less than half the journey. Do you think we could have a little less 'efficiency' and get the whole way?'.

There was no need to gloat over diesel failures and I was disturbed over the way an article of mine, describing a run from Euston to Glasgow in the winter of 1963–4, was presented in *The Railway Magazine*. I had an engine pass to ride one of the English Electric Type '4' diesels through from Euston to Carlisle, on 'The Midday Scot', and we arrived at Crewe with one of the water tanks leaking. Slight though this trouble was it rendered the locomotive a total failure, temporarily, and it had to be taken off the train. The locomotive controller gave us in exchange the first thing that was ready, a 'Duchess' Class 4-6-2. Fortunately, for that time in steam history, she was in good condition, and with a splendid pair of Crewe North men we made a magnificent run to Carlisle, the fastest I had *ever* made up to that time with any form of motive power. Against a schedule of 151 minutes for the 141.1 miles we took only 141½; and although on account of works preparatory to electrification, the diesel had brought us into Crewe 7½ minutes late, we were only 8½ minutes late on arrival at Carlisle despite the inordinately long wait at Crewe for the relief. Unhappily the article in which the run was described was 'splashed' 'RED DUCHESS TO THE RESCUE'—rather too much inclined towards 'unholy joy'. For the record the engine in question was the *Duchess of Rutland*, hauling a 12-coach train of 455 tons.

Reverting to Westinghouse troubles, the winter of 1963–4 was one of high drama for the top management. The Action against British Railways claiming £3 million damages for breach of contract was dragging its way through the High Courts, and the Defendants were in fact pleading for a postponement. Although fortunately for our cash flow situation, this was refused by the judge and an amicable agreement was arrived at between Dr Beeching and our Chairman, P. Ewen; but we had to settle for no more than £1.625 million, instead of £3 million. On top of this, the catastrophic end of the adventure of the Brake Division into the Hobbs Automatic Gearbox saw another £4 million down the drain, and with it the dismissal of the Director concerned. It was certainly time for the period of 'Baldwin Government' to be ended. Mervyn Shorter retired from the Managing Directorship and was appointed Deputy Chairman, and Leslie Thompson stepped up into his place. At once a period of investigation towards a re-grouping of activities began. It was a strange and unsettling period, with relatively junior men charged with enquiring into the activities of departments that had been steady dividend earners.

Even taking the kindest view of it the eventual reorganisation of the Signal and Colliery division was rather pitiful. No longer was the strong hand of Jack Aldridge at the helm. He had been appointed Deputy Managing Director, and the Divisional Managership passed to Douglas Shipp, his former assistant, technologically one of the most brilliant men I have ever met; but he did not prove a very effective manager, and his caustic wit, and often delicious repartee, was a cloak for a rather timorous disposition. There were times when he seemed scared of his superiors, and he always hesitated to take a firm line when subordinates chose to be awkward. There were many stories of his quick wit, one of the best of which concerned a pre-Christmas social visit to one of the British Railways Regions, prior to entertaining our friends to a festal lunch. Among the token gifts handed out to each was a pair of finger-nail clippers. The senior railway officer present said: 'These are nice. Do you use them yourselves?'. Like lightning came Douglas Shipp's retort: 'No, we bite ours!'. Amid the storm of laughter that ensured, however, I had time to reflect that there was a sad reality underlying that quick riposte, and that many a time during the four years that I served under him on the seven-man Divisional Executive, discussions on difficult points of administration drifted down to the level of a village debating society, while he sat—if not actually biting his nails—looking on from the chair, a picture of indecision and unhappiness. And yet in all matters of electrical technology he was a positive giant.

One of the most voluble of those who had participated in the investigation stage prior to reorganisation was assigned to me in my new role as Planning Manager. In the preceeding months he had so favourably impressed—I was almost tempted to write 'blinded'!—some of the senior management with his eloquence as to be commended to me as a person of exceptionally high 'IQ'. If the initials had stood for 'hot air' I would readily have agreed; but actually I felt like the Lord High Executioner of Titipu when, towards the end of the second act of *The Mikado*, he sang:

'The flowers that bloom in the spring, tra, la,
Have nothing to do with the case.
I've got to take under my wing tra, la,
A most unattractive old thing, tra, la.'

I could have coped with any amount of hot air, but what I could not stomach was disloyalty. It was a thing I had never experienced in all my 30 years of middle and senior management in the firm, and with this character it began no more than *hours* after his appointment. Fortunately he did not last long. He got a job in another company, and although his going was regarded as a 'tragedy' by some of the 'IQ' enthusiasts, it was a great relief to me to be rid of him.

One of the most delicate tasks I had as Planning Manager, and one of the most ultimately satisfying, was in negotiating the delivery programme of material for the signalling and automatic train operation of the Victoria Line of London Transport. As a member of the Joint Committee presided over by Robert Dell, the Chief Signal Engineer of LT, I had many opportunities of appreciating the marvellous grasp of every single facet of the job possessed by that remarkable man. His technology was consummate; his command of the overall situation complete, but he was also a master craftsman. There was no

South African Railways: the GEA class Beyer-Garratt locomotive 4-8-2 + 2-8-4 type that I rode from Mossel Bay to George (Cape Province).

job, in his workshops or out on the line, that he could not do as well as any of his technicians. In times of difficulty I preferred to see Dell alone rather than with an attendant delegation from the Works. When the essence of any real difficulty was put to him his grasp of production matters made him responsive and sympathetic. I shall always remember the aftermath of one such occasion when one of his top assistants, who had expected to see me flayed alive, said, as I was leaving the outer office, 'I think he's let you off very lightly!'.

Troubles apart, however, the Victoria Line was a marvellous project with which to be associated. It was a tremendous step to introduce the automatic driving of trains on the London Underground; but by the process of ingenious prototype design, and ruthlessly extensive testing, first on a short section near Ravenscourt Park, and then on the Hainault Loop, in which Harry Duckitt, who became Divisional Manager after Douglas Shipp's death in 1970, headed the Westinghouse team, the engineering finalised on the Victoria Line itself was absolutely right from the outset, and it has worked without a hitch ever since. It remains a monument to the genius of Robert Dell.

One of my last tasks of customer liaison took me into rather more exotic regions than the London Underground, to Kenya, where difficulties had arisen over some equipment recently supplied to inaugurate tokenless block working on some sections of the East African Railway. The working conditions had not been fully understood in London. In the late summer of 1968 I flew to Nairobi, where arrangements were made for me to visit some of the stations concerned. Never previously, or since for that matter, have I gone trouble-shooting in such delightful conditions. Down the line we went in a little inspection 'buggy', given mail-train priority at the various passing loops. At Nairobi and for some distance westward the altitude, well over 4,000 feet above sea level, is such that the climate is deliciously dry and bracing, with no suggestion that one is so near the Equator. We stopped at some of the stations for me to make sketches of the layouts, and eventually climbed to the escarpment leading down into the Great Rift Valley, where the tremendous prospect westward includes the great volcano, Mount Longonot. The line descends steeply, but having reached Naivasha and drawn alongside the lake of the same name, we had secured enough data on the train working for my enquiry, and there was time for a motor boat trip on the lake before we headed back to Nairobi. Next day we went eastwards as far as Athi River, and I returned on the footplate of one of the enormous 59th Class Beyer-Garratts hauling a mixed freight train of 1,050 tons, which it had brought up over the 332 miles from the coast at Mombasa.

· With my work in Kenya finished and a report sent back to London I flew south next morning getting a magnificent view of Mount Kilimanjaro, the highest in Africa, soon after leaving Nairobi. In Johannesburg I stayed briefly with my old friends, Dick and Jane Walwyn, at their beautiful home in Sandton, before joining a railway tour which took me eventually down to the Cape, and which gave me an opportunity of footplating on a 'GEA' Class Garratt—4-6-4 + 4-6-4 type—of the South African Railways. On the north-bound journey I left the tour at Bloemfontein. They were going through Natal, to Durban, but I, with a holiday booked in Malta, had to get back to the United Kingdom, with only one full day to spare in between.

When the train drew into Johannesburg Dick Walwyn was on the station to meet me, and he looked worried. While I had been away in the south a design question had been raised by the South African Railways concerning the new type of electric point machine that we had recently supplied to them. It was known as the Model 63 and was actually one of the last new designs for which I had been responsible, as Chief Mechanical Engineer. Many of them were already in service on British Railways, but in London the question raised by the South African Railways was thought to be of such a nature as to require Douglas Shipp's presence in Johannesburg. Dick Walwyn was primarily a brake man, but on the way to his home he said that Shipp was 'in a state. John's coming over later; he'll tell you more about it'. John Pryce, Dick's co-director, looked after signalling interests and, having told me what the trouble was, asked if I could stay to attend a meeting with the chief signal engineer of the SAR on Thursday morning. It was then Tuesday, and I was booked to fly back to England on the Wednesday evening, to give me a whole day to sort things out before flying to Malta with Olivia on the Friday afternoon.

I shall not forget that grisly Wednesday! The points raised on our new machine by the SAR were purely mechanical. This was far from Douglas Shipp's strongest suit, and he seemed in horror of meeting the railway engineers. While we churned the questions over and over again, John Pryce's staff were trying to get me fresh flight bookings, and trunk calls to Olivia, and Westinghouse, for altered travel arrangements in England, for getting her, and my holiday luggage to Heathrow on time. Even if the jet from Johannesburg landed punctually there would be no more than a few hours before our departure for Malta, and in that time there had got to be an extensive change in the luggage I would be carrying. On Thursday morning Shipp was still obviously in a highly tensed-up state when we were ushered in the 'Presence'; but he seemed glad enough to leave the talking to me. Their difficulties were soon resolved, but the real 'cliff-hanger' so far as I was concerned was to come. Would the complicated arrangements for getting Olivia and my holiday luggage to Heathrow work out? All the details had been settled over a rather crackly long-distance phone! When John Pryce took me to Jan Smuts airport later on that eventful Thursday there was a wealth of feeling in his laconic farewell: 'Thanks for staying'. And all turned out well in England too.

Chapter 13

Presidential year, and just after

We returned from Malta to urgent preparations for my year as President of the Institution of Railway Signal Engineers. It had been hoped that the summer convention, in 1969, would be held in Spain. The recently opened Madrid-Burgos direct line, via Aranda, was an important addition to the European railway network. It had shortened the distance between Madrid and the French frontier by 60 miles, and it included some interesting techniques in its signalling. With a Westinghouse President in the chair the company would have been proud to show it to our fellow members, and particularly those from Continental countries and from still further overseas. But in response to our letters the Spanish National Railways (RENFE) seemed in no hurry to get to grips with the arrangements necessary, and with correspondence dragging on into the summer of 1968 I felt that things were not advanced far enough to risk it for my year, and I handed over the papers to Armand Cardani, who would succeed me in the Chair in 1970. I wrote to the Belgians instead, and they immediately took it up with enthusiasm.

With my South African trip in prospect, followed at once by holiday in Malta, I was going to be out of the country for a month and, before I went, arrangements were made for the pilot visit to Brussels by the secretary and treasurer of the General Purposes Committee of the Institution. There was an element of uncertainty here, for we had a new secretary and one could never be sure how he would go down, as the saying goes. But as things immediately turned out we were supremely fortunate in getting Howard Worsley, of London Transport—'Buster' to all his friends. His gay, unflappable personality hardly concealed his outstanding efficiency in administration, and we had not gone far into the Presidential Year before we all realised that behind him too, solidly, was his charming wife, Jeanne, who was always a tower of strength on those occasions when the ladies were present.

The run-up to the actual year is traditionally one of the busiest in the life of an aspiring president, for he is automatically chairman of every single committee of the Institution. I was nobly supported by Westinghouse at this time, and it made amends for the disappointment I had felt when, under the reorganisation of 1965, the old Chief Mechanical Engineer's department had been fragmented, and the strong and loyal team that I had built up dispersed and subordinated to men of quite mediocre quality who happened then to be in favour with the new management. It was, nevertheless, gratifying in later years to see them all fight their way back, and in one case to very high level. It is still more pleasurable for

Olivia and me, 16 years after the dissolution of the CME's department, that those splendidly loyal assistants, and their wives, are still numbered among our closest family friends.

The Annual General Meeting of the IRSE at which I took office as President, was on April 9 1969 and, in addition to a goodly muster of our own members, I was honoured by the presence of Dr J.H. Jellett, President of the Institution of Civil Engineers, and the Senior Vice-Presidents of the Institutions of Mechanical and Electrical Engineers. At the Members Dinner following I was joined at the top table by Peter Ewen, Chairman of Westinghouse, L.E. Thompson, Managing Director, Eric Robson, President of the Institution of Locomotive Engineers, and Colonel J.R.H. Robertson, Chief Inspecting Officer of Railways, of the Ministry of Transport. The chief guest was my very old friend, Willie Thorpe, who I had first known when he was Divisional Operating Superintendent at Hull, but who, in 1969, had risen to the very high office of Deputy Chairman of the British Railways Board. At Hull he had instituted a stationmasters' discussion group and several times I had the great pleasure of giving them informal talks, under his chairmanship. On the following day we always had a day out, with a locomotive and inspection saloon, calling on some of the more remote and unfrequented stations in the district, while Willie himself regaled us with one hilarious railway story after another. At the IRSE Members Dinner he was in more circumspect form, though amusing enough for all that.

As it befell Presidential Year, and my last year of service with Westinghouse, we had some eventful times even before we began the serious business of the winter's technical meetings. How the trip that Olivia and I were able to make right round the world was first conceived I cannot now remember except, of course, that there were three different things that each made such a trip attractive in themselves. First of these was that Trevor, our son, was by that time well established as a chartered accountant in Melbourne whence he had gone two years earlier, only a month after his marriage to Lesley Stuart Black. Secondly, there was the happy idea of visiting the Australian section of the IRSE in my Presidential Year, and repeating the Address at one of their meetings while, if one returned via South Africa and made a slight detour into Rhodesia, that address could be given a third time, in Bulawayo. In the political climate of the day, however, this could be a bit tricky, because the Wilson government at home, incensed by the declaration of 'UDI', had imposed a form of sanctions upon Rhodesia, and British citizens entering the country without formal authority could, on their return to the UK, risk the seizure of their passports. Lastly, of course, there was the series of books on *Railways of the World* that Archie Black had commissioned, for which a trip to Australia was virtually a must.

I went to Australia House, in London, to make some preliminary enquiries and there learned, to my delight, that a separate office representing all the railways of Australia had recently been set up in London. An appointment was quickly arranged, and so I met Jack Taylor, the first man designated as plenipotentiary of all the seven independent railways in the Australian Commonwealth. Taylor himself was a Victorian, but he was the agreed representative of them all, and had particularly the staunch backing of one of the strongest personalities in the Australian railway scene, N. McCusker, the Commissioner of Railways in New South Wales. I can say at once that

Left *United once again, in Australia; Trevor with Olivia and me at the IRSE dinner in Sydney, 1969.*

Right *IRSE occasion in Sydney: the Australian section dinner in 1969. At top table, left to right, Harold Bourne, Signal Engineer, NSWGR; Olivia; the 'Old Man' speaking; Dorothy Irving; Alan Irving, Chairman of the Australian section.*

Australia could not have had a finer envoy, nor Olivia and I a greater friend. He set about the organisation of our tour with the utmost enthusiasm and efficiency. I can repeat again the words in which I introduced him and his wife as a guest at the IRSE Dinner and Dance in October of that same year, after our tour was completed:

'A journey like that, in which one has to crowd visits, a lot of travelling, functions, and goodness knows what else into a very short time, does not just happen. You cannot go to the station at Sydney and say "I want to travel up to Brisbane tonight". It cannot be done. Things have all to be organised in advance, and we are very delighted to welcome here tonight the man who made our journey in Australia so very easy, so comfortable, and so free of fatigue— Mr Jack Taylor'.

It was not, however, until August that we set out on our tour, and in the meantime there was much to be done nearer home. The annual summer convention of the Institution of Railway Signal Engineers which I had the honour of leading, in May, was a very pleasant series of meetings and visits. It is not only the Institution itself, but Westinghouse also, that has very close connections with the Belgian National Railways. In 1925 the first-ever summer meeting to be held overseas took place in Belgium, and there had been two others subsequently, in 1935 and 1955. The Westinghouse association, through our famous constituent company, Saxby and Farmer, goes back to the very beginnings of signalling in Belgium where, by the end of the 19th century, the railways were more completely equipped with interlocking and manual block signalling than those of any other railway on the continent of Europe. So far as modern developments, M Louis Devillers, Director of Electricity and Signalling, and his staff, organised a splendid programme of visits to some of the latest installations.

The explanations and demonstrations given to us during the summer meeting were notably supplemented in the autumn, when two Belgian engineers read a paper to the technical meeting of the Institution in November. Then the problems of the railways, serving the most densely populated country in Europe were admirably summarised thus:

a) To ensure transport in complete safety:
—at a speed up to and exceeding 200 km/h;
—at the highest possible frequency;
—in accordance with a programme which takes energy consumption into account.

b) To guide trains into complex station layouts:
—from a single control centre even when highly complex layouts are involved;
—at the highest possible rate and with automatic announcements at passenger platforms.

c) To ensure automatic train control.

IRSE Presidential visit to Belgium, 1969: a flashback to Westinghouse history on the State railways. The picturesque signal box and gantry of signals installed by Saxby and Farmer in the 1980s, has now, of course, been replaced.

One of the 'AD' Class Beyer-Garratts, 4-8-2 + 2-8-4, crossing the Hawkesbury River bridge with a Sydney bound coal train (C.A. Cardew).

At that time traction on the Belgian railways was already predominantly electric, when the extension of the British Railways 25 kV electrified network from Weaver Junction northwards to Glasgow was still awaiting Ministerial sanction. It was not until February 1970 that the 'go-ahead' for the latter was given. And in the autumn of 1968 railway enthusiasts had flocked to see the melancholy event of the last steam hauled train to be run by British Railways. The total ban upon the running of privately sponsored steam specials over BR tracks had not yet descended; but there was ample evidence in high quarters that such specials were looked upon with the greatest disfavour. Such was the 'home' atmosphere in which Jack Taylor and I planned the tour of Australian railways. The long air journey from London to Sydney by Qantas, punctuated by stops at New York, San Francisco, Honolulu and Fiji, seemed likely to induce jet-lag with a vengeance, and so we decided to break the journey for two days at San Francisco, which would be reached at a fairly civilised time in the early evening. We could then take breath, as it were, before the night flight, which would bring us to Sydney in time for an early breakfast. Sydney seemed an ideal point for the start of our railway tour but, before we were half way across the Atlantic, we had an amusing forecast of the reception we were likely to meet in the State Capitals of Australia.

I was privileged to spend some time on the flight deck of the 'plane, and the Captain asked where we would be going on our tour. He was a typically genial 'Aussie' and he said, 'Well, it may not be said in as many words, but I guess the first question that will be asked you in each of the cities will be along these lines: Brisbane, 'what are you going to drink?'; Sydney, 'how much money do you make?'; Melbourne, 'what school did you go to?'; Adelaide, (the only one that did originate as a penal colony) 'what church do you go to?' and Perth 'what are you going to drink?'. We laughed a lot over this, especially about Melbourne. Two years earlier, when Trevor, our son, was doing a good deal of homework in preparation for going to Australia he was advised not to stress the fact that he had been to an English public school. But he went to, and settled in Melbourne; and believe it or not, after about two months he sent home for his old school tie!

Olivia and I are not likely to forget how we first set foot on Australian soil. Travelling in early August we had left behind us in England one of the finest summers in memory, and our brief stay-over in San Francisco had also been blessed with cloudless sunshine. But, after leaving Fiji, increasing evidence of turbulence was amply confirmed when daylight came, and we saw below great banks of cumulus cloud. At one time there was talk of diverting to Brisbane, so strong was the cross wind on Sydney's Kingsford Smith Airport. But all eventually was well, and we touched down dead on time, at 7 am—in torrents of rain! Any chilliness we might have felt from a look at the weather was very quickly dispelled. Harold Bourne, Chief Signal Engineer of the New South Wales Railways, was there to meet us, together with two of his senior officers, Bill Oliver, and the irrepressible Ted McCamley, and the warmth of their welcome set a pattern that was sustained throughout our tour. Despite the weather our hosts were determined that we should have a very proper introduction to Australia, and even before lunch on that very first day we were taken to the shores of Botany Bay to be photographed beside the monument marking the spot when Captain Cook first landed in 1770.

Our initial stay in Sydney was, however, not for very long because the technical meeting of the IRSE, at which I was to give the Presidential Address, was not until the end of the month, and in between we had got to get in a visit to Queensland. We went north on the 'Brisbane Limited Express' leaving Sydney at 6.30 pm. Australian sleeping cars are luxurious and we slept well, until I was called, about 5.30 am. I was due to ride in the cab of our diesel locomotive on the concluding three-hour non-stop run from Casino to Brisbane, and there had to be time for a wash, a shave and an early breakfast before we left the former station, about 7 am. We had two locomotives, each of 1,800 horsepower, and a load of 570 tons. There was some hard climbing, in wild country, up to the state boundary of New South Wales and Queensland, and a spectacular spiral location just at the summit to avoid having a gradient steeper than 1 in 66. Although the standard rail gauge in Queensland is 3 foot 6 inches the 4 foot 8½ inch gauge of New South Wales is continued to Brisbane. Meanwhile, back in the train, Olivia was having her first sight of what an 'Australian breakfast' is. She had made her way to the buffet-dining car to have the modest Continental breakfast that we both normally take, and was astonished to see most of her fellow travellers—glamorous young things too!—tucking into enormous repasts of steaks, chops and goodness knows what else, that made the heartiest English 'bacon and eggs' look like an exceedingly light snack.

It was just after 10 am on a morning of cloudless sunshine that we arrived in Brisbane, 15 hours 38 minutes to be exact for the 613 miles from Sydney, and there to meet us were three more members of the IRSE—Frank Jones, Signal Engineer of the QSR, Dave Evans, his chief-assistant, who succeeded him in that high office, and D.G. Whisson. They and their wives certainly saw to it that our four days in Queensland were fully, and delightfully, occupied. In between railway sightseeing and social calls we enjoyed, in the company of Jean Jones and Mary Evans, a heavenly day beside the glorious beaches of the Queensland 'gold coast'; but one of the most diverting experiences was a trip northward from Brisbane on the 'Rocky Mail', as it used to be known. Our new

One of the Newcastle Flyers on the New South Wales Government Railways. It was one of these impressive 4-6-2s that I rode from Gosforth to Fassifern.

friends were a little concerned that we were going up to Rockhampton by this train, instead of by the luxurious air-conditioned 'Sunlander'; but time was not on our side, and the 'Mail' gave us an arrival three hours earlier. Actually the vintage sleeping cars, mahogany panelled and magnificently maintained, were very comfortable, though the decor was slightly reminiscent of 'Wells Fargo'! We both had a very busy day in Rockhampton. While I was watching the coal train operations, and being interviewed by a young lady reporter from the local paper, who took everything down in long-hand, Olivia was being taken on a lightning tour of the surrounding districts.

Back in Brisbane our stay was of the briefest, for we and many members of the IRSE were headed south for Sydney, by the night 'sleeper' in readiness for the technical meeting on the following day. The timing of the southbound 'Brisbane Limited Express' was fortunate for me, because it was daylight by the time we passed Gosford, and drew alongside the beautiful estuarine scenery of the Hawkesbury River. Our arrival in Sydney Central station was a masterpiece of precise timing for Olivia and me because our train drew in abreast of the 'Spirit of Progress' sleeper, from Melbourne, and stopped at the opposite face of the same platform; and then, from a carriage almost opposite to our own out stepped Trevor, our son, who had come to join us for the IRSE weekend activities—a spectacular start to a reunion after two years. He was on his own, because Lesley, our daughter-in-law, a top-class hockey player, was in Adelaide for the week-end playing for Victoria against South Australia. The inclusion of the ladies in an IRSE gathering was, we learned, an innovation in Australia, and was arranged to accord with Olivia's presence with me. It proved so popular that it has been customary ever since.

At the technical meeting in the afternoon the Institution members from New South Wales and Queensland were joined by those from Victoria—in fact the Chairman of the section, Alan Irving, was then Assistant Signal Engineer of the Victorian Railways. Delivery of the Presidential Address was a congenial task for me, followed in the evening in convivial style by a dinner at which many ladies were present at the St George's League Club. As with such gatherings of the Institution in Europe the week-end was 'all go'. Next morning the party went north to Newcastle to view installations; but, knowing my own predilections, arrangements had been made for me to go down by train, on the footplate of one of the 'Newcastle Flyers'—electric to Gosford, and steam thereafter. I had the company of a very distinguished locomotive engineer in C.A. Cardew, whose technical writings I was already familiar with, in the Proceedings of the Institution of Locomotive Engineers. He was also an expert photographer of trains at speed, and he made available to me a magnificent selection of his own results.

When we reached Gosford, and found one of the massive '38' Class 'Pacifics' waiting to take over, I was interested to find that the same crew were continuing. By that time the top-link men at Sydney and Newcastle worked on electric, diesel, and steam locomotives indiscriminately; but on this occasion Cardew himself took the regulator of No 3827, the driver did the firing and the fireman went back to the train for a ride 'on the cushions'. I must not dwell upon the technical details of the performance, which were published in *The Railway Magazine* in August 1970, except to rejoice once again in the recollection of the 'sound and fury' of a big steam locomotive, and particularly of roaring up the 1 in 50 gradient of the bank from Dora's Creek, at 41 mph. I left the train a few miles short of the journey's end at the country station of Fassifern, to which we had run the 38.2 miles from Gosford in 43¾ minutes. There one of the IRSE members met me to take me on by car to join the rest of the party for lunch. Reflecting upon the name of that wayside station, there must have been Camerons among the early settlers hereabouts, because Fassifern House, beside Loch Eil far away in Scotland, was the home of Colonel John Cameron who was killed at Quatre Bras, in 1815, two days before Waterloo. One of the highlights of that week-end for me was a quick visit to Broadmeadow running sheds, on the outskirts of Newcastle, where many of the enormous 'AD' Class Beyer-Garratts were on shed.

Trevor had to get back to Melbourne for business on Monday morning, and Harold Bourne drove us back into Sydney for him to catch 'The Spirit of Progress' express, leaving at mid-evening. Olivia and I stayed on for a few days because the New South Wales railway people had some more sightseeing for us. There was a lovely trip out to the Blue Mountains, by train right through the area to Lithgow, and then back by car, detouring to see some of the most famous mountain sights in the world. The railway itself was by that time electrified, but by car we were able to drive on the roadway that then followed the course of the famous Lithgow 'Zig Zag' location. When I last went to Australia, in the late autumn of 1979, this had been re-instated as a 3 foot 6 inch gauge steam line, and I was able to ride up the 'Zig Zag' on an ex-Queensland 2-6-2 tank engine. Another memorable day trip from Sydney was to the Federal Capital City of Canberra. All too soon, however, it was time to press on south from Sydney, and we took the 'Intercapital Daylight' express, leaving at 7.45 am for Melbourne, a journey of 598½ miles scheduled in 12 hours 35 minutes. It was only seven years previously that the standard gauge line over the Victorian section of the journey, from Albury to Melbourne, had been completed, and the inconvenience of the break of gauge eliminated. Until 1962 one had to change from a 4 foot 8½ inch to a 5 foot 3 inch gauge train at the State boundary.

On this long all-day run I rode on the footplate of the 1800 hp Class '44' diesel of the New South Wales Railways for the first long section, from the

Sydney suburban station of Strathfield to Goulburn, 130 miles, and then over the Victorian section south of Albury where the train runs non-stop over the last 196.7 miles into Melbourne, Spencer Street. Although the maximum speed did not at any time exceed 70 mph it was an impressive performance, with very smooth and comfortable riding on both NSW and Victorian diesel locomotives and in the train. I was particularly interested in the operating between Albury and Melbourne, because from its opening in 1962 this line had been controlled by a single centralised traffic panel in one of the offices at Spencer Street. A few days later I was able to watch the progress of the northbound 'Daylight' over the last 40 miles of her run to Albury, and to see, by clocking the indication lights on the panel, that she was making a steady 65 to 70 mph. It was an interesting thought that the detailed log of our journey, published in *The Railway Magazine* for March 1970, could have been compiled with equal accuracy by someone sitting in the Spencer Street control room, and watching the indication lights on the panel.

In Melbourne I began to wear my third 'hat' more frequently, because there were visits to the offices and works of the Westinghouse subsidiary, McKenzie and Holland (Pty) Ltd, and to the impresive new hump marshalling yard just outside Spencer Street station, the design engineering for which had been in progress at Chippenham for some time before I left England. The equipment included my own cherished 'baby', the Westardair retarders, which always brought back memories of visits to the Workington Iron and Steel Company, at Moss Bay, in Cumberland. When the preliminary work for the new Melbourne yard was in hand, in England, about a year before my own visit to Australia, Leslie Reynolds, one of the Assistant Commissioners of Railways, in Victoria, and himself a civil engineer, spent some time with the design staff. I found him a great enthusiast and when, rather more than a year later, he took me round the unfinished works in Melbourne, I found that he was an enthusiast for other things beside the most modern railway equipment. He took Olivia and me in his own car out to Belgrave, in the Dandenong Range for a trip on the Puffing Billy railway, up to Emerald, in glorious hill country. This splendidly managed 2 foot 6 inch gauge line is a railway enthusiasts dream, and again I was accorded the privilege of riding on the footplate. It was rather a tight squeeze in the cab of that little 2-6-2 tank, especially as the driver, with whom I had ridden only a few days earlier on one of the big main line 4-6-4s, was a giant of a man, with distinctly 'broad gauge' proportions in every direction!

At Trevor's home there were family gatherings, joined by friends who had been my kindly hosts in Bangkok five years earlier. But the days slipped by all too quickly, and it was soon time to push on, westwards. On a cold blustering Sunday night in early September, the climatic equivalent of an English March, a group of Australian friends foregathered with Trevor and Lesley, to bid us farewell from the eastern states. We were leaving by 'The Overland' express for Adelaide, on the first stage of our long journey right across Australia. The night run of 483 miles begins at 8.40 pm and this heavy sleeping car train is booked to connect with the 'Intercapital Daylight' from Sydney. As the latter does not arrive at Spencer Street until 8.20 pm, giving no more than 20 minutes interval, it is clearly expected that the 'Daylight' will not be late. On this first visit we made little more than a 'whistle-stop' in Adelaide. A more extensive sampling of the many attractions of South Australia had to wait for two years, for now we continued on the 5 foot 3 inch gauge to Port Pirie. I do not think one could have imagined a more unlikely starting place for one of the really great express trains of the world—here, out on the coastal flats of Spencer's Gulf, with no town in evidence, only miles of sidings, on three different gauges! That was before the standard gauge through line to New South Wales was completed, and the Trans-Australian express started here. It was even then the most elegant and sophisticated of trains, though it was not until the following morning that I had the well-nigh shattering experience of seeing what this amazing line looks like from the footplate.

Around 7 am we had stopped at Cook for a crew change on the locomotive, and from the cab I looked ahead along that extraordinary 'straight' that extends for 297 miles. This is not a form of words. The line is literally, and geometrically straight, over the flattest and most featureless countryside that could be conceived. The bluish grey scrub, never more than about 12 inches or so from the ground, is said to provide good fodder for sheep, except that there are no sheep to eat it, nor was there any other sign of wild life. Absolutely nothing—under an all-embracing cloudless blue sky! Even at seven in the morning it was already blazing hot, and windless, in contrast to the squally spring weather we had left behind in Melbourne. In the train, with efficient air conditioning, it was delightfully cool, and in the driving cab of the locomotive, with windows down, the moderate speed we were soon making created a pleasant breeze. I am always a little hesitant about air conditioned trains. They are all very well as long as the apparatus works; but I have grisly recollections of a long journey—not in Australia—when the temperature outside was 100 degrees Fahrenheit, plus, and in the train, unable to open any windows, we were just about cooked! One feature of the 'Trans', and the completely featureless outlook from the driving cab was the way in which buildings at the few stations first appeared. The highest points of them appeared first, and one realised that they were being sighted over the curve of the earth's surface.

Towards evening we crossed the state boundary into Western Australia, and at Kalgoorlie, where locomotives were changed from those of the Commonwealth Railways to those of the WAGR, there was time to get down from the train and have a stroll around, before settling down for the night run that would bring us to Perth about breakfast time. It was to be a short night for me, because I had to be up to ride the big 3,300 hp 'L' Class diesel from Northam, where we were due to leave at 5 am. The line from there westwards is entirely new, magnificently engineered through the hilly country of the Darling Range, with tremendous cutting and embankment works to keep the gradients down to a maximum of 1 in 200, on an alignment to permit continuous running at 70 mph by passenger trains. Indeed we covered the first 67 miles from Northam in 70 minutes. The powerful headlight of the locomotive showed up vividly the stretches where great cuttings have been hewn out of the solid rock, and all the time we were gliding smoothly along at 70 mph.

Perth is a delightful city, and we came to it in weather that was just like an English spring, with the gardens gay with flowers that are so welcome at home after the rigours of winter. Apart from the line over which the 'Trans-Australian' express had brought us, the rail gauge in Western Australia is 3 foot 6 inches and at the time of our visit there was a good deal of steam traction on the freight trains. We made a day excursion down to Bunbury, due south of Perth, by a diesel train called the *Australind* and, on arrival, I was delighted to find that the motive power depot was a veritable parade ground of steam,

Left *Presidential duties in Rhodesia: receiving a copy of the classic book,* Chronicles of a Contractor, *dealing with the life and work of George Pauling* (Rhodesia Railways).

Right *Rhodesia Railways: southbound freight, with Class '19D' 4-8-2 locomotive which I had ridden from Umtali, leaving Shangani, and passing a Westinghouse dual-control electric point machine in the foreground.*

ranging from the big modern 2-8-2s to vintage 2-6-0s and 4-6-0s. But, from my boyhood, Western Australia has always been associated in my mind with black swans, for nearly 50 years (1854–1902) the *only* emblem to appear on her postage stamps. And surely enough, as though to symbolise the identity of the State where, in a very short time, we had made many new friends, there were black swans swimming in the ornamental pools in front of the main building at Perth Airport. There we foregathered with a little group of Australians, one New Zealander and one Englishman who had come to wish us 'bon-voyage'. All at once the world seemed a smaller place. It was past noon, and we were due to dine in Johannesburg! There was just time for a few group photographs, and then the loud speakers were calling us to board the big jet—first stop, Mauritius.

At their home in Sandton, Dick and Jane Walwyn made us regally welcome, and this time they had a special treat in store for us, a five-day visit to the Kruger game reserve, some 250 miles north-east of Johannesburg, and on the borders of Mozambique. In these days of television documentaries, books like those of the late Joy Adamson, and the work of that consummate artist of wild life, David Sheppard, there is a greater familiarity with nature in remote parts than when the construction gangs of the Uganda Railway some 90 years ago were occasionally being decimated by man-eating lions! But there is nothing quite to compare with having been on the spot. Lest there should be any ideas of wild animals in a zoo the first thing that strikes one, even living in the camp enclaves, gated in from dusk till dawn, is the great distance one often has to motor before seeing *anything*. We were taken around in great comfort, in an air-conditioned 'jeep', and from what Dick and Jane said I think we were lucky to see as great a variety of animals as we did.

There is a tremendous thrill in the first sight of a giraffe on the skyline of some hillock, or of an elephant not taking too kindly to visitors; but our most vivid recollections are those of lions. We were driving slowly along one track,

when away in the scrub on our right we spotted a lioness, efficiently camouflaged but obviously stalking something. Then we saw a second. The likely victim seemed to be a warthog, nonchalantly feeding about 50 yards away. We watched, breathless. The two lionesses seemed to be working together, when quite suddenly, as if the game was not worth it, one of them turned, and came straight towards where our jeep was standing! Quite regardless, she walked so close to the car that I was able to photograph her at point blank range, as it were. She turned round and looked towards us, and then, quite unconcerned, strolled off into the bush. Then early one morning we had the dramatic sight of *five* lions at a kill, near enough to the road to make another good photograph. We had had the single lioness to ourselves, but two other cars were watching and filming the kill.

On the rough tracks in the game reserve if a slowly moving car has stopped it can generally be expected that they have spotted something within the cover of the tawny vegetation which provides such excellent camouflage for most of the animals. On our last day in the reserve we were driving slowly down the road that leads to the southernmost gate, at Komatiport, and not far abreast of this is a branch line of the South African Railways, leading to Beit Bridge on the frontier of Rhodesia. At a small stream that ran athwart our track there is a clearing in the scrub, through which we could see the line, and just at that moment a northbound freight train was approaching. We stopped, and watched it go by, and then discovered to our astonishment that three other cars had drawn up behind us, and were eagerly scanning that watercourse with field glasses. We had not the heart to tell them that we had merely been counting the number of wagons on that long train!

Last of all, in this long and exciting tour, was Rhodesia, where the section of the IRSE had invited me to give my Presidential Address. The technique of getting into and out of the country without the risk of subsequent repercussions was simple. You had a loose sheet of paper inside your passport, and the folks at Bulawayo Airport were ready enough to stamp on that loose sheet. Actually we changed planes, and flew straight to the Victoria Falls, where George Anderson, Assistant Signal Engineer of the RR, and two of his staff were waiting to show us round. From photographs I had been familiar with the general look of the Victoria Falls, and the magnificent steel-arched bridge that spans the gorge of the Zambesi River nearby; but no photograph can convey any true impression of that stupendous sight, and the sound of its falling waters. The actual flow was well below maximum at the time of our visit, and this was a good thing because otherwise the cloud of spray might have been such as to obscure all view of the falls. As it was, very lightly clad, we were both drenched to the skin, but dried off in minutes in that glorious sunshine.

We returned to Bulawayo that night on the 'up mail', on which a saloon marshalled next to the engine was put at our disposal. Olivia was entertained to dinner by members of the IRSE while I rode on the footplate of the huge 20th Class Garratt, 4-8-2 + 2-8-4 type, the largest and most powerful on the Rhodesia Railways, as far as Thompson Junction. Under a brilliant moon I could see that the bush was teeming with wild life, including some of the largest and most spectacular species. After Kasibi I saw five elephants, and then approaching Sambawizi the driver gave a shout and pointed, and there, drinking from a pool at the foot of the water column, was one of the big 'cats'. I think it was a lioness, but when picked up in the engine headlight she made off quickly enough.

In Bulawayo I saw signalling installations; we both enjoyed the most charming hospitality, and then on the last day we were taken to the Matopos region to see the fantastic, and I can quite believe, unique rock formations. But there was another compelling reason—to make pilgrimage to the grave of Cecil Rhodes, high in this strange hill country with such a prospect in every direction that it has been named 'View of the World'. At the end of that sultry day, storm clouds were gathering, and there was a suggestion of thunder in the distance. If ever there was a 'stormy petrel' among the architects of the British Empire it was Cecil Rhodes, and to visit his grave on some serene cloudless day would have been out of character to the man himself.

We returned, bronzed and a little travel-weary, with only a few weeks to regain breath for all the winter activities and technical meetings of the IRSE Presidential year. At the Dinner and Dance in October the principal guest of the Institution was my great friend, Derek Barrie, then Chairman and General Manager of the Eastern Region of British Railways, and he proposed the health of the Institution in a speech sparkling with charm and his own very pretty wit. The six technical meetings, as usual, covered subjects with which the President has been associated, and we had papers dealing with signalling in Belgium, Australia and Rhodesia; a paper on 'The Victoria Line in Operation' was the occasion of a Joint Meeting with the Institute of Transport, while J.F.H. Tyler, then Chief Signal and Telecommunications Engineer of the British Railways Board, delivered a paper that was repeated five times in Great Britain and also at the Overseas Provincial Meeting in Cologne, on 'Signalling for High Speed Trains'. At that time I should add that while there was much talk of speeds up to 125 mph, maximum speeds in Great Britain had not officially advanced beyond 100 mph. The first reading of this paper, in London on January 7 1970 was made a joint meeting with the Railway Division of the Institution of Mechanical Engineers.

Then there was Westinghouse. Despite the tremendous advances in electrical technology I felt that the great importance of having faultless *mechanical* design of the numerous components should not be lost sight of, and I asked Eric Harris, who had been my chief assistant while I was Chief Mechanical Engineer, to give us a paper. He responded nobly with 'Mechanical Design Considerations in respect of the use of Electronics in Railway Signalling'. From Westinghouse my own retirement came in January 1970, though in IRSE and other matters I remained closely connected with the company. In April I was succeeded in the Presidency of the Institution by Armand Cardani, who was then Chief Signal and Telecommunications Engineer of the London Midland Region. The negotiations I had started two years earlier for a summer convention in Spain had been brought to a successful conclusion, and in May we all went out to enjoy a delightful visit. I must admit, however, that relieved of technical responsibilities at home I found the greater interest in the magnificent cathedral of Burgos, the gigantic Roman aqueduct of Segovia, and the fortified city of Toledo. After the convention we did not return to England with the rest of the party but flew instead to Majorca, which we had not previously visited.

That holiday has poignant memories for Olivia and me for it was the last time we saw my old friend and close colleague, Douglas Shipp. He and his wife, Mattie, were staying at another hotel in the same little coastal resort west of Palma, and we had some happy times together. But he was not in good health, and shortly afterwards he was stricken by a fatal disease and died in October of that year. Of my long association with him in Westinghouse, extending back to 1928, I cannot say that it did not include some mixed memories. His was a marvellous brain. As I grew to know him better I realised, however, that his abrupt manner, and sarcastic tongue—that upset so many people—was the cloak for an exceedingly sensitive nature, and that inside he was the kindliest of men. I have always thought that his exceptional talents were not readily adaptable to the tasks of senior management in modern times, although he stuck doggedly and loyally to the task. He died while still in office at the early age of 63. The year 1970 certainly took its toll of veteran Westinghouse engineers, for in addition to Shipp, Mervyn Shorter, the former Managing Director, died in June, and his famous predecessor, Captain B.H. Peter, followed six months later. The old order was changing.

Chapter 14

World wide travels

It cannot have fallen to many men that the first five years after their retirement should prove among the most eventful and busiest of their whole life. In 1970 I thought my Westinghouse duties were finished and, although I remained a Member of Council of the IRSE, the duties of a Past-President are not usually excessive. But I had in hand that splendid commission from Archie Black for a series of books on overseas railways. The first volumes were drafted, but I had still to visit North America, India, and the countries of the Far East. There was much to do. Apart from a hernia, caused by a slight accident with a motor-mower—quickly rectified by surgery—I was in excellent health; but with the years slipping past me it seemed wise to get the more extensive travelling done as soon as possible.

The purely railway side of those five exciting years went to fill as many volumes, and there were articles in *The Railway Magazine* wherein the technical details of many individual runs were described. But thinking back to that time, now seven years ago, when Olivia and I returned from South Africa, via Angola for a change, there are so many things no more than slightly linked with railways to be recalled. I had barely started to write this book when I was struck down by a serious illness, the most critical time of which, when I was in intensive care, coincided with the approach of the festive season. Day by day Olivia brought the Christmas cards that were flowing in, and many of them came from friends far overseas whom we had first met in those exciting five years of world travel. And so my first thought is to say 'thank you' once again to all those who have made our world travels possible. It is often imagined that railway men, and particularly railway enthusiasts, are a race apart, having one track minds. I can quite well appreciate that the deeply ingrained 'gricer' can be a bore to others of a more liberal outlook; but looking back to our own experience, in four continents, I like to think of the pleasure with which we have been welcomed into the family circles of so many, of how sightseeing excursions and evening parties were laid on, at which the talk usually moved very far from railways.

In this chapter, which relates to a time when I saw so much, I have prepared some maps showing where we went, and the things we saw, rather than attempt a geographical precis of our journeys. Olivia did not come with me on all these journeys. She found the 1972 'marathon' rather tiring, especially the abrupt change of temperature from Fiji to New Zealand—40 degrees Fahrenheit in three hours!—a little too rapid, and caught a chill. Before getting on to overseas travels in earnest, however, I must mention, in passing, the decision of the Council of the IRSE in the spring of 1971 to have a definitive textbook on modern signalling. A small committee was appointed, and I was asked to act as chairman. I have always been chary of literary works in which a consortium of authors, or editing by committee, is involved; but about the textbook I need not say more than that it was almost *ten years* after that decision by the IRSE Council before the book was on sale to the public! The fact that one vital member of the committee was overseas for some time was not the least of my troubles as editor.

My Canadian tour of 1971 was very comprehensively and efficiently organised by Ray Corley, then with Canadian General Electric and a good friend of us in Westinghouse. It promised to be something of a trial of strength, so packed was the schedule he worked out for me so that I could see the absolute maximum of railway interest in the six weeks I had set aside for the job. Although tempting invitations were offered to her, Olivia decided early in the negotiations to opt out of this trip, and we arranged for quiet holidays together before and after my time in Canada. I had not gone far in studying Corley's proposed itinerary and its implications before I felt that a change was necessary from the original scheme of the series of books that Archie Black and I had worked out together. There was evidently so much of first class importance to see and describe in Canada that the idea of having an all-embracing book for North America had to be discarded; and we agreed that there would have to be separate full-length books for Canada and the United States.

To be reasonably sure of getting good weather for our holiday together in early June we decided upon the Côte d'Azur and, on the strong recommendation of Baron G. Vuillet and his wife, we stayed at a lovely little hotel on the outskirts of the fishing village of Cassis, about half-way between

Rhodesia: the overnight mail from Victoria Falls to Bulawayo, taking water at Nyamandhlovu ('the meeting place of elephants'). The engine is one of the 15th Class Beyer-Garratts.

Marseilles and Toulon. Although it was to be an entirely non-railway holiday I could not resist a driver's cab pass for the 'Mistral', as between Paris and Dijon, which produced the usual immaculate French electric locomotive performance; but what I did not expect was to see this tremendous machine, which among other things, had taken its 14-coach train up the 1 in 125 gradient to Blaisy Bas tunnel at 95 mph, subsequently brought to a dead stand by bad weather. A series of violent thunderstorms south of Valence had interfered with the power supply to the overhead line, and we stopped simply from lack of current. We stood for over an hour in open country, and at times the torrential rain was so dense that we could hardly see vehicles ploughing their way along the water-logged and windswept highway only about 200 yards away! It was a daunting prospect for our holilday, but when we reached Marseilles, about 70 minutes late, although the evening was cloudy, we seemed to have run out of the storm zone. The 'Mistral' continues along the Côte d'Azur, to Nice, but does not stop at Cassis, where the station is in any case several miles inland from the village. We had arranged for a hired car to meet us at Marseilles. Once arrived the weather and the hotel came up to our highest expectations, and we had a lovely leisurely fortnight.

Ray Corley came to England on business towards the end of July, and we spent a day together finalising the arrangements for my tour. This was to take me to the remote and quite isolated Quebec North Shore and Labrador Railway; to Arctic tidewater at Moosonee, as well as visiting many famous locomotive works, and great traffic centres. As far as I could judge there would be very little 'recovery time' in the schedule. Apart from a day in Winnipeg where there was nothing more than a lunch appointment on the agenda, there was to be only one completely free day in the entire six weeks—a Sunday, in Vancouver! Apart from a devastating, though fortunately brief spell of 'jet lag', on first arrival in Montreal I settled into the swinging programme and enjoyed it thoroughly. Ray had influential contacts all over Canada, and when he was not there himself there were delightful people to meet me and take me round. Before I had been in the country a week there had been visits to the great locomotive works of the Canadian Pacific, and Canadian National; a flight up to Sept Iles for a trip on the QNS & L to Labrador City, not to mention a quick dive into the USA to see the antiquated, though active and popular, cog railway up Mount Washington in the State of New Hampshire.

Back from Labrador, and among the big cities once again I joined Ray Corley and his friends for a weekend of miniature railroading, first at a rally of steam locomotive operators at Milton, near Peterborough, and then on the Sunday at a private circuit. There I was able to study the model engineering craftsmanship of Jack Hewitson, at that time engineer in charge of the dynamometer car of Canadian Pacific. His model work, as varied in its prototypes as it was successful, was a complete negation of the often-held idea that to have a good working model it is essential to choose a large boilered prototype. I remember so well, just before the Second World War negotiating with a world-famous British firm towards a 3½ inch gauge model of a Highland 'Duke' Class 4-4-0, and how they sought to dissuade me because of its relatively small diameter boiler. As it turned out the onset of war killed the project anyway. But Hewitson himself built a very successful 3½ inch gauge live-steam model of a Stirling 8 foot single 4-2-2 of the English Great Northern Railway, a type which, in the words of Sir Nigel Gresley, 'had no boiler to speak of, yet steamed well enough'. That

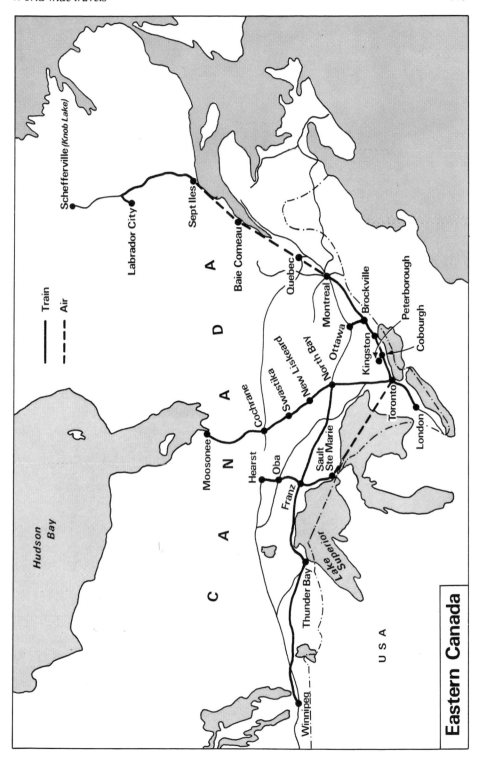

Eastern Canada

Driving the Canadian built 'Schools' Class engine, St Trinians (R. Corley).

Sunday gathering near Peterborough was enlivened by the presence of Jack Hewitson's charming wife, Ivy. I am sure she will not mind if I refer to her as a 'tom-boy', because her ebullient personality made her equally successful as a boisterous, indefatigable 'mate', helping to run steam locomotives, and as a vivacious hostess in her own home.

The most interesting locomotive of the Corley stud, which did some excellent running on those circuits near Peterborough, was a 'Schools' Class 4-4-0, a perfect external 'portrait' of one of those splendid Southern 4-4-0s that I knew so well in England. But this was a 'School' with a difference. She had two cylinders, instead of three, and her piston valves were actuated by the Baker valve gear, instead of the Walschaerts. Corley felt that she should have a name equally suggesting something out of the ordinary. The 40 titles of the original Southern 4-4-0s were scanned, without finding one that really fitted the case. Even if considered, my own 'Giggleswick' and Trevor's, 'Monkton Combe' were equally passed over. Then Ray Corley had an inspiration. His school was one with a difference—why not 'St Trinians'! Name apart, his engine performed with infinitely more decorum and reliability than the inmates of that notorious academy. Pulling three hefty adults, and scrutinised by Ivy Hewitson, she made circuit after circuit of that 200 yards oval; but as that hot day wore on the clouds began to gather, and there was every sign of thunder. I was heading north that night for Cochrane over the Ontario Northland line, and it looked as if I was in for a stormy trip. When Ray Corley drove me out to catch the night express from Toronto, at Beaverton, the western sky was lit by an almost continuous fusilade of lightning flashes.

In his fascinating book, *The Way North*, S.A. Pain has written: 'The town of Cochrane seems to have an appeal of its own, as being a magnet which draws men and their produce from east and west, particularly the west, by railroad, by thundering road transports, by trucks, cars, and caravans; and here at last they turn south on the last lap of their journey, which will take them through our ancient corridor. The town is a gathering-place and turning-point for the traffic of the North, and at the same time it always gives the impression of being a frontier town, at the limit of the familiar and at the edge of a different and largely unknown world which lies to the north again, where the continent slopes down from the 1,000 foot plateau to sea level'.

Arctic tidewater! Who could resist the urge to press on, over the 198 miles that remain; and on arrival at Cochrane, at eight in the morning, there in the station was the 'Polar Bear Express', waiting to take us on to Moosonee. The keen air, so different from the humidity we had left overnight, completely belied the fact that Cochrane lies nearer to the Equator than any part of the British Isles. But once out into the wilds, in the driver's cab of this extraordinary train the outlook makes nonsense of all such technicalities as degrees of latitude. As I wrote at the time: 'this was wilderness country in 1932 when the railway was completed, and in many ways it still belongs in spirit to the fur traders of 300 years ago. It is a land that has still been little tamed beyond the width of the railway right-of-way. It is a land of ever-continuing muskeg and scrub bush, where there are still long distances where a man can become hopelessly lost a few hundred yards from the railway; where canoes, dog teams, and snowmobiles are the family transportation, where a 'skyscraper' means a two-storey shack'. The journey was brought more vividly alive for me by the

Canada: Field Hill on the CPR in the Rockies. The westbound freight train headed by locomotive No 4242 is almost completely obscured in one of the spiral tunnels. Its own tail end and caboose is crossing its head-end at right angles! (CP Rail).

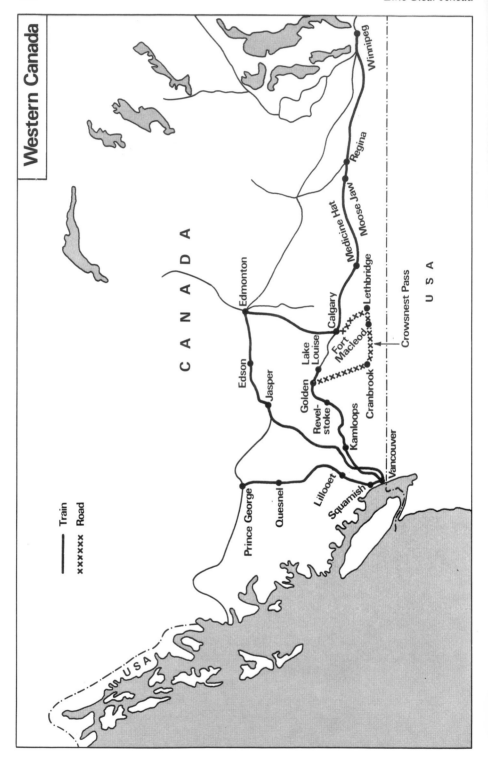

Western Canada

Train
xxxxxx Road

Canada: the 'Prairie Dog Central'. The Dubs-built 4-4-0, No 3, originally No 22 of the Canadian Pacific and which will be 100 years old in 1982, with three vintage carriages out on the prairies west of Winnipeg in 1972.

company of Bob Moore, the Trainmaster of the Ontario Northland Railway, and on the return journey also by the sprightly young train hostess, in the buffet car. I stayed overnight in Cochrane at the 'Northern Lites' hotel, (spelt thus).

There were no passenger trains on the one-time National Transcontinental line, that intersects the Ontario Northland at Cochrane, and, to resume my journey to the far west, I had to travel southwards to North Bay. There were no day-time passenger trains over this route either, but the Ontario Northland runs an excellent bus, and by this I made a day-long journey, giving me comfortable time to join that most prestigious of trains, 'The Canadian' late at night. I do not think there is any railway company name that can stir the imagination more than Canadian Pacific, nor do I think I ever looked forward to a journey with greater anticipation. Nor was I disappointed. Next morning in brilliant sunshine I saw from the driver's cab that amazing ledge hacked out of the iron-hard wall of rock on which the line is carried for many miles beside the blue waters of Lake Superior; I saw the unbelievably vast expanse of the prairies, and then there were the Rocky Mountains. Fascinated by geography from my kinder-garden school days I had looked forward, beyond anything else, to seeing these great mountains, and in my early preparations for the tour, with Ray Corley, it became clear that to see them to the best advantage a detour from the direct line would be advisable. So I left 'The Canadian' at Calgary, and after some railway sightseeing in and around that city in the scholarly company of Dr Eric Johnson, I went north to Edmonton to pick up the 'Super-Continental', of Canadian National, and go to Vancouver via Jasper and the Yellowhead Pass route.

I returned several days later by the eastbound 'Canadian', on which dawn, on the second day, was just breaking when we arrived at Revelstoke, and I joined Walter Paffard, Assistant Superintendent of the Division, in the cab of the

Canada: zero-degrees weather on the Algoma Central. A 5-engined freight train, 68 cars, 5,000 tons load, waiting in the loop at Ogidaki, for the coming of the daily northbound passenger train from Sault Ste Marie to Hearst.

leading unit of three diesel locomotives. But while the talk in that cab was of locomotives great and small, diesel and steam, I watched, simply entranced, while the pageant of gigantic mountains slowly passed by. The sky was cloudless, and the summits, all topping the 10,000 foot mark, were snow-capped. No words of mine, no superlatives could do justice to the sublime grandeur of such scenery; and after we had passed through the Connaught Tunnel and eased our way down the precipitous descent to Golden in the Columbia River Valley, there lay ahead of us the fearsome ascent of the Kicking Horse Pass, with its spectacular spirals. We were now climbing amid the main range of the Rockies. I can quite understand how some people would find the awesome proximity of such colossal heights forbidding, even frightening, especially when the single line railway takes a headlong dive into the side of one of them to gain height in a spiral tunnel. And when Eric Johnson met me at Lake Louise station, and took me by car to the lake itself, I felt I had reached the point of utter satiety in sights of mountain splendour, in seeing that vivid emerald-green sheet of ice-cold water, with a dazzling backdrop of glacier covered heights.

How we haltingly retraced our steps down the Kicking Horse Pass, with my calling for photographic stops every few hundred yards or so it seemed, and our subsequent passage down the Columbia valley, and through the Crowsnest pass, would take almost the day-and-a-half we spent on it to describe in adequate prose; but my time in Canada was drawing to a close. I cannot end, however, without recalling the Sunday I spent with Jim Brown, his wife, Ann, and their three bewitching little daughters. For having been with Jim in locomotive works, and on live-steam model circuits, they took me to see Niagara Falls, not too far away from their home on the outskirts of Toronto. It was a grey day, but the rain held off, and nothing could damp the spirits of my companions. It was a joyous family occasion, of which I shall always retain the liveliest memories.

Back home, Olivia and I managed to get ten days of holiday together before autumn activities began in earnest. We went to Gibraltar, and loved it. We were there on the anniversary of Trafalgar and witnessed the moving ceremony of remembrance at the little cemetery where so many of the sailors killed in the battle were buried. Though I had returned with several bulging notebooks I found that I had not yet finished with the railways of Canada. Visiting my publishers one day Charles Black, Archie's son and now Chairman of the company, asked if I had included anything in the book about the Algoma Central Railway. I had to admit the answer was 'no'. It is true that when Ray Corley and I had discussed the itinerary it was mentioned; but it did not seem worth spending an extra three or four days—for that was what it was likely to involve. Charles Black pulled a wry face, and said: 'That's a pity, because my father-in-law is the Chairman!'. Something had obviously got to be done about this; but I explained that I could not go to Canada again for nearly a year, and I asked whether it would then be too late to include a chapter in the book. Olivia and I were already planning a long trip 'down under' to begin in August 1972, and he said that if he could have the manuscript of the Algoma chapter not later than the end of August it would be all right. I then received an invitation to meet the chairman, the late Sir Denys Lowson, and to join him and his fellow directors at dinner, at a delightful West End restaurant 'A l'Ecu de France', in Jermyn Street. Apparently this railway company had an occasional board meeting in London and at this gathering I was able to meet Mr L.S. Savoie, the President, and J.A. Thompson, Vice-President and General Manager, and other directors.

That dinner party in December 1971 proved a momentous occasion for me, because it was suggested that, quite apart from writing a single chapter to include in my book on the *Railways of Canada*, I might like to write a whole book about the Algoma Central. At the time I must confess I knew very little about the railway; but from the general conversation and the enthusiasm of my hosts I sensed that there could be a great story. However it was agreed that on the larger project I should go, and see for myself. So on July 19 1972 Olivia and I set out a week earlier than we had originally intended, and instead of pausing briefly at San Francisco on our way 'down under' we went to Sault Ste Marie. Jack Thompson had a very effective way of showing us something of the Algoma Central. We slept that night in the luxury of a massive 12-wheeled business car, which was attached next day to the rear of the passenger train going the entire length of the line, up to Hearst, where it connects with the National Transcontinental line of Canadian National. We learned how, although the life-blood of this remarkable railway is in freight, it nevertheless runs a one-day wilderness excursion every day during the summer tourist season. The timing of the regular daily passenger train in each direction is such that the 'excursion' part of the train is detached from the northbound at Agawa Canyon, and gives a two-hour break before returning to Sault Ste Marie on the southbound train. Actually the excursion has proved so popular that the section of the train reserved for this facility far outweighs the regular train going through to Hearst. On our trip the latter consisted of one passenger car, one baggage car and two business cars, whereas the excursion portion consisted of eight coaches and two dining cars.

Jack Thompson, his colleagues and their wives were delightful hosts, and between them they unfolded a story of pioneer railroading, of business vicissitudes, of life out in the forest wilderness of Algoma, and of enterprise that has enabled the railway to achieve such an enviable position, that when we returned after our two-day 600-mile trip on its metals, and I was given a glimpse into some of its archives, I was already convinced that in its story, and of its later diversifications there was ample first class material for a full length book. The promised chapter for my general book, *Railways of Canada*, was written during our two-day stopover at Vancouver, and posted back to Sault Ste Marie for their approbation before we left for Fiji; but I also wrote to Sir Denys Lowson and told him I had no doubt that the history and present operations of the Algoma Central could be worked up into an interesting book. Stepping 1½ years out of chronological sequence to tell how, at the end of March 1974 I went back to the 'Soo'—as everyone in Ontario calls Sault Ste Marie—I can only say that the month lived on location, in the workshops, riding the trains, visiting the local industries with which it is so closely associated, and voyaging in its gigantic bulk-carriers on Lake Superior was an unforgettable enrichment of life's experience. My journeys both by rail and ship were made in conditions that we, in Great Britain, would regard as extremes of winter, when the engines of our diesel locomotives were overheating, because the ventilators were continually becoming clogged with packed up snow, and when freight cars waiting to be collected in sidings were half buried in snow up to and even above their running boards.

Going back to August 1972, however, we would have welcomed a nip of autumn, or early spring in the air when we arrived in Fiji. The Qantas jet, bound for Sydney, landed us at Nadi soon after daybreak; but this international airport was on the opposite side of the main island to Suva, the capital, and we had a bumpy flight over the mountains in a rather primitive little kite of a plane to where our hosts were waiting for us. Noel and Denise Anderson, business colleagues of Trevor's in Melbourne, and god-parents of his eldest son were 'sweating out' a posting in Fiji, he as local manager for the accountants Price, Waterhouse & Co. Until I set foot on this steamy, yet fascinating, outpost of the British Commonwealth I did not really know what humidity could mean. The dampness, together with the heat permeated everything, and already the Andersons had sent a number of their cherished possessions back to Melbourne, to await their return at the end of their term of office. We were put something in mind of 'desert island discs' on going out to a lonely beach for a lazy hour of beachcombing, but we were nevertheless secretly glad to get back to civilisation. And on the next stage of our journey Nemesis struck—hard!

At Nadi airport the temperature was around 90 degrees; when we reached Auckland three hours later it was 50 degrees, with an unexpected hazard to be surmounted. The customs authorities, scrutinising our passports, noted that we had been in Germany only three months previously, where there had been a small outbreak of foot and mouth disease. A representative of the Ministry of Agriculture and Fisheries was summoned and, beginning at 11 pm suitcases had to be unpacked and every single item of footwear examined. It was past midnight before we were cleared, meantime the New Zealand Railways officer

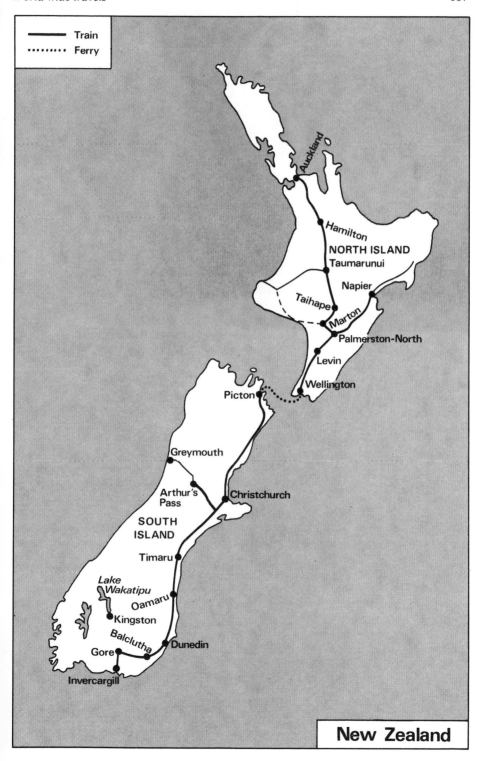

Train
Ferry

Auckland

Hamilton
NORTH ISLAND
Taumarunui
Napier
Taihape
Marton
Palmerston-North
Levin
Wellington

Picton

Greymouth

Arthur's
Pass
Christchurch

**SOUTH
ISLAND**
Timaru

*Lake
Wakatipu*
Oamaru
Kingston
Balclutha
Gore   Dunedin
Invercargill

New Zealand

NSW '38' Class, Sydney–Newcastle express with the author on board.

who had come to meet us was waiting patiently, and Olivia was shivering from the cold. At that time my publishers had intended to include a volume on the New Zealand railways in the series of overseas books, and such was actually advertised on the back jacket flap of the Canadian book; and in readiness Tom McGavin, the assistant Publicity Officer of NZR and editor of the New Zealand *Railway Observer*, had organised a magnificent programme of sightseeing. Unfortunately subsequent to our trip, the beginnings of inflation and trade recession caused some second thoughts, and market research proved unfavourable. So our travels in New Zealand were covered by no more than a few magazine articles.

Ever since I was a school-boy reader of *The Railway Magazine* the name of W.W. Stewart had been familiar to me as a photographer of New Zealand locomotives. Over the years we corresponded, and he sent me photographs for some of my own articles, but it was delightful to meet him in person at a gathering in Auckland, and to receive a copy of his magnificent book, *When Steam was King*. For Bill Stewart was not only a photographer of very long standing but an artist of rare distinction in oils. His book, illustrated entirely by his own work, includes no fewer than 31 paintings in colour, and another 18 reproduced in black and white; but he was also a painter of ships of all kinds. We travelled the length of the North Island main line in the 'Blue Streak' express railcar, in which the central part of the journey includes an ascent averaging 1 in 85 for 32 miles to an altitude of 2,647 feet at National Park, where there are several active volcanoes. The total run of 426 miles from Auckland to Wellington took 10 hours 50 minutes, but there were many stops, including the heavily graded section just mentioned.

In the gracious Capital City of Wellington I was once again wearing my

Westinghouse 'hat' when Olivia and I entertained the General Manager of the NZR and a number of his senior officers to a cocktail party on behalf of the company. But we were soon heading further south. We crossed the Cook Strait in the luxurious ferry boat to Picton, a vessel more like one of our own channel packets than a mere 'ferry', and then next day we took another railcar down the South Island main line to Christchurch. Here my dear Olivia had to give up for a while, remaining in the hotel to nurse that influenza cold that she contracted in that chilly midnight shoe-examination at Auckland. I went right down to the far-south, to Invercargill, and to the most southerly extent of rails anywhere in the world, at Bluff. There were talks to groups of railway enthusiasts at Invercargill and Dunedin; but the highlight of my trip to the far south, was a run by car northwards from Invercargill to Lumsden, the starting point of the fabulous *Kingston Flyer* steam run, to the foot of Lake Wakatipu. This very popular steam excursion had not yet begun operating, but my railway friends had arranged that one of the celebrated 'AB' Class steam 'Pacifics' should be drawn out of its winter quarters for me to photograph it. It was one of my great regrets that being so near to the magnificent mountain and lake scenery of the Southern Alps I could not penetrate further. As a stamp collector Lake Wakatipu had been a household word for me since my boyhood. The pronunciation, by the way, is 'Wock-a-tip'.

We flew direct from Christchurch to Sydney, a journey enlivened by the company, as fellow passengers, of the English touring company of the comedy, *Move over Mrs Markham*—as delightful, and highly amusing cast, off duty, as they must have been on the stage. Eric Archer and his wife, May, met us in. Eric had recently succeeded Harold Bourne as Chief Signal Engineer of the New South Wales Railways, and with them, and Frank and Jean Jones up in Brisbane, we had a very enjoyable stay in the eastern states of Australia. One of the most unusual events was the prelude to our departure for Melbourne on the *Southern Aurora* night sleeping car express. On that train passengers were permitted to entertain guests to dinner before departure, and we were glad to have Eric and May Archer with us, for a dinner party in the dining car, in Sydney Central station. Several other passengers were availing themselves of this surely unique facility, for more than an hour before departure time.

The *Southern Aurora* is a beautiful train, and in it we travelled through the night to Melbourne. Our great friend, Jack Taylor, of the Victorian Railways met us in, but we were not staying long on this occasion. Our immediate objective was Tasmania, where Trevor, our son, was then manager for Price Waterhouse & Co, in Hobart. We looked forward especially to greeting our first grandson in a country that has always intrigued me since my earliest days of stamp collecting. Tasmania was one of the very earliest units of the British Empire to issue a set of large pictorial stamps. I had one of these, and delighted in the beautiful colours and the attractive scenes depicted. From the railway point of view also, Tasmania was the birthplace of the world-famous Beyer-Garratt articulated type of locomotive. I travelled by the daily passenger train between Hobart and the ports on the north coast. It took five hours to cover the 133 miles to Launceston, and having seen the incredibly curving alignment over much of the route I found it surprising that the railway service is so fast! It carries the name *Tasman Limited*, but among Trevor's business friends in Hobart, who can reach Launceston in little more than half the time in their own cars, the train is known as the '*Very* Limited'! Much the most diverting

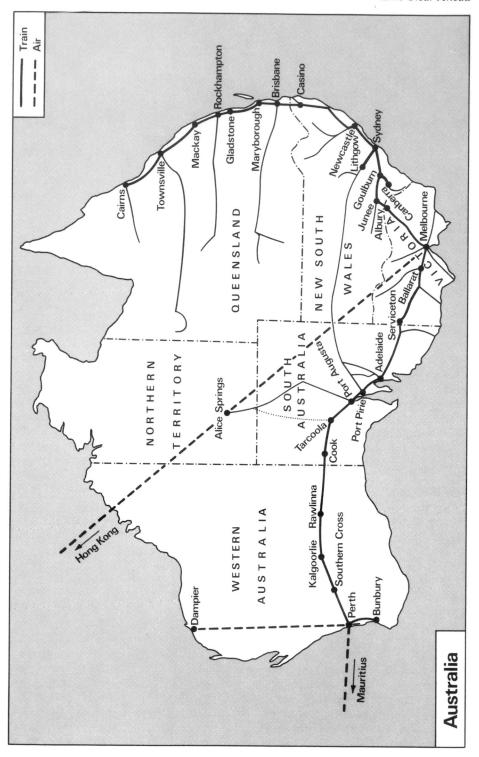

Australia

The Hamersley Iron Railway, in North Western Australia, where the ex-GWR 4-6-0, Pendennis Castle, *is now based: a maximum load iron ore train, 15,000 tons, leaving Tom Price for the port of Dampier.*

occasions for me on the Tasmanian Railways were the excursion runs up the Derwent Valley line, to National Park, on the preserved steam 4-6-2 and 4-8-2 locomotives, both gorgeously painted in a brilliant cherry red.

A few years ago railway preservationists, and particularly those with affection for the Great Western Railway, were saddened at the thought of the *Pendennis Castle*, going to an apparently permanent home in Australia—not only that, but to one of the most remote and completely isolated lines in the whole of that vast continent. I was amazed, and yet fascinated, because in 1972 I had visited the remarkable Hamersley Iron Railway, in Western Australia, and seen something of its enormous traffic, entirely in iron ore. An average pay load of 75,000 tons of ore per day was legislated for in the planning, and for economic operation, 15,000 tons per train. Having been there, and seen the working against the incredible background of near-desert conditions, with an all-pervading dust, iron-ore red, instead of sand, over the entire 182 miles of the mainline between the mines at 'Tom Price', and the port of Dampier, I have been wondering what use will be made of *Pendennis Castle* in such a terrain. When I went there transport between the two communities, for the staff, wives and families of the railway and mining folk, was by a tiny five-seater monoplane. There were no such things as passenger trains, and no stations; and to reach Dampier it is a flight of just over 1,000 miles by air from Perth. So, *Pendennis Castle* has gone very much into seclusion. The railway itself is a magnificent piece of engineering and operation, with some spectacular works on the extension of Paraburdoo, which I saw under construction; but it hardly comes within the sphere of even the most enterprising of modern rail tours.

After flying west and visiting our friends in Johannesburg and Bulawayo we arrived back home at the end of September, and I had immediately to begin thinking about my next overseas trip, to Japan, in the spring of 1973. Two pen-friends, Y. Kawakami, in Akita, and H. Uematsu, in Tokyo, who I learned were well known to each other, were full of ideas for an itinerary, while in London the Japanese tourist office were extremely helpful, immediately sending telex messages, and setting up liaison with Japanese National Railway headquarters in Tokyo. There, Uematsu, already well known to them from his photographic activities, had also been busy, with the result that what could have been a dive into the unknown was made a very smooth and enjoyable trip, with English speaking companions everywhere I went. Before leaving Heathrow I felt I was half-way there, for nearly all my fellow passengers on the 'JAL' jumbo-jet were Japanese and as soon as we were airborne most of the stewardesses changed into national costume—a delightful prelude. I cannot, however, remember a journey that played quite such 'ducks and drakes' with the time. According to my diary I see that we left Heathrow at 15.25 and arrived in Tokyo at 17.10—the same day! We flew over the North Pole, and were each given a certificate to that effect, and made our first stop at Anchorage, Alaska about eight hours later, and most of it in sunshine. It was only just getting dark when we approached Tokyo. Uematsu met me in, and although he was quite fluent in English, he confessed to being a bit confused when he heard it spoken!

The Japanese railway officers could not do enough to help me. I was presented with the enormous centenary celebration volume, giving a pictorial history of the railways, fortunately including English translations of the captions to no fewer than 1,200 illustrations; it was so massive a work indeed that even on this first day I was beginning to wonder how much excess luggage I should have to pay for on my return home. In Tokyo I did not see the oft-related spectacle of packing passengers into commuter trains in the peak hours,

The Japanese 'Royal Engine' 4-6-2, No C57 117, photographed at Miyazaki, with the flags and the symbolic chrysanthemem in place. Next day I rode the same engine, not decorated (!) on a freight train.

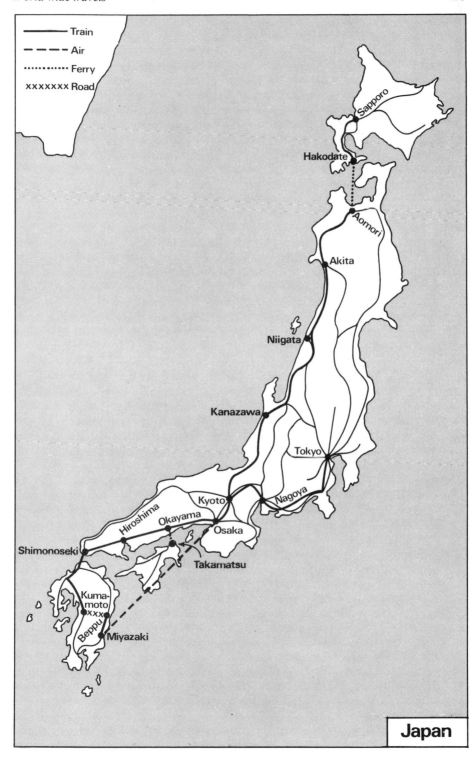

Train
Air
Ferry
Road

Sapporo
Hakodate
Aomori
Akita
Niigata
Kanazawa
Tokyo
Kyoto
Nagoya
Hiroshima
Okayama
Osaka
Shimonoseki
Takamatsu
Kuma-moto
xxx
Beppu
Miyazaki

Japan

but I did see and experience myself the precision in which the Hikari high speed trains were loaded. The passenger movement was as streamlined as the trains themselves, with the position of the doors of each car marked on the platform with numbers to correspond with the number on each passenger's ticket. Everyone was neatly queued up ready at the correct entrance place, and although the doors were not opened until about five minutes before departure time about 1,000 people stepped smartly in, and the train left dead on time. The confinement within an air-conditioned interior, and windows that are relatively small by British standards, gave little impression of high speed; yet we actually ran the first 213½ miles to Nagoya, our first stop from Tokyo at an *average* speed of 106.7 mph. For most of the way we were running at more than 125 mph, up to the maximum of 130 mph.

On the run down the east coast of the main island of Honshu, to Okayama on the Hikari trains, and then to Shimonoseki by the 3 foot 6 inch gauge express I wondered if we were ever going to run clear of heavily industrialised areas; and it was in fact not until we were away from Kumamoto, on the island of Kyushu, that we saw some real country, highlighted at one of my staging points, Miyazaki, by the presence of the steam-hauled Japanese Royal train. When next morning I had an engine pass to ride a freight train into the mountains to the south they put on the Royal engine, the 'C57' class 4-6-2 No 117, though naturally divested of its special decorations. To save time I flew back from Miyazaki to Osaka, prior to making the long run up the west coast of Honshu. It was then that uncertainties entered into my schedule. There were disturbing labour troubles, including the all-too-familiar tactics of 'go-slow'. Nevertherless, nothing could damp the enthusiasm of my hosts, and the fact that my train was going to be late gave them a chance to prolong their lunchtime hospitality! My companion on the northward run to Akita told me how the Japanese refund fares if the train is more than an hour late. When we arrived at Akita, 1¾ hours late, all passengers alighting made straight for the booking office. There was no argument or delay; the queue seeking refunds was dealt with as promptly as one intent on booking tickets at a London Underground station.

Next day there was a general strike of railwaymen, and instead of railways, Kawakami, who had met me in on that delayed arrival at Akita, had organised with JNR a road tour of some of the beautiful country in the neighbourhood, including a sight of the fishing village of Oga, where all the ships were gaily and flamboyantly dressed with flags to show that they had secured a record catch. Uematsu rejoined me for the northmost continuation of my journey, by the night ferry across to Hakodate, on the island of Hokkaido. There, at its Capital City of Sapporo, I received the greatest of VIP welcomes, from Mr Hata, the Vice-President of JNR in Hokkaido. He saw to it that my days there were full, and he bade fair to make the nights equally so. A dinner party, Japanese style, was attended by a bevy of geishas, and while there was a great deal of railway 'shop' talked with Hata and his colleagues these ladies, interspersed between the men round the table, sat wide-eyed in rapt attention. Only one of them, however, could speak any English, and towards the end of the evening when some of them had sung to us, she startled me by suddenly saying: 'now Nock-San make music'! It is a long time since I sang in public, but in a rather croaky voice I did my best.

It was not until nearly two years later that I set out for India. This was to be a tour with a difference. The earlier ones referred to in this chapter took me to

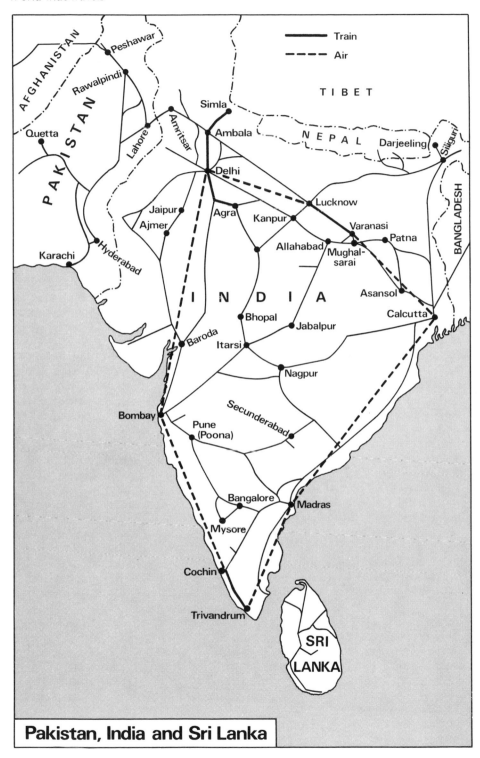

Train
Air

Pakistan, India and Sri Lanka

places on which the railway literature in English was not extensive, and of which I had not much prior knowledge; but from my first days with Westinghouse I was involved in work for Indian railways. My new-found colleagues were then constantly coming and going, bringing with them stories, and incidents while, of course, my interest in locomotives had already extended to the products of the North British Locomotive Company, the Vulcan Foundry, and other British builders, who were, in the 1920s between them the only suppliers of motive power to the Indian railways. In London I had worked on apparatus for large contracts in Bombay, and later for single-line token instruments for many parts of India, so that when I set out for Delhi, in January 1975, it was very much a case of going to a country where I was familiar at least with the railway scene. My good friend, Jack Brown, representative of Westinghouse in India, had secured introductions for me in the highest quarters, and he accompanied me on many of my journeys. The January weather was beautiful in Delhi, temperate with serene sunshine, though home-studied statistics had not prepared me for the incredible sights of a big Indian station, with its crowds, and the maelstrom of vehicular traffic outside. It was Bangkok again, though many times multiplied.

I was soon to experience a violent change in climate, for an early expedition took me up to Simla, where we were not only trudging about in deep snow, but very conscious of remaining memories of the British Raj. While in Simla, and in conversation with two Englishmen in one of the shops, I learned of the disaster to the Tasman Bridge, across the estuary of the River Derwent at Hobart. It was not until later that I also learned of how narrowly Trevor himself had escaped being involved. From Simla it was a characteristically quick transition, scenically, as well as temperature-wise, to Bombay, to see the majestic Gateway of India, memorial arch on the sea wall, marking the spot where King George V and Queen Mary landed prior to the ceremonies of the Imperial Durbar, in 1911. It was the first and only time that any of the five Emperors of India have visited the country in person, during his or her reign. Then again, among all the ornate and grandiose railway stations of Europe and America there is surely nothing in sheer magnificence to equal Victoria Terminus, the Bombay terminal of the Great Indian Peninsula Railway. A water colour painting of 1878 which shows, in breathtaking detail and beauty, the station as it was, before becoming hemmed in with building of the developing city, forms the frontispiece of a beautiful recent book *Railways of the Raj*, by my friend Michael Satow, and Ray Desmond. It was a privilege to give a talk to a gathering of Indian railway officers in such superb surroundings.

From Bombay I flew south to Cochin to see the gauge-conversion works on the line southwards to Trivandrum. The South Indian Railway in this region was originally built on the metre gauge, but traffic is now such that the line is being upgraded to the broad, or 5 foot 6 inch gauge. But of the far south—not quite the southern-most tip of India, but very near it—I have especial memories of the hotel where I stayed near Trivandrum. It was only six days since I had been at Simla, in deep snow, and here was I, now, sitting out by the sea in my shirt sleeves at near midnight. I was up and about early next morning to take photographs of this gorgeous tropical beach in all its colour before my railway friends called for me, and the programme continued—'all go'! There were a few days in Madras, and then on to Calcutta. I have the most incredibly mixed impressions of this extraordinary city: of poverty, dilapidation, of supremely well-run commuter train services, and perhaps most surprising of all, the utterly magnificent Victoria Memorial, standing alone, huge, majestic in appropriately vast grounds, and within immaculately maintained. It is not only a brain-child of Lord Curzon's Viceroyalty, as a monument to the first Empress of India, but today verily a salute to the British Monarchy itself, with a portrait gallery extending back to much earlier sovereigns than Victoria, and brought forward to the present day. It was impressive to see this gallery, thronged with Indians of every estate passing attentively from one picture to the next with every sign of the utmost respect.

Heading back towards Delhi our next call was at Benares, or Varanasi as it is now known. There the contrasts that India can show are most vividly apparent, when one came out from the modern diesel locomotive works into city streets where elephants were being used as beasts of burden, and hand-drawn rickshaws jostled with other vehicles hauled by camels. I went on to Lucknow by train on the footplate of the diesel hauling the Amritsar Mail, and there, in addition to much railway activity, I saw the famous Residency, preserved in a semi-ruined state, exactly as it remained after its heroic defence in the troubles of 1857. Back in Delhi there were lectures to be given; thanks to be extended, particularly to M.N. Bery, then Chairman of the Railway Board, and to Manuel Menezes, then Director of Railway Planning, who were entertained by Jack Brown and his wife, Thelma, at a dinner party in Delhi.

The Indian Railways had one more treat in store for me, a day trip to Agra, travelling there on the footplate of the big steam 'Pacific' hauling the *Taj Express*. It was an easy run from the locomotive point of view, involving no higher speed than 60 mph on a level road, with a load of less than 400 tons; but once arrived in Agra we set out on a lengthy circular tour, visiting many temples and shrines in the neighbourhood. The itinerary was skilfully arranged so as to bring us to the climax at the end. From the Fort, our last stop but one, we looked over the battlements, down the course of the Jumna River to the 'Taj' itself; and now, as I saw it, dazzling white, in the clear air and mellow afternoon sunshine, I wondered if after all it would live up to expectations, as the most famous and beautiful tourist sight in the world! I was not disappointed. Although so familiar, from photographs, coloured prints, and posters, in reality it transcends them all by so much as to be positively stunning. I could have sat for hours just quietly contemplating its serene and matchless beauty. One could not have had a more perfect ending to my journey round India.

Above *Great Anniversaries: the replica* Rocket *built for the Rainhill sesquicentenary, including the 'pipe of port' water barrel on the tender, which my friends in the wine trade obtained from Spain, as told in my book,* Rocket 150.

Below *Two famous participants in the 'Rocket 150' cavalcade of which I have vivid memories: the Gresley 'A4', No 4498,* Sir Nigel Gresley, *and the ever-memorable* Flying Scotsman.

Chapter 15

The great anniversaries

When I was in Calcutta in January 1975 one of our guides taking Jack Brown and me round the railway installations of Howrah was a very enthusiastic Anglophile who delighted in airing his command of colloquial English. Learning of my age he remarked that 'if he ever got thus far he would be nothing but a bloody dried up old fossil!'. I must admit that in the six years since that visit there have been occasions when I have felt a bit of an old fossil myself; but in the steam shed nearby he found an old BESA 0-6-0 with a date plate reading January 1905, and had the two septuagenarians photographed together. From this very minor occasion I had returned to preparations for the great anniversary of the year 1975, the sesquicentenary of the opening of the Stockton and Darlington Railway.

I was greatly honoured to receive an invitation from the Institution of Mechanical Engineers to collaborate with Roland Bond in the presentation of the James Clayton Memorial Lecture, of which the title was to be '150 years of Uninterrupted Progress in Railway Engineering', and which was to form one of the evening attractions to the Conference.

To mark this event the Institution of Mechanical Engineers organised a mammoth International Engineering Conference, to take place in September, which was jointly sponsored by the Institutions of Civil, Mechanical, Electrical, and Railway Signal Engineers, and which included no fewer than 72 papers, by authors from many parts of the world. Later, on that evening of the lecture, those attending the Conference were invited to a conversazione at the Science Museum and, to minimise transit time, the lecture itself was held in the main lecture theatre of the Sherfield Building of Imperial College, nearby—a nostalgic memory of my own college days, though by then, of course, the old City and Guilds had been completely rebuilt. The organisers were taking no chances with that lecture of ours, and we were required to attend for a full rehearsal a week previously.

Roland Bond and I had a great time putting that lecture together, and choosing the hundred or so illustrations that were to be shown on the screen. It was obvious that we could not go into any minute detail, for within the scheduled time of about 1½ hours we had to cover all the four disciplines represented by the sponsoring institutions, and to make it interesting to the many ladies who were expected to attend. It was arranged that the lecture should be delivered in two sections, Bond doing the early half, and I the modern part, with a vintage film of 1937, *The Coronation Scot*, in between. On

September 23, at Imperial College, we had a very appreciative audience of about 800, and subsequently in 1975 we gave the lecture in Bath; in 1976 in Manchester, Newcastle, Glasgow, Hull and Liverpool; in 1977 in Rugby, and in 1978 in Cambridge and Ipswich. The latter presentation, on November 14, was on the eve of my departure for another round-world trip, in the course of which I gave the lecture on my own in Brisbane, Sydney, Melbourne, Hong Kong and New Delhi. By that time I knew the second half almost by heart!

The year 1975 was not past before I was involved in preparations for another forthcoming anniversary—that of the Settle and Carlisle Railway, in the early summer of 1976. Looking back on these and subsequent events, with which I became personally involved, it is pleasant to reflect upon how, in the early evening of my life, some links with earlier associations that had become tenuous with the years were notably strengthened again. This proved especially the case in respect of Giggleswick School, the City and Guilds, and my time at Westinghouse; while links with three of the professional Institutions became much more than the routine paying of a subscription every year.

For some time the Settle Civic Society had been looking towards the great anniversary that was to come in 1976, and with the formation of a Railway Centenary Committee, including in its membership two Giggleswick School masters, it was, inevitably, perhaps, not long before I was roped in to help. The run-up included several meetings in the winter of 1975–6, and I spoke at meetings in Carlisle and Ingleton. We had great fun in planning the exhibition of historic models, pictures, and other relics to be staged in The Shambles, in Settle market place; but all the time the million dollar question remained: 'Would British Railways relax the prevailing ban, just for one day, and allow the centenary special train to be hauled by steam?'. To try and help the committee I pulled all the strings that I could think of at Euston, and elsewhere. The obstacle was the business of turning the engines at Carlisle, and avoiding their passing under the overhead electric wires. There were suggestions that steam working should terminate at the old Durran Hill shed location and that the train should be hauled thence into the Citadel station by diesel; but the only concession eventually made was that the engine which had worked the special across from Carnforth in the morning should be allowed to proceed up the Carlisle line afterwards, as far as Settle, and be on exhibition during part of the afternoon.

I shall never forget that week-end. On Friday, April 30, using the M4, M5 and M6 motorways in succession we drove up to Giggleswick, and on arrival we were horrified to learn that *both* engines booked to haul the centenary special from Carnforth to Hellifield on the following morning had failed! We were to have had the Midland compound No 1000, and a 'Black Five' 4-6-0 which had spent much of its active life on the Settle and Carlisle road. Nigel Mussett, one of the Giggleswick masters involved, and secretary of the Railway Centenary Committee, told us that arrangements were being made to get *Flying Scotsman* across from the National Railway Museum at York, to provide the main haulage for the special, while at Carnforth the historic LNWR 2-4-0 No 790, *Hardwicke*, was in good trim, and would act as pilot to the big 'Pacific'. While feeling relieved to hear that there would be steam locomotives available to haul the special, it was ironic that, on so predominantly Midland an occasion, recourse had to be made to London and North Western, and Great Northern engines to help out.

Olivia and I had the privilege of riding in the VIP saloon, and of the return journey from Carlisle there is a good story to be told. At the Citadel station my good friend 'Bobby' Howes and his wife had joined us. He, as Assistant General Manager of the London Midland Region, was to be one of the speakers at the banquet to be held at Settle station on our return, and he was appropriately dressed. Eric Treacy and I, and our wives, were dressed for a day in the country. We had been assured beforehand that although official proceedings would begin as soon as we arrived at Settle there would be plenty of time to change, and that rooms had been set aside in the station house at Ribblehead for us to do so during a scheduled photographic stop of 30 minutes or so on the journey back. But the day had turned very wet, and from one cause or another the diesel hauled special became very late. When we eventually got to Ribblehead, not only were the conditions pretty hopeless for photography, but the organisers decided to cut the stop to less than ten minutes, to make up as much time as possible. There was no question of the four of us going to the station house to change; it had to be done in the saloon, with only 11 miles of fast downhill running to go before our arrival in Settle. May Treacy and Olivia were one after the other accorded the seclusion of the 'loo', while Eric and I shielded from public gaze by a ring of fellow guests changed our trousers in the open saloon!

The hilarious incidentals of this occasion were not ended with our arrival in Settle. The banquet was held in a large marquee in the station yard. It had been raining all day, and by the time we sat down to dinner it had degenerated into a downpour, and the ground inside the marquee behind the top table was rapidly becoming little less than a quagmire. The caterers and their staff, however, were magnificent, and the motherly old Yorkshire waitress who was looking after us, excused herself for a moment to go and put on a pair of 'Wellies', in which she afterwards padded up and down on the sodden ground. Olivia was sitting next to Eric Treacy, and she has often recalled the running commentary that accompanied her very efficient serving of the meal. It began in earnest after she had changed into gum boots. In broadest Yorkshire dialect she told Eric and Olivia how all that week she had prayed for fine weather, but she was disappointed that the Good Lord had not answered her prayers. Then, without seeing his 'front' she continued, patting Eric affectionately, and commenting upon what a fine pair of shoulders he had. (Shades of our Rugger days!). Then he turned to speak to Olivia. He was, of course, in full clerical regalia, and she saw! When she had recovered her breath she gasped: 'Oh, my God: oh my Lord: oh your Grace . . .'. But he put the old dear completely at her ease, with the charm and spontaneity that was so characteristic of his whole life.

At the end of May that year Olivia and I went down to Cornwall for an early holiday, at the Budock Vean Hotel near Mawnan Smith. There is something uniquely charming about a secluded creek on a Cornish estuary, especially when the path leading to it is flanked by an absolute riot of rhododendrons in full bloom. While we were there we were able to meet once again, in Falmouth, some surviving members of the family of that great Chief Mechanical Engineer of the LNWR, C.J. Bowen Cooke, whose eldest daughter, that grand old lady Mrs Faith Harris, was then approaching her 90th birthday. She, her brother and her surviving sisters, had helped me with many reminiscences of their father in connection with the book I was working upon describing his locomotives and their history. I am glad that the book was finished in time for her to receive an autographed copy on her own great anniversary.

There was another amusing flash-back to earlier days during that holiday of ours in Cornwall in 1976—Great Western this time, instead of LNWR. Proofs of another literary assignment had been late in coming and I had to give the publishers my holiday address. We arrived back to lunch one day to find a telephone message: 'Proofs consigned to you by Red Star on 11.30 from Paddington. Please collect at Redruth'. The 11.30 was then the 'Cornish Riviera Express', and old associations came crowding: *Red Star* on the Limited; the very first time I saw the train when I came to London to begin my engineering studies in 1921 the engine had been the 4-cylinder 4-6-0 No 4006 *Red Star*, and my mind went still further back to the many times I had seen the up Limited with 'Star' Class engines in those far-off days when we lived at Mortimer Common and I used to wait for the Basingstoke 'motor', on Reading West station. We drove to Redruth that afternoon to await the coming of the 11.30 from Paddington; but when it arrived, hauled by a travel-stained Class '50' diesel, there was little to remind one of the spacious days when there would be a 'Red Star' at the head of the train, instead of a parcel in one of the vans.

My book on the Bowen Cooke locomotives came out in 1977, but that was only one of the highlights of a very eventful year. One day in March, when I was away from home briefly, G.E. Gelson, an old student of the City and Guilds rang and asked Olivia if she thought he might nominate me as his successor on the General Committee of the Old Centralians. The name, by the way, is a living reminder of the time it used to be known as the Central Technical College—long before my student day, I might add. She demurred, suggesting that I 'might' be too old, but he brushed the objection to one side saying he was three years older than I. So, towards the end of April I met him, and his fellow Old Centralian in the same age group, W.J. Fenton, for lunch at the Athenaeum Club, to learn something about what membership of the General Committee of the club would involve. The duties, as it turned out, were very light, but I welcomed the opportunity of strengthening my links with the college, and the meetings and social functions proved, as I expected, most enjoyable.

Another link with old associations was also developing fast at the same time. The year 1981 would see the centenary of the formation of the Westinghouse Brake Company, in England. Certain other constituents of the firm I joined in 1925, such as Saxby & Farmer, and McKenzie & Holland were much older, but they had existed as trade partnerships rather than limited companies. In 1977 it was felt that the centenary of the Brake Company should be adequately celebrated, and I was invited to write a book covering the hundred years between. The moving spirit in this project was my former chief assistant and great personal friend, Eric Harris, by 1977 an executive director of the Westinghouse Brake and Signal Company Ltd. Needless to say I had jumped at the chance of such an assignment and, after some preliminary negotiations, at the end of April Eric and I went down to Newton Abbot to conclude details of the contract for the book with David St John Thomas, Chairman of David & Charles Ltd. The title was to be *A Hundred Years of Speed with Safety*.

Less than a month later I left England for a month's tour of the USA to collect data for the last of the books on overseas railways commissioned by Archie Black. It had proved a difficult trip to organise and, although there had been a mass of preliminary correspondence, the responsible officers seemed strangely reluctant to finalise travelling arrangements, and there were Transatlantic telephone calls right up to the day before my departure. When I actually arrived in the States, and met some of them face to face it transpired that they did not think I, or anyone else for that matter, would have the staying power to go through with the programme I had outlined; and while according me the fullest facilities had left the actual making of reservations to me when I had crossed the Atlantic. My first call was at Providence, Rhode Island, to visit the family of a young lady who had been an across-the-road neighbour of ours in Bath. When we moved from Sion Hill to 'Silver Cedars' Jill Siqueland (née Godfree) had been a vivacious senior schoolgirl, so energetic and so full of good neighbourliness that she mowed the grass verge in front of our house, before our arrival. She met me off the plane at Boston on the Friday afternoon, and I enjoyed a delightful week-end with her family before starting in earnest on the railway tour.

One of the first things I had to do on the Saturday morning was to get those elusive reservations settled. It was simplicity itself. Jill took me to the Amtrak station in Providence, and in less than one hour I had reservations all round the USA on the days that I had originally planned. Business concluded so speedily, she and her husband then proceeded to show me the sights. Jill had established herself as a house and estate agent, and believe it or not her English accent had brought much business to the firm. Apparently clients were thrilled 'to hear the English lady talk', and indeed she interspersed one of our sightseeing tours by a visit to a property on the seashore, duly clinching a very profitable deal. On the Sunday afternoon we went to a 'clambake', a kind of barbecue in which roasted clams were the principal delicacy. But it was an occasion 'for all the family', as the saying goes, with outdoor games for all ages and sexes. Mixed 'softball', baseball with a soft ball, was especially popular.

Next morning I caught an early train for New York. My stay there was of the briefest, merely to take the measure of the railway passenger facilities, and I saw the great city in one of its worst aspects. The line of the one-time New York, Newhaven and Hartford is not one of the most interesting, and the general air was one of thinly veiled dilapidation, with poor running, many delays, and an approach to New York through rather dismal suburbs and eventually a dive under the East River to reach the Pennsylvania station underground in Downtown Manhattan. I should imagine that the best way to appreciate the remarkable geographical location of New York would be from a helicopter, flying in from the bay, when the whole array of skyscrapers massed together on Manhattan Island would be displayed to the best, most dramatic effect. I came to the surface in the midst of them, and on a hot, steamy afternoon the effect was well-nigh overpowering. I drove to my hotel, and lay down for a considerably longer afternoon nap than usual!

Next day I went on to Philadelphia to call in at Conrail headquarters, and to confirm to them that I really *did* want to ride a freight train eastbound from Pittsburgh on my homeward journey, so as to see the far-famed Horseshoe Curve in daylight. Even before I left England I had come to realise that passenger trains are few and far between in the USA, except in the North-East Corridor. But the Conrail people became thoroughly caught up with my own enthusiasm, and were most helpful. Real railway sightseeing began, however, when I reached Baltimore and the men of the Chessie System took me into their care. It was the first taste I had of what American railroad hospitality can really mean; and re-reading the book I wrote subsequently, more than 300 pages of it, I am reminded not only of the thousands of miles I travelled, nor of the vast amount of data I collected, or the photographs I took, but of the men themselves who made me so welcome in their various spheres, and who 'put-across' their experience and accumulated expertise with such enthusiasm. With some of them it did not stop 'out the line', as the Highland Scots would express it. I was taken to their homes, entertained at their clubs, while a wealth of books, pamphlets and entertaining correspondence followed me home to England.

After lunch with one of them, on the biggest coal carrying railway in the USA I wrote: 'The dedicated railroadman is an international character. It matters not whether the scene be set in Norfolk Virginia, in Toronto, Kanazawa, or Bangkok; in de Aar Junction, Sydney, or Invercargill, in Vienna, Amsterdam, in Crewe (England) or in Aberdeen. By the sheer force of his enthusiasm, his expertise, and his pride in the job, he channels ones thoughts on to a single track, and I am inevitably caught up in the stream and carried happily along with it. But', I continued, 'over lunch that day I recalled that bed for me that night was in New Orleans, just about 1,000 miles away, and that I had to "do" the Southern Railway in the meantime!'.

Although I could well have felt like the most superficial of tourists, it was not really so; because, with modern signalling and control methods on the various control panels and track diagrams in the headquarters building at Atlanta, I could see, by their indication lights, practically every train on the system. And so I went round America—New Orleans, Cairo, St Louis, Chicago, a trip down to Louisville, and back, Rock Island, Salt Lake City, and over the unforgettable Rio Grande to Denver, where Dick Kindig a pen-friend of nearly 40 years standing was waiting to greet me. Then down to Pueblo, and a night car journey to La Junta to catch the *South West Limited* for Los Angeles. Up the Pacific Coast to San Francisco, and on to Seattle; eastwards then, in a 2½-day train journey to Chicago, and a brief retracing of steps to Milwaukee, to meet the distinguished editor of *Trains* magazine, David Morgan, and then by night to Pittsburgh, for three memorable days with Conrail. When I met Howard Gilbert for the second time at the Philadelphia headquarters, and thanked him for all he had done, and I called John Ragsdale, and thanked him too for all the facilities Amtrak had given me, I felt I was thanking them both on behalf of all the railways of the USA, and I hoped they were all pleased with the 300-page tome I wrote about them.

Then for my last days in the States I donned my Westinghouse 'hat', and went out to see Westcode Inc at King of Prussia. For here, in Pennsylvania, our English company has a subsidiary concerned mainly with freight train brakes, and in view of that important literary commission from the parent company, I was interested to see something of its establishment. But 'King of Prussia'—what an extraordinary name for an American township! Its origin can be traced back to the War of Independence, when George Washington was encamped at Valley Forge, keeping watch on the English army under Lord Cornwallis, in winter quarters in Philadelphia. Among the foreign mercenaries sent to help Washington, and embarrass England, was a certain Baron von Steuben, a Prussian. He was an able soldier, and helped to reorganise the rebel armies and contributed to the eventual defeat of the British. In acknowledgement of the part Von Steuben had played, one of the inns in the hamlet of Valley Forge was named 'King of Prussia' and, although the inn itself has since been retitled, the district assumed the historic name, and it was there that the factory of Westcode Inc was situated when I first went to see it. The activities of this American consitutent have now been transferred to larger premises nearer Philadelphia.

While I was there Jim McLean, President of Westcode Inc, took me to lunch at a restaurant with the unlikely name of 'Victoria Station'. It is one of a chain of establishments in the USA, all bearing the same name, and offering a quality and nature of cuisine recalling the greatest days of the British railway station dining rooms, with a menu that travellers of earlier days would associate with the dining room beside the Great Hall at Euston, or with the Silver Grill on No 10 platform at Kings Cross. In King of Prussia the fare was certainly as ample as it was excellent; but I was equally interested in the wealth of pictures, station signs, relics and other memorabilia of earlier days on the railways of Britain. I gathered that all the other 'Victoria Stations' in the USA are decorated in the same way. McClean, himself a frequent visitor to Chippenham, was as pleased to have the particular significance of some of the exhibits explained as I was to do so.

I flew back to England that same night, and was very soon involved in another exciting project. The BBC in Scotland were examining the possibility of making a feature film of the 'Race to the North', concentrating on some of the more dramatic episodes of the race of 1895. Michael Marshall, their producer, came to 'Silver Cedars' armed with a copy of my book, and together we discussed the possibilities of a script. At such a prospect it can well be imagined that my brain was working at a rate of '19 to the dozen', and when he left I

Memories of the USA; the 'South West Limited' of the Santa Fe in the desert lands of Arizona (Tim Zukas).

feared that he might have been overwhelmed by my enthusiasm and with the factual documentation that I loaded on to him. The proximity of the National Railway Museum, and the presence within it of two of the actual types of locomotives involved, suggested scenes depicting the change of engines from Great Northern to North Eastern in York station, at eleven o'clock at night; and then, of course, for the rival line, there was *Hardwicke*, in good running condition. To get such scenes would, of course, require the closest co-operation from British Railways, and from the Science Museum, in London, of which the NRM at York is an out-station. Marshall went away to do some costing and other investigation; but by the end of the year I was delighted to learn from him that the project had been authorised.

The filming at York was fixed for Saturday night–Sunday morning of March 18/19, 1978. British Railways had risen magnificently to the occasion, and made two out of the four through lines under the great arched roof of the station available exclusively to us from about 10 pm onwards, and diesel shunting locomotives were assigned to us for moving the museum pieces as and where we needed them. We were fortunate, too, in having Eastern Region headquarters of BR only five minutes away, and a scholarly assistant in the public relations and publicity department, J. Rankin, deputed to help. He was invaluable. Before the actual night of filming there was much 'to-ing and fro-ing', to ensure that accuracy of detail essential in a programme that would come before the critical eyes of many thousands of dedicated railway enthusiasts. For example, we had to titivate the Stirling 8 foot single No 1 to make her pass as No 775, a later engine of the same type that actually worked the racing train from Grantham to York in 1895. It was not only a matter of changing the number. On the later engines the very distinctive open-slotted splasher over the great 8 foot driving wheel had been closed in; and this had to be done, temporarily.

It was a bitterly cold night and poor James Cameron, the veteran narrator for the programme, caught pneumonia in the process. I went round to the museum to see 'No 775', and the genuine 1621 of the North Eastern, extracted and I rode on the footplate of the former as the BR diesel drew the two of them gently out and propelled them into the station. In the actual film John Belwood, Chief Mechanical Engineer to the Museum, was the 'driver' of No 775, while No 1621 was 'driven' by Peter Semmens, Assistant Keeper of the Museum, who three years later succeeded me in the authorship of 'Locomotive Practice and Performance' in *The Railway Magazine*. The firemen were museum staff. Only one period carriage was available, and great care had to be taken in filming to exclude the diesel locomotive that was propelling the 'train' from the rear.

The night at York was, however, less than a fraction of the total job. Michael Marshall's script was to include scenes from some of the railway conferences at the time of the race, and episodes from the memorable run of the East Coast train on the night of August 19/20, 1895. Three very versatile actors had been engaged, and filming took place in the Glasgow studios of the BBC in June 1978. Versatile indeed! One of those actors had to portray such diverse characters as Matthewman, Stirling's chief clerk, Welburn, Superintendent of the Line of the North Eastern, and Charles Rous-Marten, while another had to play Stirling himself, F.P. Cockshott of the GNR and the Rev W.J. Scott. The make-up was marvellous, and it was fascinating to me to sit at the control panel, with the producer, John Macpherson, invigilating on the performance being enacted before us. It took two whole days, during which the scene was changed (and the costumes and make-up likewise) from the NER headquarters offices at York, and Stirling's holiday hotel at Scarborough, to the racing train of August 19/20, 1895, and to a realistic portrayal of the terrific shake-up they all received when the Portobello S-curve was rounded at 80 mph! Although the filming in Glasgow was not finished until June 6, Olivia and I were invited to a pre-view of the whole thing in London on June 14. It was certainly worth all our days and nights on location. Less than a week later it was shown on BBC2.

There had been a felicitous prelude to those busy days of filming in Glasgow, for on the preceeding days I had been at Giggleswick, for Old Boys' Day. Some months earlier I had been asked if I would stand for the vice-presidency of the Old Giggleswickian Club. I felt it was a great honour to be asked; for although I had always felt a deep debt of gratitude to the school, and all it stood for, and not least for the sturdy northern climate that had contributed so much to the robust health I have enjoyed all my life, my connections had really been no more than slight since I left, in July 1921. But retirement from daily business, and especially my involvement with the Railway Centenary celebrations in 1976, enabled my links with the school to be greatly strengthened once again, and I was proud to accept the nomination, which would lead to the presidency of the club in 1979. Before that time, however, Olivia and I had decided, sadly, that some considerable contraction of our property was essential. Beautiful though 'Silver Cedars' was, and cherished for all we had done there, we were neither of us getting any younger. We began to think in terms of a labour-saving bungalow, with a much smaller garden. It would, of course, mean the dismantling of the model railway and the disposal of much of the equipment and, sadly, the landscaping (viaducts and tunnels based on the countryside around Giggleswick) would have to go. But, we reflected, there are many good things that must inevitably come to an end; and after a disconsolate fortnight I began to scheme out space in the bungalow we were planning where a static model railway exhibit could be located, with a scenic background reminiscent of the Craven countryside.

Mindful of the Westinghouse centenary volume, on which I had already started work, arrangements had to be put in hand to visit the overseas companies; while the fact of my going to Australia and India suggested still further presentations of the Clayton Memorial Lecture of the Institution of Mechanical Engineers to branches overseas. Roland Bond and I already had a commitment to give the lecture at Ipswich on November 14, and my tour had to be squeezed between then and Christmas. In fact I returned to London the same night, and by 3.30 pm next day I was in Philadelphia. There was a quick call in at 'Westcode'; dinner, once more, at 'Victoria Station', and a visit to the Pennsylvania Railroad Museum at Strasburg before taking to the air once more and crossing the States to San Francisco. The next fortnight, 'down under', was crowded with a positive whirl of engagements. For Westinghouse, I saw signalling in Brisbane and Melbourne; the brake works at Concord West, Sydney, while Noel Reed, secretary of the Australian Section of the IRSE, had two railway treats for me, in visits to the 3 foot 6 inch gauge steam line on the Great Zig-Zag, near Lithgow, and to the New South Wales Railway Museum at Thirlmere. The I Mech E Clayton Lecture, also, was given to railway audiences in Brisbane, Sydney, and Melbourne. Apart from the short footplate ride on one of the ex-Queensland 2-6-2 tanks on the Zig Zag there was no time for any railway travelling in Australia. All my inter-city journeys were made by air and, on arrival in Melbourne, I was delighted to find my third grandson, Andrew (one year old), with Trevor and Lesley at the airport to meet me in.

Westinghouse hosted a delightful dinner party one evening at which Bill Gibbs, Commissioner of Railways, Victoria, was the principal guest. It was also grand to meet once again my great friend, Jack Taylor, and his wife Diana, who did such a marvellous job in organising my first trip to Australia, as told in Chapter 13, and no less, Mervyn Lawton and his wife, Rosemary, with whom I had first become involved in my travelling in Bangkok in 1964. Mervyn, a high standing officer of Qantas is a nephew of a very old friend of ours from Sion Hill, Bath, and has a way of arriving on her doorstep, and sometimes ours too, at 'Silver Cedars', without the slightest warning, from the other side of the world! I sat next to Bill Gibbs at that dinner party, and he, hearing that I had a son in Melbourne immediately began organising a lunch in his private dining room at Spencer Street station for the next day, which in due course Trevor thoroughly enjoyed. I spent the week-end with my family, at their home in Cheltenham, meeting once again Noel and Denyse Anderson, who Olivia and I had last seen in Fiji, six years previously.

Australia was plagued with industrial unrest at the time. On the day of my departure there was a general strike of railwaymen in Victoria, and air services

An occasion at Platform 3, Blackpool south station: the celebrated bookshop owned by Irving Scott in 1979. Olivia and I were presented with a beautiful picture looking down the Pentonville Road towards Kings Cross, in celebration of my 100th book. Irving Scott is on the left; on the right is Jim Slater, Chairman of the North Western Branch of the Locomotive club of Great Britain.

throughout the Commonwealth were disrupted by a strike of ground staff—fortunately not total. I was flying *Cathay Pacific* to Hong Kong, and while I was assured that the booked flight would actually go there was a warning of delay. When we were called to board, less than half an hour after scheduled time I was handed a card from Mervyn Lawton. It read: 'I enjoyed cleaning out your aircraft, bon voyage!'. That, however, was only the start of our adventures that day. We got to Sydney, only to be asked to vacate the aircraft and join many hundreds of bewildered and frustrated passengers in the transit lounge, most of them awaiting no better news than the cancellation of their flights. There we stayed for four sweltering hours, until suddenly there came the call to board for Hong Kong. Once in flight we were told we were going back to Melbourne (!)—to refuel; but it was after seven in the evening before we took off in earnest. For me the flight was not without interest because we flew direct, passing over Alice Springs, which I had never seen before. At Hong Kong our movements had been carefully monitored and, although it was after 1 am before we touched down, instead of 7.35 pm, Humphrey Jones, bless him, once a draughtsman in my Kingwood office and now resident on the great Mass Transit project in Hong Kong, was there to meet me.

Although the primary object of my visit to this most fascinating place was to see the progress of the Westinghouse works on the Mass Transit Railway, and on the modernisation of the British section of the Kowloon-Canton Railway, the sheer beauty of its spectacular geographical location gripped me from the moment I looked out across Victoria Harbour from my hotel bedroom window next morning. Tower blocks may not be the most beautiful form of architecture but the massed effect of them against the majestic background of the mountains of Hong Kong island, silhouetted against the dawn sky, was tremendous. A full account of the things I saw and the people I met in the week that followed would fill many chapters, instead of a few paragraphs. I had demonstrated to me the efficacy of the technology that ensured the safe automatic driving of the trains on the Mass Transit Railway; I was taken on the footplate of one of the Kowloon-Canton trains to the Chinese border at Lo Wu, I lunched with the Hong Kong branch of the Old Centralians, and I gave the Clayton Lecture to a meeting of the Permanent Way Institution. But the event to which, perhaps, I looked forward more than anything was a motor-boat trip around to the east side of Hong Kong island to Aberdeen harbour, where the junks, most of them residental, are so tightly packed. I made several journeys to Victoria Peak by the tram—local name for the cliff-side railway—to enjoy the magnificent prospect in all directions; but the real 'cliff-hanger' of the whole four-weeks tour was presented to me by Air France on the first leg of my homeward journey.

Arriving at Delhi at midnight, to be met by Jack and Thelma Brown, it was to find that my luggage had been wrongly routed through to Paris, and that here I was in India with no more than a small briefcase and the clothes I stood up in! This was Wednesday midnight. On Saturday afternoon I had to give the final presentation of the Clayton Lecture to the Indian branch of the Institution of Mechanical Engineers, and the suitcase containing the script of the lecture and the slides was winging its way to Europe. Frantic telephone calls on the following morning, and a visit to the city office of the air line produced nothing more than the stolid reaction to a personal emergency that one expects from officialdom, and all day we awaited the vaguely promised telephone call with information, in vain. We re-opened the barrage on Friday morning, still with no effect, until we were just sitting down to lunch. Then came a ring from Air France to say that my case had been located, and had been sent on to London—momentary gasp from all of us who heard!—to catch a plane that it would get it back to Delhi quicker. And I received it just *one hour* before I left to give the lecture!

I returned home to the ice and snow of an English Christmas, and then Olivia and I faced the daunting prospect of house moving. It had, of course, become generally known that we were proposing to do so, and that the railway would have to be dismantled; and early in February 1979 a BBC camera and sound recording team, with Glyn Worsnip as commentator, came for an all-day session. I do not think our tracks and rolling stock have ever had such intensive usage. Recalling earlier visitations, however, we did not expect to see anything on our screens for many weeks, perhaps months. A week later I was in London for the annual dinner of the Old Centralians. Eric Harris was to be my guest, and we were having a quiet cup of tea together in the lounge of the Great Western Royal Hotel at Paddington when I was called to the 'phone. It was the BBC; they had been on to 'Silver Cedars' and discovered my whereabouts, and told me that 'End of the Line' was to be on Nationwide that very night! We were due at the Mansion House at 7 pm. There was only one way to see it, to get into our dinner jackets first, see it on the television in one of our bedrooms, and then chance getting a taxi quickly afterwards and a clear road!

We enjoyed the programme, and we enjoyed the dinner, but neither of us gave a thought to what was happening at 'Silver Cedars'. The programme had scarcely finished before Olivia was subjected to a perfect barrage of telephone calls. They seemed to be queueing up: 'Can we come and see it', 'Has it been sold?', 'How much is it?', 'Will you bequeath it to our museum?' and many more like it, going on for more than four hours! Poor Olivia: it was late before she got her own supper that night. The years 1979 and 1980 were hectic for both of us. Quite apart from the trauma of house moving I was putting the finishing touches on three books timed to coincide with the celebration of the 150th anniversary of Rainhill, including the special *Two Miles a Minute*, while Olivia was experiencing all the worries and vexations of the domestic side of such an upheaval. There were many times when the 'downs' seemed to outbalance the 'ups'. Although fit enough in myself I felt that having passed the three-quarter century mark in January 1980 it was time to ease up a little, and I decided to relinquish the authorship of 'Locomotive Practice and Performance' in *The Railway Magazine* after 22 years. I was glad that the 'Invitation Run' of the Advanced Passenger Train came on October 3, in time for me to include a log of the run from Euston to Stafford in the last of my contributions.

I shall never forget—and neither will my dear Olivia!—the last two months of 1980, for several times it did seem I was very near the 'end of the line'. Having for a short time, had signs that all was not well with the plumbing, but otherwise being as fit as the proverbial fiddle, I decided to have the operation that is generally regarded as no more than a routine job for men passing beyond middle age. I went into the Nursing Home in mid-November, had the operation, and was home again within a week. I will not dwell upon what happened subsequently, except to say once again a very big 'thank you' to the scores of friends who rallied round, and were such a comfort to Olivia, when anxiety stretched her nerves almost to breaking point. In retrospect, it was rather a pity that I was too ill to note details of two record runs in which I was involuntarily a

Into the 1980s at 'Two Miles a Minute'—one of the already celebrated 'Inter-City 125' HSTs passing through Sonning Cutting on its Bristol–Paddington dash.

passenger—by ambulance. The first was from my home back to the Nursing Home, when by the aid of flashing lights and sirens, we got through *non stop* in the thick of the morning rush-hour traffic. The second was late on a freezing cold Sunday night when I was similarly rushed into 'intensive care', for an immediate operation performed around midnight. But when I was released from intensive care just before Christmas and returned for a spell of convalescence to the Nursing Home it seemed that at last the signals were changing up from 'single' to 'double yellow'. After a couple of months they changed joyously to 'green'. Once again, it was *Line Clear Ahead*.

Bibliography of works by O.S. Nock

Historical studies
Scottish Railways, London, Nelson, 1950.
The Great Western Railway, an Appreciation, Cambridge, Heffer, 1951.
The Railway Engineers, London, Batsford, 1955.
Branch Lines, London, Batsford, 1957.
The Great Northern Railway, London, Ian Allan, 1958.
The London and North Western Railway, London, Ian Allan, 1960.
British Steam Railways, London, A & C Black, 1961.
The South Eastern & Chatham Railway, London, Ian Allan, 1961.
The Caledonian Railway, London, Ian Allan, 1962.
The Great Western Railway in the 19th Century, London, Ian Allan, 1962.
The Great Western Railway in the 20th Century, London, Ian Allan, 1964.
The Highland Railway, London, Ian Allan, 1965.
The London & South Western Railway, London, Ian Allan, 1966.
Steam Railways in Retrospect, London, A & C Black, 1966.
History of the Great Western Railway, 1923–1947, London, Ian Allan, 1967.
North Western: a Saga of the Premier Line of Great Britain 1846–1922, Shepperton, Ian Allan, 1968.
The Lancashire and Yorkshire Railway, Shepperton, Ian Allan, 1969.
Underground Railways of the World, London, A & C Black, 1973.
150 Years of Main Line Railways, Newton Abbot, David & Charles, 1980.

Biographical
Father of Railways: the Story of George Stephenson, London, Nelson, 1958.
Sir William Stanier: an Engineering Biography, London, Ian Allan, 1961.
The Railway Enthusiast's Encyclopaedia, London, Hutchinson, 1968.
The L.N.W.R. Locomotives of C.J. Bowen Cooke, Truro, Bradford Barton, 1977.
Out the Line, London, Paul Elek, 1976.

Locomotive history
Locomotives of Sir Nigel Gresley (with a foreword by O.V.S. Bulleid), London, Longmans, 1945.
Locomotives of the L.N.E.R. Standardisation and Renumbering, London, the LNER, 1947.

Kings and Castles of the G.W.R., London, Ian Allan, 1949.

The Premier Line: the story of London & North Western Locomotives, London, Ian Allan, 1952.

The Locomotives of R.E.L. Maunsell, 1911–1937, Bristol, Everard, 1954.

Locomotives of the North Eastern Railway, London, Ian Allan, 1954.

Steam Locomotive: a retrospect of the work of eight great locomotive engineers, London BTC, 1955.

Steam Locomotive: the Unfinished Story of Steam Locomotives and steam locomotive men on the Railways of Great Britain, London, Allen & Unwin, 1957.

Historical Steam Locomotives, London, A & C Black, 1959.

The Midland Compounds, Dawlish, David & Charles, 1964.

The British Steam Railway Locomotive, 1925–1965, London, Ian Allan, 1966.

Southern Steam, Newton Abbot, David & Charles, 1966.

The L.N.W.R. Precursor Family, Newton Abbot, David & Charles, 1967.

The G.W.R. Stars, Castles and Kings, Part 1, 1906–1930, Newton Abbot, David & Charles, 1967.

The Caledonian Dunalastairs, Newton Abbot, David & Charles, 1968.

L.N.E.R. Steam, Newton Abbot, David & Charles, 1969.

LMS Steam, Newton Abbot, David & Charles, 1971.

The G.W.R. Stars, Castles and Kings, Part 2, 1930–1965, Newton Abbot, David & Charles, 1971.

G.W.R. Steam, Newton Abbot, David & Charles, 1972.

Engine 6000: the Saga of a Locomotive, Newton Abbot, David & Charles, 1972.

The Gresley Pacifics, Part 1, 1922–1935, Newton Abbot, David & Charles, 1973.

The Gresley Pacifics, Part 2, 1935-1974, Newton Abbot, David & Charles, 1975.

Locomotion: A World Survey of Railway Traction, London, Routledge & Kegan Paul, 1975.

The Southern King Arthur Family, Newton Abbot, David & Charles, 1976.

Standard Gauge Great Western 4-4-0s: Part 1: 1894–1910, Newton Abbot, David & Charles, 1977.

The Royal Scots and Patriots of the LMS, Newton Abbot, David & Charles, 1978.

Standard Gauge Great Western 4-4-0s: Part 2: Counties to the Close, Newton Abbot, David & Charles, 1978.

The G.W.R. Mixed Traffic 4-6-0 classes, London, Ian Allan, 1978.

The Last Years of British Steam, Newton Abbot, David & Charles, 1978.

Signalling

Fifty Years of Railway Signalling, London, the Institution of Railway Signal Engineers, 1962.

British Railway Signalling: a Survey of Fifty Years Progress, London, Allen & Unwin, 1969.

Railway Signalling: A treatise on the recent practice of British Railways, London, A & C Black, 1980.

History (specialised)

The Railway Race to the North, London, Ian Allan, 1959.

Historic Railway Disasters, London, Ian Allan, 1966.

British Railways at War, 1939–1945, London, Ian Allan, 1971.

Speed Records on Britain's Railways: a Chronicle of the Steam Era, Newton Abbot, David & Charles, 1971.
Rocket 150: a Century and a Half of Locomotive Trials, London, Ian Allan, 1980.

Locomotive working
British Locomotives at Work, London, Greenlake, 1947.
British Locomotives from the Footplate, London, Ian Allan, 1950.
Four Thousand Miles on the Footplate, London, Ian Allan, 1952.
Fifty Years of Western Express Running, Bristol, Everard, 1954.
British Steam Locomotives at Work, London, Allen & Unwin, 1967.
Rail, Steam and Speed, London, Allen & Unwin, 1970.
Sixty Years of Western Express Running, London, Ian Allan, 1973.
Sixty Years of West Coast Express Running, London, Ian Allan, 1976.
Railway Reminiscences of the Inter-War Years, London, Ian Allan, 1980.

British railways, operating
British Railways in Action, London, Nelson, 1956.
British Railways in Transition, London, Nelson, 1963.
Britain's New Railway (the LMR electrification), London, Ian Allan, 1965.
Electric Euston to Glasgow, London, Ian Allan, 1974.
Two Miles a Minute, Cambridge, Patrick Stephens, 1980.

Overseas railways
Continental Main Lines: Today and Yesterday, London, Allen & Unwin, 1963.
Railway Holiday in Austria, Dawlish, David & Charles, 1965.
Single Line Railways (for United Kingdom Railway Advisory Service), Newton Abbot, David & Charles, 1966.
Railways of Southern Africa, London, A & C Black, 1971.
Railways of Australia, London, A & C Black, 1971.
Railways of Canada, London A & C Black, 1973.
The Algoma Central Railway, London, A & C Black, 1975.
Railways of Western Europe, London, A & C Black, 1977.
Railways of Asia and the Far East, London, A & C Black, 1978.
Railways of the U.S.A., London, A & C Black, 1979.

Archaeology
Railway Archaeology, Cambridge, Patrick Stephens, 1981.

General
Railways of Britain—Past and Present, London, Batsford, 1947.
The Boys Book of British Railways, London, Ian Allan, 1951.
British Trains—Past and Present, London, Batsford, 1951.
Main Lines across the Border, London, Nelson, 1960.
British Steam Locomotives (in colour), London, Blandford, 1964.
Steam Railways of Britain in Colour, London, Blandford, 1967.
Railways at the Turn of the Century 1895–1905, London, Blandford, 1969.
Railways at the Zenith of Steam 1920–1940, London, Blandford, 1970.
Railways in the Years of Pre-eminence, 1905–1919, London, Blandford, 1971.
The Dawn of World Railways 1800–1850, London, Blandford, 1972.

The Golden Age of Steam, London, A & C Black, 1973.

Railways in the Formative Years 1851–1895, London, Blandford, 1973.

The Majesty of British Steam (paintings by G.F. Heiron), London, Ian Allan, 1973.

Railways in the Transition from Steam 1940–1965, London, Blandford, 1973.

The Railway Picture Book (paintings by Jack Hill), London, A & C Black, 1975.

The Pre-Grouping Scene (G. W. R.), London, Ian Allan, 1975.

Railways in the Modern Age, Poole, Blandford, 1975.

Railways Then and Now: A World History, London, Elek, 1975.

Pictorial History of Trains (colour), London, Sundial, 1976.

Great Steam Locomotives of all Time, Poole, Blandford, 1976.

Encyclopaedia of Railways, London, Octopus, 1977.

Great Western in Colour, Poole, Blandford, 1978.

World Atlas of Railways, London, Mitchell Beazley, 1978.

The Pre-Grouping Scene (G.N.R.), London, Ian Allan, 1979.

The Pre-Grouping Scene (L.N. W.R.), London, Ian Allan, 1980.

Serial articles

Locomotive Causerie, 186 articles, monthly in *Railways/Railway World* from 1940 to 1956.

Railway Signals: standard semaphore types used in pre-grouping days, 31 articles, with working drawings, in *The Model Engineer* at intervals between September 1940 and March 1942.

Railway Interlocking Frames, a series of articles with working drawings, in *The Model Engineer* at intervals between March 1946 and August 1947.

Locomotive Working in Great Britain, a series of articles (with varying subtitles) in *The Engineer* from 1945 to 1957, at varying intervals.

Locomotive Practice and Performance, a continuous monthly series of 264 articles, from January 1959 to December 1980 in *The Railway Magazine* in the series inaugurated by Charles Rous-Marten in September 1901.

Index